Sheldon Amos

The Science of Politics

Third Edition

Sheldon Amos

The Science of Politics
Third Edition

ISBN/EAN: 9783337134310

Printed in Europe, USA, Canada, Australia, Japan

Cover: Foto ©ninafisch / pixelio.de

More available books at **www.hansebooks.com**

THE

SCIENCE OF POLITICS

BY

SHELDON AMOS, M.A.

BARRISTER-AT-LAW ; AUTHOR OF 'THE SCIENCE OF LAW' ETC.; LATE PROFESSOR
OF JURISPRUDENCE IN UNIVERSITY COLLEGE, LONDON, AND TO THE
INNS OF COURT ; LATE EXAMINER IN CONSTITUTIONAL
HISTORY TO THE UNIVERSITY OF LONDON

THIRD EDITION

LONDON
KEGAN PAUL, TRENCH, TRÜBNER, & CO. Ltd.
1890

PREFACE.

I HAVE done my best to avoid the temptation of constructing an ideal polity founded on mere guesses and hopes.

That there is an ideal polity for each State, if not one for all States, I steadfastly believe. But it is only to be discovered in the paths of history and observation.

In passing from the 'Science of Law' to that of Politics, some change of method is inevitable, owing to the superior complexity and larger range of the subject-matter. But the exercise, once become familiar in the narrower field, of applying a severe terminology and logical process to ethical notions will be found of the highest service in the wider field.

A two years' journey round the world, in the course of which I visited the chief centres of political life, ancient and modern, in Europe, America, Australasia, Polynesia, and North Africa, has not only helped me with illustrations, but has been of no small use in stimulating thought.

ALEXANDRIA.

CHAPTER VIII.

THE GOVERNMENT OF DEPENDENCIES 311

CHAPTER IX.

FOREIGN RELATIONS 342

CHAPTER X.

THE PROVINCE OF GOVERNMENT 371

CHAPTER XI.

REVOLUTIONS IN STATES 427

CHAPTER XII.

RIGHT AND WRONG IN POLITICS 447

INDEX 485

THE
SCIENCE OF POLITICS.

CHAPTER I.

NATURE AND LIMITS OF THE SCIENCE OF POLITICS.

THE progress of the strictly physical sciences in modern times has had a two-fold influence on the advancement of those branches of knowledge which deal less with physical than with moral, social, and political facts. On the one hand, the exact methods and indisputable conclusions of the sciences concerned with matter have inaugurated modes of study and enquiry which are believed to be of universal application. On the other hand, the standard of rigorous logic in all studies is so far exalted that those subjects of thought or investigation which do not conform to identically the same standard as that maintained for the study of matter are thought to be not worth pursuing with any regard to the claims of a severe logical process. This sort of antipathy between the physical and the ethical regions of search and argument has been intensified by the coexistence of two opposed orders of minds, the ardently speculative and the persistently practical. The former

B

are discontented with the notion of a so-called Science of Politics because of the complexity of the subject matter, and the intrusion, at all points, of such seemingly incalculable factors as the will and passions of mankind. Practical statesmen, again, immersed in actual business and oppressed by the ever-recurring presence of new emergencies, almost resent the notion of applying the comprehensive principles of science, and still more the conjectural use of foresight, in respect of subjects which, for them, are in ceaseless flux, and can, at best, only be safely and wisely handled by momentarily adjusted contrivances.

Between these two extreme classes lies all the large portion of society composed of persons with minds less distinctly determined and trained in one direction or the other, and therefore all the more open to be impressed by influences derived from sound thinkers and energetic workers, but experiencing these influences only in a loose and diluted form. The aggregate result is that the subject of Politics floats in the public mind either as a mere field for ingenious chicane or as a boundless waste for the evolutions of scholastic phantasy. If Politics are to be vindicated from the aspersions cast upon them from the opposite quarter here indicated, and are ever to be erected into a science with its own appropriate methods and limitations, the foundation of these sceptical suspicions must be investigated and their real value strictly assessed. The investigation will proceed as follows.

1. One obvious class of objections to the possibility of applying rigorous scientific methods to Politics is founded on the number and nature of the component and preparatory studies which are presupposed in

all strict enquiries into the theory of Government. Assuming that the physical sciences,—beginning (say) with astronomy and ending with physiology or psychology,—have reached a strictly scientific stage, there yet remain, as properly leading the way to the study of Politics, all those branches of knowledge which depend on the composite nature of man both as isolated and as in society. Such are Ethics in the Aristotelian sense, comprehending as topics decorum and propriety as well as duty; political economy, which deals with the conditions under which national wealth is produced, accumulated, and distributed; law and legislation, (sometimes comprised under the general head of jurisprudence) which deal with the essential nature, logical distribution, and historical growth of the general rules of conduct which all Governments maintain and enforce; and lastly, the somewhat novel science of Sociology, which deals with the inherent problems to which the aggregation of mankind into groups gives rise, so far as these problems can be abstracted and treated independently of Government.

This list of studies, which might be multiplied and varied to any extent according to individual proclivities, encloses large areas of knowledge over the subjects of which the human will and human passions must have, at least in the course of ages and in passing from country to country, an amount of influence which seems to set scientific precision at defiance. Nevertheless, and in spite of all the controversies waged among those who prosecute these studies, there is no doubt that in all these pursuits the most searching and exact methods, so far as they are applicable, are beginning to be used, and the certainty and universality of the sequence of cause and effect,—that is, of Laws of Nature,—to be recognised as a premise.

The extension of the like severity of process to political studies is mainly delayed by the constantly disappointing incompleteness of the constituent and preparatory studies just enumerated. A Science of Politics, indeed, has its own special sources of embarrassment, owing, among other things, to the necessity of co-ordinating in one view all the conclusions deducible from those other, and as it were introductory, researches. Of course this process of combination abounds with its own manifold opportunities of error; but this fact need no more produce despair than the composite quality of physiology leads the student to be sceptical of the scientific character of enquiries into the constitution of the animal world.

There is a vast difference between calling a branch of knowledge a science, because it can only be profitably studied by the use of the same logical methods as are indispensable in the mastery of the best-established physical sciences, and being, as yet, scientifically cultivated, or advanced in outward form to the full proportions of a maturely developed science. It may be, indeed, that, from a number of causes to be shortly adverted to, Politics will always present an appearance neither homogeneous nor, in one sense, exact. But these defects neither impair the genuine truth of the universal laws to which the topic is submitted, nor ought to convey any imputation on the only methods serviceable in treating it.

Admitting as a provisional and practical postulate the freedom of the human will, it might indeed seem to be impossible, on the face of it, to bring within the domain of stringent scientific methods any class of materials largely conversant with the direct actions and emotions of mankind. But there are certain corrections which reduce the significance of any sceptical conclusions which might be drawn.

In the first place, the more extensively and minutely historical studies are carried on and the investigations of travellers pursued and recorded, the more uniform does human nature appear, and the more calculable are the actions, sentiments, and emotions of large classes of mankind, when the antecedents and surrounding conditions are ascertained. So far as political enquiries are concerned, it is more with classes, groups, and assemblages of men, and with considerable stretches of time, than with any individual men at a given moment that the investigator is occupied. Thus the historical method, in proportion as it is extensively pursued, contains in itself its own correctives.

But in the second place, if the researches of historians and the reports of travellers contain an endless and boundless mass of facts which seem rather to increase the list of human eccentricities than to reduce it by discovering a dominant order and an integral unit of progress and purpose, yet here again the problem of finding a scientific form for the theory of Government is on the whole simplified rather than otherwise. As explorations of all sorts are multiplied and extend, they take the place of the logical instrument of experiment; and the result of them is that a limited number of propositions are evolved which admit of being announced with a fair assurance of their universality. If the area of observation be limited, the truths reached will, indeed, be proportionately restricted in number, but within this area they will be none the less valid.

Thus, in the science of Political Economy, it is not universally true that, in all conditions of society, population tends to increase out of proportion to the means of subsistence; for the effective desire of individual self-enrichment constitutes in certain conditions a reparative and compensating force. So in Law, it is not everywhere true that a human being is, in a legal sense, a person and not a thing; or that laws proceed from a consciously acting Political Authority; or that it is recognised as an axiom that taxation and representation go together. The several propositions here chosen by way of illustration from two of the component sciences which, with others, go to constitute the complete range of political studies, and help to convert those studies into a separate science, are only partially and relatively true at certain places and periods. But, within these limits of time and place, their truth, and the truth of all like propositions, is invariable and incontestable.

Thus if the composite nature of Politics impairs the universality of the majority of the propositions with which it is concerned, this only establishes the relativity of these studies, and in no wise detracts from their usefulness or supersedes the employment of those rigorous logical methods which in other respects continue to be applicable.

2. Another reason which accounts for the unscientific aspect under which political studies usually present themselves is that it very rarely happens, or has happened, that conscious attention to the true character of Governmental problems, to their difficulties, and to the modes of their solution, is aroused in any nation till

long after a practical solution of some kind has been instinctively resorted to, and a considerable advance in the art of administration achieved.

An exception might be supposed to exist in the case of colonies and dependencies, at the first foundation of which all the materials seem to be within the conscious control of the parent or governing State. But it is just on this very account that theoretical truths have here their most hopeful platform, and are habitually applied in practice to an extent which, because of unnoticed but vitiating errors of calculation, is often fraught with serious hazard. The Cornwallis settlement in Bengal, the early land policy of the Australian Colonies, and the attempted central taxation of the American Colonies by the British Parliament, are all instances of the over-hasty application, to materials believed to be malleable, of firmly fixed political principles. The principles themselves, indeed, in all these cases, needed re-examination and re-statement.

The obstacles to at once applying even the best-established principles of Government in all conceivable emergencies, so soon as conscious attention happens to be awakened to the national needs, are sufficiently obvious. It is not only that the principles themselves usually demand modification in view of the circumstances of the people and of the day, but that the greatest allowance must always be made in all political reforms for the influence of fixed sentiments and habits. It also may happen that bad institutions, —such as a bad poor-law system, or, in the criminal law, a falsely conceived relationship between crimes and punishments,—may have generated a vast and complex web of affiliated ideas, customs, institutions, and laws, which can severally be neither defended in principle nor yet rudely disdained and cast aside.

For not only do custom and habit enable a people, or classes of a people, to work in long established grooves with the smallest amount of friction and obstruction; but the mere fact of the long existence of a familiar usage so far fashions in its own image the mind, and even the conscience, of a people, that a critical reformer has a hard and unpopular task to perform in assaulting even the most indefensible abuses. The large mass of the people, if disused to political change of any but the most cautious, slow, and tentative kind, have their sentiments of loyalty and reverence outraged by the sudden introduction of what is new and unfamiliar. Their mind has been trained and pruned in such a way as to be unable to conceive, as a mere intellectual notion, a better ordered world than that in which they live. Where too great a disparity both in sentiments and in intellect exists between the reformer and the people, or even between different classes of the people in the same community, it may show that the times are not yet ripe for changes recommended by deference to the claims of logic and of justice.

Instances in point are supplied by the difficulties experienced by the British Indian Government in dealing with such patently immoral institutions as polygamy; by the attachment of the Scotch to a law of marriage which notoriously facilitates the most cruel of frauds; and by the obstacles in all countries to any comprehensive reconstruction of the systems of land-tenure and inheritance, and of civil, and still more of criminal, procedure. These last-mentioned institutions have seldom been radically altered in any country by any process short of revolution, however persuasive the voice of right, of reason, and of utility, in favour of change. So vast is the number of individual persons interested in these classes of matters, so well habituated are they, and consequently so deeply attached, to the recognised forms, usages, or even gestures, customarily in use,—many of which are of a public nature and are daily witnessed by all men,—that any vital re-construction seems little short of sacrilege, and the most conclusive reasons in favour of it are scarcely comprehensible.

3. It is needless to point out that the conception of Politics as a Science is much affected by the imperfections of Politics as a practical Art. It is not only by reason of the existence of ineradicable institutions and ideas that the scientific development of political studies is hampered and delayed. There is another reason of a still more commanding importance which operates in the same direction with a still more signal force. It is that, at any given moment, when the legislator, or administrator, would otherwise most desire to govern with due regard to well-established principles dictated by abstract political science, he is imperatively urged on to the front, and impelled into action, by the pressing necessity of instantly choosing between a limited number of possible alternative courses. Most of all is this the case in what are sometimes called constitutionally-governed countries,—that is, countries in which representative institutions have reached a tolerable degree of advancement, and political knowledge and interest are widely diffused. In these circumstances a spontaneous organisation of political leaders

and their respective followers into parties for the purpose of uniform and combined action is sure to have taken place.

The result is, that an artificial effort will be made, at each critical occurrence which seems to call for the intervention of the Government, to narrow the possible courses of action to a very few immediately intelligible expedients, recommended rather by their rough conformity to some pre-existing schemes or ideals in favour with the different contending parties than by their intrinsic harmony with scientific requirements. No doubt the party leader who is himself imbued with a scientific spirit, and is personally disposed to do as little violence as possible to his cultured instincts, will do his utmost to bring all his measures into the shape which his logical and historical training, applied to all the circumstances of the special case, leads him to desire. But action at once and without farther delay is unavoidable. A decision can only be deferred at the cost either of letting go the opportunity for providing a remedy of some sort for a possibly crying abuse; or of openly confessing impotency; or of surrendering to others a leadership which, with all its demerits, is probably believed to be, on the whole, fraught with good rather than with evil. Thus the peremptoriness of political opportunities, and the necessity of instant action, withstand, in a country with free representative institutions, every effort to impart to political action through a long period a comprehensive, consistent, and scientific character.

It is no wonder if the same class of facts re-acts on the intellectual conception of the position of Politics as a subject of study and of knowledge.

The topic is naturally relegated to the region of caprice and accident, or to that of tentative experiment and spasmodic contrivance. This intellectual consequence is intensified by the fact that all Governments, —and not least those known at the present day as the freest and, on the whole, the soundest,—are habitually made the arena of purely ambitious contention, of selfish aspiration, and even of corrupt conspiracies against the public well-being. The wider the territorial area of any particular Government, and the more complicated and extensive its essential mechanism, the more opportunity there is for the exhibition of personal or, at the most, of local selfseeking. So far as this prevails, Politics become degraded into a mere vulgar struggle for money, office, or power. All actual reference to scientific considerations is excluded. The tone of public thought and sentiment becomes proportionately infected, and all the claims which might otherwise be asserted on behalf of Politics to take its place by the side of other sciences dealing with such moral elements as the human Will meet with a sceptical repudiation.

Where free representative institutions are not found, and absolutism of one type or another prevails, the way is more open for a deliberate choice of the policy to be pursued in any sudden emergency. Such a case has presented itself, again and again, on the occurrence of famines in British India. Could such a casualty occur without being long foreseen in a country enjoying a popular constitution, the question of remedies would be instantly debated in every kind of public assembly, and by all the organs of public opinion, with a ferment of party zeal which would daily gain in heat and vehemence, and would impel statesmen to select with over much precipitation between the limited number of remedial measures which enjoyed, for one cause or another, the popular favour.

The legislation demanded in the case of a failure of the potato-crop in Ireland has more than once illustrated this position. One party advocates the institution of public works, of a purely wasteful or superfluous kind, on an enormous scale; another is in favour of indiscriminate outdoor relief; a third recommends, with the late Lord George Bentinck, the construction at the public cost of railways, with the purpose at once of employing labour on a large scale and of distributing food. However much a judicious statesman may be opposed to all these views, yet for fear of being reduced to nullity, and of having to give place to opponents, he can only connect his own name with, and invite the adhesion of his followers to, what seems on the whole the least objectionable of the popular alternatives. The utmost he can do is to combine different courses in such a way as that some special evil of one may neutralise some greater evil of another, and to introduce modifications which may escape general attention, but which none the less go some way, at least, to qualify the mischievous operation of the scheme, a professed adoption of which cannot be evaded.

It will depend, of course, very largely on the constitutional circumstances of the country how far, even in the case of a pressing emergency, the art of politics may be made to comply with the requirements of scientifically ascertained laws. Where a large and promiscuous population has to be satisfied or must be appealed to by statesmen for political support, the measures must be instantly intelligible and not too far removed in their conception from the average ken of mankind as represented then and there. The ulterior objects proposed must not belong to a too distant future: the pursuit of them must not involve what seem to most people excessive or disproportionate sacrifices: they must easily and obviously connect themselves with the common wants and feelings of the many at the moment, rather than with the (seemingly) problematical aspirations of a few in the indefinite future.

The case is different where popular government has not yet established itself, and where, in consequence, none of the above obstacles, even at a critical juncture calling for the immediate intervention of the legislator or administrator, are presented. But the exemption of the statesman or ruler from the checks of popular control of a constitutional kind by no means ensures a deference to purely scientific demands. Timidity, rashness, prejudice, personal rivalries, and the still less worthy influences of calculating self-interest or of a narrow ambition, dwarf and vitiate a policy not less surely than do the impediments due to popular ignorance and incompetence. The statesman, in the one case as in the other, is bound to act,—and this too without delay; and, though a scientific resolution cannot be excluded, yet, from one cause or another, the temptations to deviate to this or that side are numerous and urgent. There have indeed been statesmen who have so far impressed their own personality on their policy, and communicated their views and aspirations to the bulk of the governing population that, at special exigencies, the public confidence previously won has enabled them to dictate a course scarcely comprehended by the people at large. Such a position was occupied on certain occasions by Count Cavour in Italy, Presidents Lincoln and Grant in the United States, even to some extent by Prince Bismarck in Germany, to a still greater extent by M. Thiers in France, conspicuously by the Duke of Marlborough for a time in England, and in modern times by Sir R. Peel, Lord Palmerston, and Mr. Gladstone.

So also in Governments not controlled by representative institutions,—such as those of almost all the States of Europe except England, up to very recent days,—there have always been found exceptional rulers who, in spite of all temptations to indulge selfish prepossessions in favour of ease or aggrandisement, have availed themselves of the peculiar felicity of their situation to pursue a consistent and far-sighted policy, undisturbed by all casual occurrences or misadventures. To this class have belonged many well-known administrators of British India and of the Crown Colonies of Great Britain, as well as certain absolute sovereigns in ancient and modern times.

It appears, then, that not only does the imminent necessity for immediate action present serious obstacles to the pursuit of a policy founded on the teachings of critical observation and a wide-reaching experience—that is, on science,—but the mere fact that statesmen are constantly impelled to act at once in directions which very imperfectly correspond to their own conceptions of what is really best throws a shadow of doubt and uncertainty over the scientific character of the studies concerned. It is felt, not unreasonably, that if those who are most concerned to be acquainted with the best methods of political research forbear to turn these methods to account at the moment of the utmost need, this is at least as likely to result from the inherently imperfect and illogical nature of the branch of knowledge in question as from any other cause. To this comprehensive scepticism some of the classes of facts above adverted to may be held to supply an answer. The unscientific character of a policy adopted at any crisis has often been an exact measure of the amount of external pressure applied through the competition of factions, or through the impetuosity of a populace only jaded into an unwonted attention to political affairs by exceptional events. Where this pressure is not at hand, rulers still may, indeed, through unworthy influences and motives, prefer the worse to the better way; but enough instances of the persistent maintenance of a deliberately adopted policy in the face of the most seductive allurements to fluctuation have been exhibited to show that it cannot be fairly alleged that politics must necessarily be unscientific because few in the real business of life have time, or liberty, or tenacity of purpose, sufficient to withstand the impetuous torrent of popular zeal generated by sudden crises or catastrophes.

Probably the most real and enduring objection to the claims of Politics to assume the rank of a true science is the confessedly immature and imperfectly developed character of the component or preparatory studies, apart from which, in their combination with each other, the study of Politics cannot be pursued. It has already been noticed that the complex and composite nature of political studies is of itself a presumption against the facility, if not against the possibility, of ever imparting to those studies the rigorous certainty essential to Science. But this presumption is greatly increased by the fact that in such broad but indispensable preparatory studies—confessedly of a scientific aspect—as Ethics, Economics, and Jurisprudence, there are to be found only the very smallest number of uncontroverted propositions. And even as to the logical methods applicable in each branch of knowledge no generally assented-to decisions have yet been accepted.

There is thus afforded to the sceptically-minded a wide opening for treating as unscientific a study which, like that of Politics, must be built up on conclusions yet to be established in those other regions of knowledge, but none of which are as yet established with a certainty which is beyond debate. Nevertheless, if it be admitted that those component studies are capable of being placed on a strictly scientific foundation, and only wait for longer time and attention to assume scientific exactness, at least as much may be claimed for Politics, and the composite study may advance in logical perfection at an equal rate with the elementary studies.

The general result of these considerations is that there are a variety of solid reasons which account not only for the reputation acquired by Politics of being an inherently unscientific study, but also for the study itself having advanced only a very short way towards scientific completeness. But most or all of these reasons have been seen to be of a kind which hold out a good promise for the future, and thereby afford an ample encouragement to the use of a strictly logical method in political investigations, and to the attempt to create a scientific structure of ever-increasing completeness in this region as well as in other more familiarly associated with the name of Science.

A science need not be built on universal, nor even upon general, propositions; and partial, particular, or probable premises may justify conclusions, drawn with logical correctness, which may be a firm basis for action. Where truths are by their nature restricted in time and place, or where evidence is yet lacking to demonstrate their actual generality, the assemblage of such truths will carry with it a fragmentary and hypothetical character which may to some seem incompatible with the rigid demands of Science. But where the investigator himself proceeds in strict accordance with the severest logical requirements, conducting his ratiocination with the utmost precision, and distinguishing at all points the possible or probable from the certain, the universal or general from the particular, and proof from plausibility or mere conjecture, it matters little what name is given to the branch of enquiry concerned. It lacks no one of the essential elements and recommendations of the best and earliest-established of the physical sciences. Its terms are submitted to the same process of definition, its subject-matter to a like arrangement into groups and classes, genera and species, and the resulting propositions are reached by a course of reasoning as logically irrefutable.

There are, indeed, certain plain indications that the study of Politics is already, even by practical states-

18   THE SCIENCE OF POLITICS.

men, being placed on a platform of far higher scientific exactness than ever before.

One of these indications is the large and discriminating use made of statistics. The collection and due use of statistics belong to very modern times; and owing to popular prejudices and social obstacles—such, for instance, as still exist in England with regard to the collection of agricultural and religious statistics—they have not yet received anything like the extension of which they are capable. Nevertheless, it has become the fashion for all the more advanced Governments to rival each other in the breadth, fullness, arrangement, and clearness of the numerical information they obtain on all the groups of national facts which are susceptible of being tabulated in a systematic shape. These tables of statistics are periodically furnished by the Government, not only for purposes of contemplated legislation, but independently of all thought of immediate use. The fallacious use to which purely numerical facts can be put, with only too seductive a show of plausibility, is beginning to be fully acknowledged and guarded against. But the assurance that the registered number of births, deaths, and marriages, within a given period and area, as well as the periodical records of crime and disease, and, even more obviously, the tabulated increase or decrease of commerce, shipping, and manufactures of different sorts, may serve to point to the presence of general laws—that is, of permanent sequences of cause and effect—is a sufficient justification of the labour and expense involved in obtaining the severally-relevant statistics. The comparison between the numerical results obtained at one time and place and another, and between those presented in different countries, is becoming a political method increasing in prevalence and repute. In many quarters, indeed, the value of purely numerical estimates has been much exaggerated, and its peculiar liability to error, when made a basis of political reasoning, has been too much ignored. But when its limits of application are duly recognised, and care is taken to distinguish legal and political causes from those which are purely ethical or sociological, the study and use of statistics must be regarded as a most valuable ally, and an unmistakable proof of the scientific character of political studies.

Akin to the token which the enlarged use of statistics affords of the growing recognition of Politics as a true science, is the ever increasing disposition, at the present day, to await, at any political crisis, whether legislative or administrative, the result of a patient examination of evidence as to the state of the facts and the previous history of the question.

It is now the practice in the more advanced countries to take, in the path of serious political change, no step which seems to be other than the next step onward in a course which has become habitual, without first nominating, by one process or another, competent persons to conduct a critical examination and to deliberate and report upon the matter. The most searching powers are often entrusted to this body of persons to enable them to inform themselves not only as to all the interests, in their several proportions, to be affected by the new policy, but as to the history of the general policy pursued in the past, and occasionally even as to the practice in other countries.

It often, indeed, happens that after a laborious investigation, lasting for months or even for years, the popular interest in the once-advocated policy is found to be exhausted, or diverted into new directions, and the thought of new legislation is abandoned, and a voluminous, costly, and invaluable report cast on one side. Such are among the inevitable accidents which retard the progress of Government.

But what is of importance to notice in this place is that the growing disposition to consult past and surrounding facts before inaugurating change belongs to the strictly scientific habit of mind; and if it is true that much laborious investigation seems for the time to be thrown away, yet it seldom happens that complicated and far-reaching changes are encountered without the assistance of a previous impartial and deliberate enquiry of the kind here adverted to. The scientific method, in Politics as elsewhere, is slowly and surely getting the better of the empiric.

It will serve to throw some light on the scientific aspect of political studies if some attention is bestowed on the several writers who, at different periods and in different countries, have endeavoured to elucidate the subject by formal treatises. These treatises—so far as they have survived—are not numerous,—a phenomenon which of itself is some indication that a theoretical handling of the problems of Government is not a popular occupation either for authors or readers. But whether this be so or not, so far as past literary experience goes, it certainly seems to be the case that the reflective or self-conscious condition of mind which alone admits of theoretical dissertations on Politics, as well as on other matters, is itself the product of a combination of partially accidental circumstances. For instance, no such treatise has ever appeared in the entire absence of pressing political problems, everywhere reckoned to be at once difficult and important. Nor have such writings emerged in countries depressed under the hand of a simple and irresistible despotism; nor, again, in times and places disturbed by the actual presence of revolution, or even of violent and systematic change.

Such treatises, indeed, are the expression of far more than the casual opinions of an individual speculator. They are the outcome of the national needs and instincts. They often register the conclusions of more or less distinctly organised schools of thought. Their language can generally be traced, either in the way of cause or of effect, in the political oratory, diplomatic and state documents, written laws, or popular literature of the hour. They thus act as the most precious, because the most unconscious, sort of historical monuments.

For the present purpose, however, they are mainly noticeable, first as substantiating the truth that there is a veritable Science of Politics, and then as illustrating the special difficulties which the cultivation of that science has to contend with.

It is worth while to make a selection, however arbitrary, of the leading political writers who in ancient and modern times have treated the subject in a systematic way, and to determine how far the shortcomings of these treatises were due to fortuitous circumstances, and what was the contribution made by each in succession to the elaboration of a true Science of Politics.

The writers on Politics who on these grounds may be fitly enumerated are the following:

1. Plato and Aristotle.
2. Cicero, Plutarch, and the historical writers of the early Roman Empire.

3. Machiavelli; Hooker; Bacon.

4. The Schools of the English Revolution.—The Declaration of Rights; Hobbes; Locke; Burke.

5. The School of the American War of Independence.—The Declaration of Independence; the Federalist.

6. The School of the French Revolution.—Montesquieu; the Declaration of the Rights of Man: Thomas Paine.

7. The Positivist School.—Auguste Comte.

8. The English Utilitarians.—Bentham; the Mills; John Austin; Sir G. C. Lewis.

1. The warmest admirers of Plato will not claim for his 'Republic,' or—if it be genuine, as Mr. Grote, at least, concludes it to be—his 'Laws,' the character of a treatise on Political Science. Plato indeed availed himself of the political phenomena everywhere conspicuously present before the eyes and minds of his readers, and of the active spirit of political curiosity which those phenomena generated. In the 'Laws' directly political objects would seem to be the end in view; but even here the main notion is that of advice or aspiration, and not that of research or exact demonstration; and the objects in view relate to individual reforms rather than to systematic construction or re-construction. Indeed, Plato's writings, though not without their suggestiveness on many points of great importance to the statesman—such as education and the mutual relation of classes—belong properly to the literary department of 'Utopias.' Sir G. C. Lewis, in his 'Methods of Observation and Reasoning on Politics,' has devoted a special section to the con-

sideration of this subject; and the invention of such political ideas is sometimes of real logical service, by furnishing a comprehensive framework for the joining together of a number of hypotheses. But while aspirations, counsels, and hypotheses no doubt hold a place in political discussion, they are, at the most, only the complements of the science, and not its essence.

To Aristotle and his political treatises,—especially to the lost one, which dealt with the constitutions of nearly 200 Greek cities,—a very different kind of importance attaches. The backward condition of the physical sciences in his day prevented Aristotle,—as, even in comparatively modern times, it prevented Bacon,—from rigidly applying inductive methods to ethical enquiries. Nevertheless, the comprehensiveness of application which belonged to these methods was fully apprehended by the earlier philosopher; and he set an example of inexhaustible value in the courage and consistency of purpose with which he followed out true methods to what he concluded to be their legitimate results. There were several reasons, however, which rendered the political investigations of Aristotle rather tentative and partial in their results than final and conclusive.

It is true that, by Aristotle's time, not only had a vast number of Grecian communities passed through, externally at least, all the main vicissitudes which separate absolute despotism from democracy of as liberal a type as was possible in those ages, but also there were conspicuously presented to every thoughtful mind the alternative constitutions of the Kingdom of Macedon and of the Empires of the East. The recently terminated struggle between Athens and Sparta had, while it lasted (as appears abundantly in Thucydides), stimulated incessant comparisons between the very different institutions of the rival States; and the orations of the great orators had, at a later date, accustomed the Grecian mind to calculate what would be gained and what lost by submission to the claims and encroachments of Philip of Macedon. Furthermore, it was, of course, vastly in Aristotle's favour that deductive logic and the practice of dialectic, in Plato's hands and, more systematically, in his own, had very recently undergone an unprecedented expansion; and that he himself had, by his physical investigations and accumulated collections and recorded observations of all sorts, laid the indispensable basis of an inductive logic capable of an unlimited reach of application.

Thus the way was undoubtedly well prepared for the construction of a genuine Science of Politics; and it was inevitable that Aristotle, after applying his newly systematised critical method to the simpler relationships of man as a member of society, should proceed to employ an equally rigid method of enquiry to the relationships of man as a subject of Government and a member of the complex organism entitled a *State*. But Aristotle must have been prevented from exhibiting the Science of Politics in an adequately finished form by certain distinct obstacles even had the habit of applying strict logical methods to ethical topics been then as familiar as it has of late been made by the increased attention bestowed on physical studies as a sequel to the vast discoveries and inventions of modern times.

(1.) In the first place, the diffused existence and

public recognition of slavery must have gone far to confuse the minds of even the clearest thinkers, and to prevent them from discriminating how far this institution was a casual result of certain fluctuating causes, and how far it was a necessary, permanent, and universal characteristic of human society. The consequence of this confusion or doubt must have been to impair the clearness of vision with which the scientific observer would contemplate all problems relating to personal liberty, and even, to speak more generally, all human rights of a purely moral kind. It will be seen later on that each of the leading political revolutions which have subsequently taken place has, by bringing into relief the fact of some class of human rights being habitually violated, given a renewed impetus to the study of theoretic Politics, and brought about some important accession to the Science in its systematic form.

(2.) In the second place, the size of the States of Greece,—even when it reached beyond the confines of a single city,—was so small, that even under the most popular Government the need for representation, in the modern sense, was scarcely felt. Not only in Attica, were all males of full age out of every city entitled to attend the public assembly and bound to serve in rotation as jurymen in the Courts of Law, but so large a preponderance of the numerous members of the Assembly and of the Jury panels were close at hand and could attend in person, that the main difficulty of modern politics, occasioned by vastness of territory and decentralisation, was not appreciated to an extent which called for scientific recognition. Representation, indeed, in the form of agency, can be traced in many institutions, as for instance in the Amphictyonic Council, in the management of certain international festivals, and in the conduct of federative alliances. But the mere fact of occasional recourse being had to the machinery of representation differs widely from the habitual use of representation as the main instrumentality for the support of the very fabric of Government. It was not till the doctrines of human equality and of individual right had to be deferred to, in connexion with extended areas of territory and an equable diffusion of territory, that the subject could take the place in all political enquiries which it occupies at this date. It needed, in fact, the experience supplied by the enormous breadth of the Roman Empire, by the organisation of the Christian Church, and by the essential character and usages of Feudalism, to prepare the world to attribute to the problems of representation their true place in any scheme of scientific Politics.

(3.) In the third place, the economic conditions of the States in the midst of which Aristotle lived, upon which alone his political experience must needs have been founded, were such as to exclude the consideration of the problems which, for statesmen in the present day, are at once the most important and the most arduous of those they have to grapple with. This class of problems relates to providing for a vast pauper population; to adjusting the principle of political equality to the fact of an unequal distribution of wealth; and, in a word, to maintaining the unity and integrity of the State amidst the dislocating and centrifugal influences of an intense struggle for existence at a variety of points, and especially at the extremities, of the body corporate.

In the political communities known to Aristotle, it was not possible that—apart from the slave class—wealth should be as unequally distributed as in modern times; and from all that is known of those communities it appears that the corresponding political problems did not press upon the attention of statesmen. No doubt there were great differences of wealth incident to the various professions, trades, and industrial occupations; and there was abundant opportunity, by saving money, or by accumulating it as capital and investing it productively, to anticipate the modern distinctions between the leisured and luxurious citizen and the citizen actively engaged in producing or manipulating wealth. To what extent the accumulation of capital through the medium of banks, companies, loan societies, and the like, was possible in the ancient world is an interesting question which belongs to the department of antiquarian or, at least, historical research. But, making the utmost allowance for the presence of monetary and circulating expedients the true character and extent of which we can only conjecture, it is impossible that anything can have found place in the older world corresponding to the scale on which capital is, in modern States, concentrated, accumulated, and assiduously transferred from investment to investment.

That no parallel in these respects exists between the circumstances of ancient and modern States is sufficiently proved by a mere glance at the enormous monetary transactions which the industrial, commercial, and even military enterprises of modern times presuppose. The spent capital commemorated in gigantic national debts; the past and current expenditure on railway and telegraph communication; the contributions to joint-stock adventures for every class of engineering and mercantile undertaking; as well as the enormous amount of corporate property, circulating or hoarded, represented by the shipping trade and by international exports and imports; not to mention the national resources diverted, in all the leading States, to the organisation, in peace as well as in war, of the Army and Navy;—these are a series of economical phenomena some of which, almost within the memory of living men, have reached inordinate proportions, and each of which has no equivalent before the sixteenth or seventeenth century of the present era.

But it is not the mere existence of such facts, or their portentous magnitude, which constitutes the difference between the political materials of the modern and the ancient world. The real difference is that in modern States population keeps increasing fully in proportion to,—and, in some States, in a degree out of all proportion to—the growth of wealth, while no natural machinery exists either for ensuring an equable distribution of the new wealth, or even for preventing it from being massed together in a very few hands. It requires the utmost administrative sagacity and energy as well as legislative inventiveness on the part of statesmen to remedy the consequences of this unequal diffusion of vast wealth, and, as far as may be, to promote a more equal diffusion. Questions relating to taxation, pauperism, inheritance and succession, entails, mercantile partnerships, bankruptcy, and free trade, have all to be handled in view of these pressing requirements; and nothing but the sudden spring and development of manufactures, together with the ever fresh occupation of territory in America and the Australian Colonies, could have prevented the occurrence of disastrous famines, and revolutions, and other like adversities, which it is the main purpose of the statesman to keep at a distance.

In Aristotle's time wealth was, undoubtedly, unequally diffused, and checks to population, both natural and artificial, abounded. But it was not till the New World had been discovered, mechanical contrivances inordinately expanded, public and international credit established, and innumerable devices for providing media of exchange invented, that the corresponding political problems could have come to light, or at least have attained the prominence they now have.

(4.) In the fourth place, the scattered extent of territory subject to the leading modern States has of itself given rise to two classes of political problems of the highest degree of importance, and yet of a distinctly novel kind. These problems relate to Local Government and to the Government of Dependencies. It needs no comment to show the importance of both these topics, the place they both occupy in modern legislative discussions and administrative schemes, and the absence of anything which can fairly be said to correspond to them in the political world open to the observation of Aristotle.

To Aristotle, the primary if not the absorbing topic was the form of Government. It is to be noted that the smaller the political community in numerical extent the more pressing,—in appearance if not in reality,—is this consideration; because, the relative proportion of the actual administrators to the numbers of the population being greater as the aggregate mass of the population is smaller, the question as to the most fitting number of administrators is a more significant and pressing one. Where the disproportion between the administrators and the numbers of the population is very great, as in the leading modern States, it matters less whether the number of the administrators be great or small. In this way one element, at least, of calculation in estimating the value of forms of Government has lost the importance it possessed in Aristotle's day. At the present time,—as will be seen later on,—it is impossible to oppose, with the sharpness of distinction which Greek experience admitted of, the monarchical to the oligarchical or, again, to the democratical form of government. Modern experience has shown that tyranny and absolutism are not incompatible with the forms of democratical government; and that under monarchical forms political and personal freedom may find adequate protection. It is discovered that new constitutional devices of a kind undreamed of in Aristotle's day, and which may be applied under any external form of government, are needed to withstand the inroads of injustice, corruption, and anarchy.

In this way, again, the Science of Politics could not have been elaborated by Aristotle, with all his logical perspicacity, his knowledge, and his prescience, simply for want of materials out of which to form it. Greek experience was widely diversified, but always in a narrow field and in the midst of exceptional and transient conditions. Greek communities were small, with a large slave population, the means of subsistence being easily supplied, and the main political problem being that of the rival advantages of placing the supreme power in the hands of one, of a few, or of many purporting ostensibly to be identical with all.

2. The next epoch in the history of Political Science is that of the historical, philosophical, and ethical writers of the last days of the Roman Republic and the early years of the Roman Empire. To this class belong such writers as Cicero, Plutarch, Tacitus, Suetonius, and (incidentally) the Jurists of the times of the Antonines.

It is more difficult to characterise the political speculation of this age than that of the age of Aristotle, because no single representative treatise,—not excepting Cicero's lately recovered work on the 'Republic,'—occupies any such place as the 'Politics' of Aristotle. But this very silence and absence of speculative writers on politics is in the highest degree instructive. In the world of the Roman Empire there could be no question of constitutional change otherwise than through the avenue of revolution. All policy was concerned with keeping things as they were; that is, with defending the frontiers of the Empire, preventing organised revolution in the army or anarchy in the provinces, keeping in restraint the horde of slaves of many nationalities, providing food for the metropolis, and establishing satisfactory relations between the reigning Emperor and those who were, or might prove, competitors for his throne. For years together the only acts of policy strictly so called,—excepting the extension of the rights of citizenship by Caracalla,—related to comprehensive improvements in the system of administration, such as took place successively under Augustus, Constantine, Diocletian, and finally Justinian.

This abeyance of political objects which is the characteristic of the Empire was compatible with a professedly high standard of political ethics, with a rigid regard for, and logical perception of, individual legal claims, and with sound and ingeniously contrived methods of provincial administration. But there was, at heart, a radical discrepancy between the principles of personal morality which, in connexion with novel theories of man's nature and destiny, were disclosing themselves in some parts of the Empire, and the universal oppression under which the slaves and the provincials were all, in a greater or less degree, suffering. It would have been the first aim of a genuine Political Science to trace how far these evils were connected with the existing system of government, or how far they could be removed by political reforms. But no such Science was forthcoming, or could be forthcoming. The only practical choice was between absolutism and anarchy; and such thinkers and writers as appeared were only free to express themselves under the cloak of satiric poems, cynical history, and critical biographies of the heroes of old.

It would be untrue, however, to conclude that the time of the transition from a republican to an imperial system of government, and of the establishment of the Empire, contributed nothing to advance the theoretical treatment of Politics. In many ways the reverse was the case; and, under a variety of disguises, and assisted by the rapid development in some directions of the Art of Politics, the corresponding Science was making achievements for which the modern world continues to be, in an increasing rather than in a diminishing degree, a debtor.

The difficulties of administration as applied over an almost unlimited area; the problems presented by the necessity of preserving order and contentment as well as, if it might be, promoting prosperity among subjects of divers nationalities, creeds, and political antecedents; the arduous questions relating to taxation and military service, as well as those due to the need for organising agriculture and land-tenure in a way likely to favour production and prevent famines; were all obviously present, if not to the mind of the Emperor himself, at least to that of his more competent advisers, on whom the safety and tranquillity of the Empire depended from moment to moment. Add to this that the silent effect of the even and generally impartial administration of justice, based on an inimitable system of equitable private right—a system developed with a logical precision which scarcely knows a parallel—was constantly discovering the nature and the necessity of stable political institutions. Municipal creations and arrangements, again, were relieving the local organs from the pressure of the central mass; and it was only when the central authority unduly encroached, by way of taxation and enforced services of all sorts, on the local bodies, that the dissolution of the Empire was threatened by causes quite independent of external aggression.

It is not only that, through the experience of the political vicissitudes which the history of the fortunes of the Roman Empire supplies, political knowledge has been increased and rendered serviceable for the instruction of future ages, but a more scientific view of the conditions of all good government was inevitably impressing itself on the thought of mankind. During these ages, indeed, it happened that most of the conscious intellectual energy of the world was absorbed in Christian controversy and speculation; and the very nature of the prevalent governmental absolutism was inconsistent with an indulgence in unrestricted political discussion. But even from a political point of view the thought of the age was not wholly wasted. Politics were almost inextricably involved in the very language employed, in the sentiments entertained, and in the reasoning adduced, in the course of the more prevalent avocations and studies. Even the Fathers of the Church, while contrasting the secular society around with the new moral kingdom the claims of which they were engaged in recommending, talked political science without knowing it. The Emperors, in the Recitals prefixed to their laws, confessed the nature of the two-fold problems presented by the Church and the exigencies of their enormous State. The lawyers, in their most technical language on private right, could not avoid admitting or rejecting dominant political theories. In fact, though the period was one of political being and suffering rather than of conscious thinking, yet an incubating process was going on which, after the confusions and the sleep of ages, was destined to produce a not unworthy progeny.

3. Historical investigation has long ago eradicated the notion that the ages which intervened between the fall of Rome and the fall of Constantinople could only be denoted by such images as sleep and death. But so much, nevertheless, is true, that it was not before the definite reconstruction of Europe after the shock of the collision between the tribes of the North and the Empire of the South that Political Science could recover its place

in the consciousness of mankind. The notion of territorial sovereignty was partly introduced and partly reinforced by three contemporaneous institutions or influences:—the Church, succeeding to the territorial claims of the Imperial Government at Rome; the Municipalities, which survived the ruin of what was more brittle or ephemeral than themselves, and persisted in maintaining a well-understood relation between public office and corporate property; and Feudalism,—inclining either to a mere military device or a mere form of tenure, according as it borrowed more from a Teutonic or a Roman source. These institutions, operating in the generation of fresh facts, and as influences on the minds and imagination of men, preserved a clear field for a system of territorial government the limitation of which was determined by geographical, linguistic, military, and even mere diplomatic and dynastic causes.

The history of the Holy Roman Empire, especially in its relation to the Church of Rome, is the history of the way in which the process of delimitation between State and State was carried out in detail, in subservience to the preponderant idea that the German Empire was a true perpetuation of the Roman Empire and that there was only one State, as there was only one Church, in the Western world. If it was the Church which, in concert with other institutions, had preserved the territorial element in the existence of the State, it was again the same Church, which, in a reflex way and by the reaction it called forth on every side against its own usurpations, helped to sharpen and define the notion of the political integrity and independence of a true State. The mercantile cities of Northern Italy were among the first to draw distinct political advantage from the rivalries between the Church and the Empire; and while the theoretical battle of Investments was being fought, as it were, in the gorgeous but unreal cloud-world of Popes and Emperors, the genuine notions of political right, duty, independence, self-government, representation, and corporate action were being noiselessly but triumphantly evolved by the tradesmen, manufacturers, and merchants of the Italian republics.

The writings of Machiavelli, both as a patriotic historian and as a scientific politician, are significant of this new and memorable epoch at its culminating point. In fact, the great author seems almost conscious himself that he is called to prescribe for an era of decline. No one knew better than he that it was not by fraudulent diplomacy or astute craftiness that Florence had attained her incomparable renown. He no doubt felt that the era of private liberty and of political independence for Italian cities had really passed away; and that only by personal adroitness in the ruler could the enemies of his country, whether French or Roman, be temporarily kept at a distance. Therefore the Political Science of Machiavelli must be sought in his History of his own city; his Political Art in his 'Prince.'

It must be observed that the conscious prosecution of political studies in Northern Italy in the fifteenth century was due to more general causes than the appearance of a race of educated statesmen, called into existence by an oligarchical constitution under republican forms—a race of which Machiavelli was the most conspicuous type. There were, indeed, contemporary statesmen of no mean calibre in England and in France; there were free self-governing cities scattered throughout every part of the Western world, and the

Hanseatic League was scarcely distinguishable in any particular from a sovereign and independent State. But in Italy alone all the conditions converged for the study of Politics according to deductive and inductive methods. These conditions were, the variety of experience which the fortunes of all the Italian republics supplied; the close neighbourhood to, and assiduous contact with, States differently governed; the legal and historical studies fostered by the great Italian Universities; the incessant diplomatic activity which characterised the relations of the Republic with Foreign Powers; and lastly, the political reflectiveness kept in constant use by the internal and never ceasing conflicts between the popular and the oligarchical parties in the towns.

The disruption of Feudalism, in the case of all the countries in which it had prevailed, was attended by a breach in the long subsisting relations between the King, the Aristocracy, and the People. It was of the essence of Feudalism to unite these persons and classes together in the well-understood and familiar relations comprised in reciprocal services and in the tenure or the occupation of the soil. As Feudalism collapsed, these relations were disturbed or destroyed. In some countries, as in France, the King profited at the expense of the nobles and the people; in other countries, as in Germany, the subordinate feudal lords profited at the expense of their feudal superiors; while in England the people at one time, by the help of the King, prevailed against the nobles, and at another time, by the help of the nobles, prevailed against the King. There needed a new fusion of classes, or rather, a new ground of political union, to take the place of obsolete facts and a decaying faith. And, so soon as revolution against the subsisting order was threatened, political theory came to the aid of society, and the doctrines of Divine Right on the one hand, and of the Social Contract on the other, were brandished with all the energy which belongs to an era of active social change.

Sir Thomas More's Utopia occupies the same kind of place in reference to later political speculation in England that Plato's 'Republic' occupied towards the 'Politics' of Aristotle. Like the earlier poem of 'Piers Ploughman,' the Utopia traced certain confessed evils to their easily recognised causes, and, with more or less outspoken freedom, demanded reform. But such utterances are rather of the nature of bitter laments or pious aspirations, dictated by the spectacle of social collapse, than a comprehensive and patient survey of the whole political field, such as belongs to science.

The struggles of Elizabeth's reign between the secular State and the mutually-opposed religious parties, which were endeavouring to divert to their own purposes the national forces, prepared the ground for a thorough theoretical discussion of one great department of Politics, the relation of the State to the religious beliefs of its component members. The treatise of Hooker on 'Ecclesiastical Polity' marks not merely an important stage in national literature, but also a freshly discovered capacity in English thought to refer legal and political institutions to their necessary origin in human and common social needs. The transition from an age of mere complaint, remonstrance, and recrimination, to an age of argument based on admitted premises of the most general kind was, in truth, effected by the practical intelligence urgently called for to settle all the constitutional and ecclesiastical questions of Elizabeth's day. Among these questions, even that of the Queen's title to the throne was involved, and still more that of her leading prerogatives.

The recent and still progressing reformation of religion, the increasingly rapid dissolution of the ancient social ties which bound class to class, the dawning of a new literary era, the speculative and adventurous spirit due to the novel prospects opening to commerce and discovery in the New World, formed a cluster of phenomena which were too distinct and portentous not to have their reflection in the mirror of Politics and to supply legislative and administrative problems of a wholly new order of importance. One and another of these problems was courageously grappled with at once —such as the poor-law system, the law relating to fraudulent debtors, the constitutional aspect of monopolies, and, more especially, the relations of the State in its secular character, as well as those of the National Church, to independent religious communities within the realm and to Churches having their centre of loyalty and allegiance outside it.

The discussion of these problems was, for the most part, conducted in a piecemeal way, with reference either to the pressing necessities of the moment or to what were believed to be well-established and long practised usages of the English Government. But, as in all great crises, when competent statesmen are at the head of affairs, the practice went beyond any known precedents, and new principles were evolved under the guise of a more logical development of old ones. Thus Hooker's great work not only went far to ascertain the past and existing relations, civil and religious, of a State Church to schismatic persons and corporations, but furnished a fresh starting-point for the conduct of the controversy in future times. So with Jeremy Taylor's 'Liberty of Prophesying.' The question is argued in view of a practical emergency. The basis of the right of free speech is laid in what are believed to be admitted Biblical, ecclesiastical, and constitutional principles. But in this open citation of implicit dogmas there was contained far more than a mere registration of prevalent ideas. The wise and erudite author was compelled by the exigencies of argument to trespass beyond the strict limits justified by his own authorities; and the consequence was that the 'Liberty of Prophesying' was in fact an anachronism, only to become adapted to the times when principles identically the same were re-asserted by Milton in his 'Areopagitica,' or at a still later date, by Mr. John Stuart Mill in his essay on 'Liberty.'

In the meantime Francis Bacon was laying the foundations of a true inductive method of reasoning, and heralding the brilliant future which lay before it. For the moment, indeed, the physical sciences were alone comprehended in the philosopher's ken. But the method announced admitted of no limitation in the subject-matter, except such as must come from a confined experience or defective means and instruments of observation. As to Politics, there were the further obstacles supplied by long fixed usage, and the general objections to all theorising which might dispose mankind for easily entertaining projects of political change. But the appeal to strict logical methods made by Bacon, in every branch of enquiry which dealt with matters cognisable by the material senses, must have ushered in sooner or later a novel and organic reconstruction of political and ethical theories. The partial speculations of such men as Hooker and Jeremy Taylor co-operated in the same direction, while the remarkable events and needs of the hour prompted men's minds to demand a central basis of thought for their mainstay and consolation amidst changes of incalculable magnitude.

Thus, the impulse to strictly scientific investigation once being given, and the political and constitutional questions astir being of a kind to arouse all the best thought of the day, it needed but the situation, the theoretical assumptions, and the conduct of the Stuart Kings, to call forth the political philosophy of the early part of the seventeenth century.

The leading political topic which dwarfed all others was that of the Prerogative of the Crown. Even so early as the reign of Edward IV., Chancellor Fortescue had been led by current events to discuss in his treatises 'De Laudibus Legum Angliæ' and 'De Monarchiâ,' the attributes of the English King, and his subjection to the law of the land, in contradistinction to the Imperial Sovereign as contemplated by the Civil Law. But, in that early day, speculative political thought was not advanced enough to admit of the enunciation of principles broader than the partially settled maxims of the English Constitution. By the time of the Stuarts the political as well as the speculative world had undergone a notable transformation. For the purposes of the Courts of Law it was sufficient to argue from acknowledged usages and decided cases that the King had or had not a right of raising money without the assent of Parliament, of maintaining a standing army, of granting monopolies, of suspending Acts of Parliament by proclamation, and of inflicting fines and imprisonment by the instrumentality of Courts not known to the Common Law. But when such questions accumulate, it is a sign that more is in debate than mere controversies of uncertain right. Men's minds must rest in some intelligible theory which can either bring into mutual harmony existing facts or can introduce new facts capable of being placed on an unassailable foundation. It has been seen that through the experience, political and intellectual, of the reigns of the Tudors, men's minds were ripe for a purely theoretical solution of pending controversies; and the main representative of the new era was Hobbes.

4. Hobbes' intrinsic merit, in respect of the history of Political Science, was that, in contrast with all his eminent English predecessors who had handled special departments of Politics in a logical spirit, he addressed himself to discover and propound principles of the most comprehensive kinds, from which all doctrines then recognised as needful might be deductively inferred. The principles adduced by Hobbes were not barren truisms founded on a rancorous despondency or a pious optimism. They were based on a careful and accurate survey of the whole field of Government; and every portion of the mechanism of Government, and each of its essential functions were regarded in the light of the central and dominating idea. Thus the foundations of a veritable political Science were for the first time surely laid; and if the superstructure has not followed as rapidly as might have been hoped, it has been only because it needed the fresh discoveries result-

ing from the later revolutionary movements in England, America, and France, to furnish the materials requisite for an adequate scientific development.

It must be noticed, too, that in other directions and by other agencies the elements of a true political science were coming into relief during the reigns of Elizabeth and the Stuarts. The incidents of English maritime adventure led to assumptions in the narrow seas which, whatever their value—as contested by Denmark and Holland, at least—went far to substantiate the notions of territorial sovereignty and of national independence. The untenable assumptions of extra-territorial maritime rights, defended by Selden and justly resisted by Grotius, drove the public conscience to criticise the nature of the relationship between State and State for some other purposes than (as heretofore) those of war alone. In the same way, the peculiar dynastic relations of James I. to the still distinct kingdoms of Scotland and England raised a congeries of legal questions bearing on the nationality of citizens of the two countries before and after the King's accession to the English throne. These questions, though primarily only of constitutional import, tended to popularise and enforce political doctrines as to the true and necessary situation of the citizen in the State to which he belongs.

Thus a series of influences were converging to bring every separate portion of the political machinery under critical review, not merely in order to test its condition and efficiency, but to determine its place and order in the whole system, and thereby to estimate the circumstances and wants of any and every State generically, as subjected to definite conditions, and not merely those of England at that time.

There were certain special circumstances which conduced to impart to all the acts and events of the English Revolution (covering, under this term, the whole of the period between the accession of Charles I. and that of William III.) a peculiarly legal character. Among these circumstances may be noted the habit of theological controversy which was abroad; the eminent lawyers of the stamp of Clarendon and Selden who took so prominent a part in the purely constitutional struggle; the secondary influences of an expiring Feudalism which had at the first been based upon the strictly legal relationships implied in reciprocity of tenure and service; and the fact that the revolution began in Parliament and not outside it,—which involved a precise technical assignment of the points of difference between the Crown and the Parliament, such as expressed itself in the Petition of Right, in the Grand Remonstrance, and, finally, in the Declaration of Rights.

This straining after legal forms and legal justification is conspicuous throughout the whole history even of the Commonwealth, and was congenial to the minds of all the principal actors. It was thus not unnatural, even when the re-settlement under the Houses of Orange and Hanover had finally taken place, for the apologists of the Revolution to cast their arguments rather in a pedantically legal than a liberally political mould. In fact, the position of the Whigs of the Revolution (as Burke abundantly showed, in his 'Appeal from the New Whigs to the Old,' and elsewhere) was characteristically legal; and in this they differed both from their more emotional opponents, the High Church devotees of the excluded dynasty, and from the non-conformist radicals who were prepared to accept,—in a generation or two if not at that time,—the broadest interpretation of the maxim *Salus Reipublicæ suprema Lex*.

Filmer's defence of the Patriarchal basis of Monarchy, and Locke's repudiation of that basis by reference to a legal and subsisting contract between a monarch and his subjects, both rested, in the last analysis, on a gratuitous legal postulate: namely, that fathers have a legal claim to obedience on the part of their children, and that all agreements must be kept on both sides, or that breach on one side justifies breach on the other.

It has been repeatedly pointed out, of late years, how insufficient were these legal metaphors to support the weight of argument cast upon them. Nevertheless, their prevalence from the times of Locke to those of Blackstone, and in such various hands as those of Hume, Montesquieu, Rousseau, and Burke, is a remarkable proof of the ease with which men's imagination—partly through indolence and partly through inadvertence—accommodates itself to legal imagery. A similar and illustrative caution is supplied by the history, at one epoch after another, of the evolution of Christian doctrine.

The notion of a 'Social Contract' was unfortunate in every aspect, historical, ethical, and even legal; and its only virtue was that it served as a convenient formula to express important and neglected truths. Historically, it postulated a primitive but imaginary condition of society in which a people and their designated rulers stood face to face with each other, and, after fairly contemplating all the circumstances, and the nature of the acts promised on each side, without misunderstanding, fear, or fraud, bound themselves and their descendants to all time. Ethically and legally there could be no more reason for keeping a contract than there is for loyalty on the part of the subjects, and good government on the part of the King, in the absence of any express or understood promises. Thus the notion of a contract, fictitious in itself, added nothing to the fact of obligation on either side, while it led to political confusion by withdrawing people's minds from the real grounds and moral foundation on which the reciprocal duties of the Governor and the Governed rest.

5. The American Revolution which resulted in the birth of the United States, while it contained many new political elements, had in it much in common with the previous revolution in England. This is especially manifested in the appeal made at the outset, and again and again in public documents of constitutional significance, to legal principles supposed to be inherent in the English Constitution and to which it was alleged that the English Government, by imposing a Parliamentary tax on the Colonies, was unfaithful. But for a period of some two hundred years the thirteen Colonies had been achieving, each for itself, an independent political existence, by the help of their original charters, (which embodied many of the most cherished but hitherto unwritten doctrines of the English Constitution, in the same form in which they subsequently re-appeared in the Constitution of the United States,) of the English Common Law, and of their own administrative system, acting in harmony with the English Parliament and the Government at

home. Thus, when the moment of revolution came, the legal points at issue between the Colonies and the British Parliament were only a part of the main question. Another equally significant question was how far, and in what way, the Colonies could co-operate among themselves so as to present a united front, not only for purposes of physical resistance at the moment but for those of permanent political organisation.

There had been temporary confederations of several of the Colonies for definite purposes on several occasions during the previous hundred years. But these coalitions implied no more than mutual temporary concessions for the purpose of securing joint and consistent action. So soon as a durable project was entertained of severing all the Colonies from their connection with a strong State bent on holding them fast,—or, as seemed likely, on recovering them at the earliest opportunity--some principles of conciliation must needs have been discovered which could go deeper than the disintegrating differences which accidentally separated, or tended to separate, Colony from Colony. The enthusiasm of the revolutionary war helped towards the acceptance and diffusion of such principles, though it was not without repeated trials and failures,—some of them only recently enacted and redressed,—that they became translated into a new Constitutional structure. Thus the broad and emphatic truisms of the Declaration of Independence must be read side by side with the new written Constitution in its successive forms, and are, in fact, its truest commentary,—especially when illustrated by the constitutional charters of the several Colonies. Among the greatest additions made to political experience by the American revolution, and recorded in the Constitution, are the doctrines, first, that a competent judicial authority is the proper and final test of the constitutional validity of a new law; and secondly, that every people, when deliberately and solemnly appealed to, is competent to revise to any extent its own system of Government.

At the time of the outburst of the American war, revolution implied federation, and federation implied revolution. The mode in which federation was alone possible in the circumstances of the American Colonies supplied a series of arduous problems, for the theoretical as well as practical solution of which there existed or arose a class of statesmen who, taken altogether, have been for political sagacity and acumen without parallel in political history. If the writers in the 'Federalist' and their worthy successors, who have critically examined and expounded every clause and almost every phrase and term in the American Constitution, have failed to construct a Science of Politics, it must be remembered that it was not their purpose to do so. Properly enough, they wrote for the emergencies and needs of their own country; though it happens that according as, in the progress of civilisation, good institutions become increasingly prevalent, the conditions of good government tend to become identical everywhere, and he who writes for any one State writes for all.

It is certain that the lessons to be learnt from the American school of politicians, especially in respect to the working of institutions on a Federal basis and scattered over an enormous breadth of territory, are by no means exhausted. Indeed, there is no Government the experience of which is more constantly cited in illustraticn of every species of political theory, and about the true nature and bearing of which more misapprehensions are afloat.

6. It might have been expected that such a cataclysm as the first French revolution, directly affecting, as it did, the fortunes of so many countries and Governments, would have had a conspicuous influence on the theoretical handling of all political topics. It needs but to read Burke's 'Reflections,' and to contrast them with Thomas Paine's more brilliant reply, to estimate the changed point of political vision effected by the events in France. Rousseau and Voltaire, and the school of the Encyclopedists generally, are usually referred to as having prepared men's minds for the Revolution and facilitated its course. It is rather the case that the appearance of this class of thinkers and writers was the first step in the Revolution itself. When once conscious thought was turned upon the institutions of the old Régime, they must have been peremptorily condemned. The ultimate revolt was successful, not merely because the whole people suffered and public justice was set at nought, but because the political institutions were one and all so rotten at the core that there was no rallying point round which the defenders of things as they were could assemble themselves to save the Constitution. There were, no doubt, a great number and variety of keenly appreciated interests; but there was no common faith or loyalty. Thus the fall of the Bastille surely betokened the fall of the Monarchy; and, because the Monarchy was the Constitution, great was the fall of it.

Hence the most notable political mark of what may

be called the school of the French Revolution has been, on the one hand, an indifference to the teaching of experience, and, on the other, an undue sanguineness as to the mechanical influences of Constitutional forms. This is the worst side of the picture. The best side is, that the same school is eagerly receptive of schemes of political improvement, hopeful of the possibilities of human nature, and generally exempt from prejudice, or prepossession with fixed ideas. The result is that what is truly national in French politicians, having no natural root to adhere to, is apt to be narrow, exclusive, and selfish, though often concealed under a show of cosmopolitanism; while in American, and, it may be said, in English politicians, what is national is a necessary condition of all political thought, and therefore implies no narrow-minded and irrational preference for any particular country, but recognises as the first duty of a State the obligation to contribute, with all other States, towards a central and common aim, to the accomplishment of which all human life tends.

The secondary and indirect influences of the French Revolution on political thought and knowledge have been more efficacious than the primary and direct. English political speculation, since the Revolution of 1688, had been oscillating between a defence of what were held to be the principles of the Revolution,—which usually degenerated into a purely legal argument proceeding from some assumed premises, true or not,—and vague dissertations on ideal forms of Government, constructed without reference to the nature of man as properly interpreted, or to the historical antecedents of the only States on whose behalf such hypothetical creations were devised. The lessons of the

EFFECTS OF THE FRENCH REVOLUTION. 51

French Revolution in its later stages, when constructive work was called for to fill the place of what was abolished, were serviceable to teach and drive home the truths, that there is no one form of Government or of political organisation which can at once be fitted to every people at any and every period; that when a decided breach with the past has been made by a nation, it needs a tedious and, usually, lengthened experience for the people to become habituated to fresh institutions and to obtain for themselves the advantages of stable constitutional order; that, in the case of an hereditary monarchy, the dynastical pretensions of excluded members of the royal family interpose special obstacles in the way of comprehensive change, but that these obstacles decrease with the lapse of time; and finally, that the most volcanic upheaval of the outward structure and form of Government may still leave the hidden vices of a centralised administration, especially as conducted by a network of police, just where they were.

These and similar lessons are, of course, only partially taught at present, but the contagious influence of popular institutions has been radiating to a wider and wider circle throughout the present century, and especially since 1848. Even the most conservative and the most despotically governed States, as Austria, Prussia, and even Russia, have submitted to the process of internal change which political events, wars, and legal reforms—as facilitated by the diffusion and popularity of the *Code Napoléon*—have contributed to bring about. A corresponding impulse has been given to the theoretical study of the chief departments of political knowledge, such as Political Economy, abstract Jurisprudence, Social Ethics, and Constitutional as well as International Law. The novel attention directed to such studies as these is a sign and consequence of the ferment in action as well as in theory which has pervaded European politics during the last thirty years; and the proximate causes of this ferment must be sought for in the social and political disruption in France at the close of the last century.

7. There has to be characterised one notable contribution to the Science of Politics in the present century, which in many respects recals the treatise of Aristotle, though it has the advantage of that treatise in being based on an additional experience, lasting over some 2000 years, of political vicissitudes, and in being constructed after the inductive method of reasoning in all its possible extensions had attained complete development.

M. Auguste Comte clearly descried two leading truths, to which, as taken together and as tracked out with all their consequences, no sufficient justice was done by any previous writer. These truths were :— the one, that the constructive politics of the future must be based on the history of the past; the other, that political science was a composite study and presupposed the complete apprehension of every other branch of science, beginning with the physical, such as astronomy, and ending with the moral, such as ethics and sociology. It is in the collocation of these two truths, and in the laborious and detailed illustration of the mode in which the new method ought to be conformed to, that M. Auguste Comte's characteristic contribution to the Science of Politics consists.

There are, however, in his political treatises other features little less important than these. There is written on every line of them the assertion that the claims of order and of progress can be reconciled by the use of good political institutions; but that these institutions can only be made to work duly and produce their legitimate fruit by the use of a diffused system of education and continual moral discipline reaching to all classes of society and based on the most advanced knowledge of the day. If M. Comte has failed to complete the task he so grandly inaugurated, it has only been because the work was too great for a single man or for a single country. It is others, and not he, who upon these foundations have built wood, hay, and stubble.

M. Comte's Treatises are the latest contribution to the Science of Politics in its true and comprehensive form as a fully reasoned out department of knowledge. But the present century,—especially the last half of it,—has witnessed the production of certain tentative and partial political systems which have had a noticeable influence on public thought, and have for the most part been useful contributions towards the erection of an edifice more complete than themselves. To this class of thinkers belong the schools of Mazzini, of the Continental Socialists, and of the English Utilitarians.

The influence of all these schools has been deep and extensive, and at present shows no signs of early exhaustion. But in spite of the undoubted merits of each one particular school, and notwithstanding the valuable ethical protests and discoveries made by each, they have been, universally, the products of violent political reactions. They are the efflorescence of passing political circumstances, and not the ultimate fruit of accumulated thought. Great and noble as were the aspirations of Mazzini, republican institutions were for him primarily a repudiation of Austrian and priestly tyranny, and the expression of a belief in the doctrine of a Divine calling for men and for nations, rather than a scientific enquiry into facts either past or present. In the same way the various modifications of Socialism which have manifested themselves in Germany, Russia, and France, are nothing more than partial and one-sided protests against the unequal distribution of wealth, the usurpations of privileged classes, the impostures of ecclesiastical officials, or the administrative cruelty which is so frequently the offspring of a highly centralised system of Government,—whatever its name and form. In its various phases and according to special national conditions, what is known by the generic name of Socialism appears as the enemy now of private property, now of aristocratic and kingly privilege, now of centralised administration, now of the institutions of the Christian Church. Thus, while the possibility, and the actual existence, of so highly organised a remonstrance against prevalent ideas and facts must needs be noticed and accounted for by the scientific political inquirer, it cannot be said that Socialism in itself constitutes an independent school of scientific Politics.

8. The attitude of the English Utilitarians, being more allied than that of the Socialist schools to the position of logical and comprehensive reasoners, would seem, in itself, favourable to the creation of a true school of scientific thought. The men who have mainly repre-

sented the Utilitarian system in England,—of which more will be said in the chapter which deals with Ethics in their bearing on Politics,—that is, Jeremy Bentham, the two Mills, John Austin, George Cornewall Lewis, and George Grote (the historian)—are a race of thinkers who could not have failed to exercise a conspicuous influence in the region of practical and of theoretical politics,—to whatever school they might have inclined. But, with respect to most of them, a vehement reactionary spirit has been more noticeable than a simple and uncomplicated search for scientific truth. They have thus been usually indifferent to the necessity of patient historical investigation, on the results of which alone a sound inductive process could be based; and furthermore, have been antipathetic, if not hostile, to every form of religious belief. Considering the place that religious belief holds in the national affairs of every existing State and has occupied in the evolution of modern Christianised society and Government, it is an obvious disqualification in a thinker or a school of thought if there is an absence of all sympathy with, or recognition of, the religious emotions of mankind. Utilitarianism is by no means, in itself, bound up with religious indifference, but, owing to intelligible causes, the English school of Utilitarians have undoubtedly manifested marked repugnance to the religious sentiment in all its phases. This indicates an unphilosophical state of mind and has been a serious bar in the way of the creation of an English school of Scientific Politics.

CHAPTER II.

POLITICAL TERMS.

THE first step in establishing the scientific claims of a department of knowledge is to show that its leading terms admit of being precisely explained and of having their meaning definitely fixed. What is or is not a true 'definition' has been a matter of so much dispute, if not of verbal quibbling, that it is safer to forego at the outset all attempt to construct a list of definitions. But it is of the utmost importance to use all terms which repeatedly occur in the treatment of a Science with all the attainable consistency, and to explain with complete clearness the facts and ideas which the terms denote.

There are some special reasons why language is peculiarly subject in political speech and discussion to flux and vacillation of import, and therefore, why the processes of definition and explanation are peculiarly difficult. In the first place, political terms are largely in use among classes who either are habitually inexact in their use of language or who have a positive motive, —good, bad or indifferent,—to be inexact themselves or to encourage inexactness in others. Popular speech is at every moment handling the common words which are, of necessity, pressed into the service of political speculation and debate. These words therefore carry with them, wherever they go, the looseness and variability of meaning they contract in the market-place and by the domestic fire-side.

Political science can never claim for itself a separate terminology possessing only technical terms with a fixed and unswerving meaning. These advantages are monopolised by the physical sciences, especially by those of a more recondite nature and which are least distorted by the vulgar dialect. The studies of Ethics, Law, and Politics are so near to human and social life, in respect of their subject-matter, that they incur the fate of having all their leading terms infected by those current sentiments and prejudices which impress themselves so deeply on the popular words and conversational forms most in use. It is impossible wholly to rescue political terms from the quagmire of misuse into which they thus habitually fall. The most that can be done is to ascertain the various meanings or shades of meaning which an important term, needed for scientific use, bears in the common speech of the people, and to select one meaning or a limited number of meanings for scientific recognition. The next step is to be consistent in adhering to this meaning or meanings and to allow no further metaphorical or analogical diversions.

But political terms do not merely suffer in fixity of meaning from the abuses common to words in familiar popular use. They are, furthermore, peculiarly exposed to a special liability to abuse from the practice of rhetorical argument conducted either on the public platform or in the popular legislature or in the columns of the public journal. The terms *republic, democracy, aristocracy, centralisation, liberty, self-government,* and the like are all capable of a favourable or unfavourable use, and it can only be on a fair examination of all the circumstances of the case to which they purport to apply that the sense in which they are employed in any special case can be determined. It, unfortunately, is often for the apparent and momentary interest of the speaker or writer to wrest the meanings of political terms and to hide from the hearer or reader one of its undoubted significations, while forcing into undue prominence another. This is done habitually in the case of all excited speech or persuasive appeals, and political terms such as *right, freedom, equality, crime, government,* and the like are the first and most constant victims of this form of abuse.

In the second place, political terms are liable to distortion from a cause which is the opposite of the one just described. For legal, diplomatic, and certain administrative purposes, political terms are often employed with an inflexible rigidity of meaning which is at once diverse from their lax popular use and also from the less rigid though definite signification needed by the requirements of a true Political Science. For instance, in a political discussion, orally conducted, in reference to a proposed land-law, those who take part in the debate will have repeated occasion to use such words as *land, tenure, landlord, tenant, rent, improvements, compensation, notice, letting,* and *hiring.* For the purposes of the discussion immediately in hand it may be sufficient that the speakers all understand each other, and it is desirable that no speaker should be stringently confined to a pedantic exactness in the use of his words. Something more precise is demanded than in occasional talk, proportionate to the gravity of the issue and the presumable mental training of the speakers; but an over refined circumscription of the use of common words would defeat its own purpose, and would rather impede than advance the discovery of truth and the reconciliation of opposed opinions.

But every one of the terms above adduced by way of illustration has contracted a strict legal meaning. Most of them have been imported into written law; and all of them have formed the subject-matter of closely-reasoned arguments in Courts of Justice, and of consequent judicial decisions. It happens too, often enough, that the very persons who are called upon to use these terms in political assemblies, in view of contemplated legislation, are the same persons who in Courts of Justice,—it may be the same day,—are under the necessity of attributing to each of those terms an import of the utmost attainable precision and fixity. Thus it comes about that while the terms of political science are peculiarly exposed to abuse and vacillation through conversational laxity, they are likewise exposed to the risk of ambiguities owing to the simultaneous functions they perform in the technical language of law, diplomacy, and administration.

In the third place, political terms suffer in a peculiar degree from a cause which is the enemy of all fixity of meaning in terms,—incessant, though imperceptible, changes in the nature of the things and facts which they are used to denote. History is full of illustrations of this phenomenon, and sometimes the consequence is even widespread misunderstandings. This is especially the case when the people of one country try to acquaint themselves with the political condition, wants, and controversies of another country.

For instance, the term *constitutional* is a peculiarly modern product. It had no corresponding term in the States of the Ancient World. It would seem to express an outgrowth of the basis of reconciliation on which it was possible for feudally opposed classes and persons to live side by side. It is a matter of mere curious research to attempt to fix the period in which the term *constitution* was first habitually used in its modern sense. But it was, undoubtedly, the contests,—always conducted on an assumed basis of reciprocal right,—between the English Commons and the Feudal Monarch, with or without the mediation of the Peers of the Realm, that first gave relevancy to the notion of a State's constitution. What was in accordance with the subsisting and well-understood relationship between the classes of persons whose political claims against each other were expressed in that relationship was *constitutional*,—what violated or threatened to violate that relationship was *unconstitutional*.

In the Ancient World, the notion of large classes of persons having indefeasible moral rights as against each other was wholly absent. There were interests, and there might be temporary compacts; and there was always organised force; but there was not, even in democratical Athens and in republican or oligarchical Rome, at their best, a settled and publicly confessed reconciliation of the mutually opposed and conflicting claims of large classes of the population to which the name *constitution* alone belongs. There was a good substitute for a constitution in the fortunate discovery or natural development of wise, equal, and well distributed systems of Government in due subjection to popular scrutiny and control. But this result was fortuitous and implicit, the transient exhibition of an equilibrium of competing forces and not the stable and consciously maintained platform for the adjustment of antithetical moral claims. It was possible enough for Aristotle to enumerate and describe all the subsisting forms of Government in the Greek cities. But had he attempted to describe, with his inimitable capacity for ethical analysis, the real foundations on which political stability in the several States rested, the want of anything corresponding to constitutional rights would have been at once apparent. The mere prevalence of slavery, —as was shown of late years in the case of the United States,—must have either proscribed the notion of a constitution or exhibited such palpable anomalies as to bring about what might have been premature revolutions.

The history of the word *party*, and, still more, that of special party names, is a further instance of the flux of political language through political events often of a silent and scarcely perceptible kind. It may be said, indeed, that such terms as these are in themselves too inexact, and that they denote phenomena which are in their nature too evanescent, for them ever to become incorporated in a system of Political Science. But a recognition of the facts of which the organisation into parties is an expression forms part of that general political experience on which the truths of the science, if there be one, are built up. Therefore in discussing, say, the modern devices for facilitating popular representation and rendering democratic institutions compatible with stability and unity of administration, an analysis of the essential mechanism of party Government must take place. But parties, though retaining the names once stamped upon them, often undergo the most complete transmutations. The 'Whig' in the politics of the United States has little relation to the modern Whig in England; and the 'democrat' and 'republican' on one side of the Atlantic are still less akin to the 'democrat' and 'republican' severally on the other. Parties in the representative Assemblies of the British Colonies are organised on entirely different principles from those which have originated, and which maintain in being, the political parties at home. The parties, again, in the French, German, and Italian Parliaments can only be understood by reference to historical facts studied in view of the particular constitutional organisation to which the facts relate.

What has here been said about 'party' and 'constitution' might be further illustrated by reference to a train of words such as *Parliament, prerogative, Crown, franchise, Church, State*, which,—however definite in meaning at a particular moment for a given State,—must be investigated and defined afresh if the reasoning be transferred to another State or to a different epoch.

The peculiar dangers and perplexities incident to Political terminology have thus been adverted to. It fortunately happens, however, that a distribution can be made between the terms which are of more general importance, as denoting facts of the highest degree of universality and significance, and those of less importance for scientific purposes, as denoting facts peculiarly liable to change and diversity in their manifestations. As to this latter class of terms it is useless in a scientific treatise to attempt any enumeration of them. Such an enumeration could only be based on transient facts and phenomena, and at the best would be only descriptive of what has existed or happens now, in fact, to exist. As to these terms, the most that can be done is to interpose cautions of the kind already alluded to and founded on the intrinsic liability of all this class of terms to flux and variability of meaning brought about in the most subtle and unsuspected way. But as to the other class of political terms of the most universal kind, inasmuch as they denote conceptions not less general than Government itself it is possible to attach to them an exact meaning which need experience no change with the progressive changed condition of human affairs. There is needed only an exhibition of the primary and essential composition of a State, in its strictly political aspect, and all the necessary conceptions, with the terms needed to express them, at once come into relief.

1. *State.*

The most central notion in Political Science is that of the *State*; and if it were once clearly ascertained what is and what is not comprehended under this term, many of the most harassing misunderstandings appertaining to the subject would be avoided. The notion of the *State* as a distinct political unit is, in fact, a product of purely accidental development, and on this ground it might be doubted whether the notion is not in itself too ephemeral and fluctuating to become the subject-matter of scientific reasoning. But it is the inherent peculiarity of political phenomena that the experience on which a knowledge of them rests has to be gathered from a very circumscribed field, and that the mere existence of any such field at all is a special attainment of advancing civilisation. Thus the *State* in the stricter modern signification of the term as a political integer, differs at once from the Grecian city (πόλις), the Roman republic (*respublica*) and the German Feudal Empire which attempted to reproduce the symbolic unity, the titles, and the pretensions, of its great Roman type.

The modern notion of the State was, indeed, not brought into clear consciousness till a number of parallel States presented themselves side by side, and each of them, by enforcing its own claims against one and another of the rest, manifested to itself and to the world its own personality, independence, and integral unity. In this sense no one State existed before there was a plurality of States. The invading barbarian tribes settling upon the sharply marked out Roman provinces developed the essential relationships of Feudalism. These relationships comprised the hierarchical subordination of persons and classes, the recognition of territorial ownership and conditions of occupation, and the existence of a variety of quasi-moral ties pervading the family and other social groups and expressing themselves in such terms as *allegiance, fealty, loyalty*, as well as in their counterparts *felony* and *treason*. Thus inside the nascent communities there were nurtured ideas, customs, practices, institutions, and associated conceptions, all tending to arrest the centrifugal impulses of a wandering and purely military life, and to create two poles of national existence—a king and a fixed territory.

But the only reason for insisting strictly on territorial limits was the juxtaposition of a series of competing and similarly organised societies, each of which was engaged in appropriating to its own uses a determinate portion of land. Agricultural needs, revenue considerations, and the commercial advantages attaching to special routes, harbours, and productive districts, tended to impart emphasis to the practice of territorial demarcation, as loosely and extensively inaugurated by the provincial distribution of the Roman Empire. Dialectical peculiarities and affinities, race sympathies, and instincts of fellowship generated by neighbourhood and by the reciprocal ties of military command and service, helped to bind together, for purposes both of internal organisation and of resistance to external pressure, the inhabitants of a clearly defined territorial area. Add to these the influence of the ecclesiastical institutions of Christendom, the local episcopacy and presbytery, the representative synods and councils, the territorial bases, small and great, of Church administration and service, and the functions of international arbitrator gradually assumed by the Bishop of Rome.

There was nothing wanting to the complete birth of the modern State but the final dissolution of the antiquated feudal tie between State and State expressed in the evanescence of the Holy Roman Empire, and the formation of a new principle of centralisation within the State itself, brought about by the constitutional action and reaction between a modern monarch and his subjects. The *State*, in the modern acceptation of the term, carries with it the ideas of territorial limitation of population past, present, and to come, and of organisation for purposes of Government. Thus a series of affiliated ideas and terms at once come to the surface, such as *Government, Law, Legislation, Administrative, Executive, Right, Prerogative, Liberty*.

It might be asked why the accidental re-arrangements of the countries of Europe which followed on the fall or transmutation of the Roman Empire should dictate, for ever, the notion of a true State. To this it may be replied that the Geographical area to which the Science of Politics extends at present is limited—as will be seen farther on—to the countries of Europe and of North America and to those countries which are directly subjected to the influence and dominating control of Europe and the United States. Thus it is not saying too much to allege that, for all purposes of practical politics and, therefore, of that Science on which all sound practice must rest, the State is that integral unity which has been discovered by the accidents of European development.

It might further be argued that the definition or explanation of the term *State*, which has just been propounded, is no mere accidental product of a casual development, but encloses a permanent and necessary conception. The nations of Europe would seem to have by no means as yet completed the process of their transformation, and the novel claims in favour of so-called 'nationality' point to much further re-construction still going on and yet to come. But it is to be noticed that all the changes are in one and the same direction,—that of defining a national area of a size large enough to promote and admit of all the economical and constitutional re-actions needed for the adequate evolution of human powers and relationships, but not large enough to swallow up all individual and national idiosyncrasies in an over-centralised dominion. Where the limit of the true State is to be fixed must be matter of experimental struggle rather than of philosophic vaticination.

It is scarcely necessary to advert to the abuse of the term *State* both in the popular dialect and, less excusably, in the speech of professed politicians or political orators. Thus the *State*, at one moment, means the Governing authority as opposed to the governed; at another, the secular authorities, legislative and executive, as opposed to the ecclesiastical. Sometimes the *State* is contrasted with the existing or temporary mechanism for governing the State, that is, with what is called the Government. At other times the *State* implies the body politic, that is, the nation regarded as a subject of Government; and this last meaning is most in accord with the results of the historical analysis just concluded, though serious omissions in the full and proper connotation of the term,—as in respect of territorial limits, and of continuous identity in point of time,—are not avoided. Lastly, there is the special meaning of the term appropriate to the constitution of the United States of North America, and the technical meaning known to International Law, according to which the State is an entity having certain recognisable predicates, such as independence of other entities like itself, and the power of self-government in respect of determining upon and controlling its own internal organisation.

2. *Government.*

The history of the European State has been seen to presuppose the fact of Government. Had the tribes which overran the provinces of the Roman Empire been essentially anarchical, or had the result of their irruption been to produce limitless and lasting anarchy, no true States could have arisen. There could have been no demarcation of national territory; no national self-consciousness based on well-preserved customs commemorative of the past and on more and more luminous anticipations of the future; no cherishing of the dislocated relics of Roman law, municipal institutions, and administrative discipline. But habits of Government, however rude, were well formed among the tribes before invasions and a variety of favourable circumstances conspired to rivet and develop these habits, while the amalgamation of native and Roman inhabitants of the newly occupied lands was being effected.

These habits of Government imply far more than a mere actual subjection of a multitude to the will and physical control of one or of a few. An actual subjection such as this may co-exist with all the elements of disunion and of mutual repulsion ready to disclose themselves at the first chance opportunity. Habitual deference to the commands of an authority elevated above the heads of the populace is a result of slow growth, and, usually, of arduous struggles and disappointing retrogressions. It grows out of tardily formed incrustations of religious ritual, social manners, military usages, and family sentiments. It is enforced by joint enterprises, military and civil, on an ever widening scale of magnitude, and is recommended by more and more prevailing considerations of economic advantage, and, at a later stage, of international rivalry. This habit of submission to orderly Government, when once formed, becomes its own chief cause. The practice of unconscious obedience to law begets desire for law, impatience of anarchy, and indignation against casual breakers of the public peace.

The demand for Government simultaneously calls

forth, first, a ruling class, and afterwards a profession of politicians in the highest sense of this sometimes abused term. The phenomenon of Government is only to be accounted for by supposing the presence of a number of contributory circumstances. It is not enough, with Hobbes, to assume that it is the mere product of usurpation and violence, or, at least, of mere superiority of physical strength; nor, with Filmer, to deduce it from no more complex an origin than the analogies of parentage; nor, again, with Locke or even Blackstone, to base it on legal arrangements formally entered into with each other by the governors and the governed. The phenomenon is rather a product of a congeries of favourable conditions, including, indeed, some or all of those which were once accepted as solely sufficient explanations, but by no means confined to them.

3. *Law.*

Though the phenomenon of *Law* is intimately bound up with that of *Government*, yet modern criticism and research have gone far to establish the existence of important differences between the two orders of ideas. For instance, antiquarian investigations into the condition of primitive societies have brought to light almost unsuspected stages of existence in which Law may be said to have existed without Government, while nothing is more familiar than the fact that in all countries a settled Government subsists for many ages before the conscious manufacture of Law. But both in the one case and in the other,—that is, whether there is, strictly speaking, no Government at all and no true State, or whether Government has merely not yet advanced to the legislative or law-making stage, all the essential characteristics of law may be present. All the supplementary aid which Government can give is to ascertain and fix the rules of law actually in force, to lend its physical aid to the maintenance of their authority, and, as occasion suggests, to modify, amend, and even annul the rules themselves.

When it is remembered that the formulated usages which take the form of law affect every part of the social framework at its most sensitive points,—as, for instance, the family relationships, the ownership of land and of all other things, the business transactions of the shop and the market place,—it ceases to be a wonder that a new Government, suddenly introduced, by conquest, cession, or alleged right of discovery, into a country already possessing stable institutions, can do little, for years to come, to change those institutions, and rarely has the chance of introducing radically new ones.

Some conquering nations have understood these truths by instinct. Others have learnt them by failure and suffering. Alexander and the Ptolemies vindicated them with notable success in their administration of Egypt. To a large extent the Romans acted upon them in provincial administration, at all events in intention; and to that extent they were, on the whole, in the best days of the Empire, successful in their provincial government. The Northern invaders of the Roman Empire pursued a similar policy, as the invaluable so-called Barbaric Codes, prepared for the Roman subjects of the conquered provinces, testify, and with a success demonstrated by the rapid development of a new national life on the ruins of the old. The Arabs in their conquests generally pursued a like policy, while the triumphs of their religion as well as of their arms brought about, in an incredibly short space of time, a total moral and legal reconstruction of society in those countries which they succeeded in permanently occupying.

The English in India have found it to be one of their main difficulties to understand the prevalent legal rules, especially in regard to inheritance and the occupation of land; the more so as these rules differ widely from village to village, and still more widely from province to province. The obstacles to having any uniform rules, whether framed from a comparison of all the chief existing groups of regulations and usages, or on some new principle recommended by general expediency, and not out of harmony with current facts and ideas, have proved hitherto all but insuperable. Nevertheless, way has been made in the direction of settled and uniform law congenial to the habits of the people, by the institution of central Courts of Justice, by special land legislation for particular districts, and by codifying such parts of the existing law in an amended form as, from time to time, it has seemed possible to codify.

It need not be said that in Ireland the English pursued a policy exactly the opposite of that adopted in India; and the results have been such as are only too notorious and might almost seem to be irreparable.

The force of those spontaneous usages, which operate as nascent law in primitive communities, is much intensified and concentrated by the co-existence of a variety of religious sanctions. It has often been noticed that in early society religious and secular ordinances of all sorts are inextricably mixed together. Not only in ascertaining the forms of marriage and the modes of discharging purely religious obligations, but in the protection of boundaries; in the use of the oath in judicial enquiries; and in the solemn rites which accompany the more notable legal acts, especially in respect of inheritance, the intervention of a priesthood is conspicuously called for. Besides this, no certain line of distinction is drawn between sins, crimes, and civil injuries; and consequently the whole forces of the growing society are directed towards repressing each and all of them with impartial zeal and generating an habitual tone of thought and opinion unfavourable to transgression.

It is this tone of thought and opinion which the Government secures on its side when it forbears to innovate, except by slow and tentative degrees, on the fixed habits and dispositions of the people. It is impossible to over-estimate the force of custom in human affairs, and the serviceableness of its potency when rightly turned to account. To defer to the actual prevalence of certain classes of ideas, rules, and institutions, is by no means to organise stagnation and immobility. It is only to recognise that men must be governed in accordance with the laws of their nature at a given time and place; and that much of this nature is the product of inherited habits and accumulated associations of all sorts. These habits and associations may be slowly and gradually deflected into new directions and refashioned afresh. It is the province of a wise Government to bring this about, and here and there, especially in respect of cruel and inhuman practices, it may be necessary to prune with a strong and firm hand. But as a rule it is prudent to employ custom as the ally of Government rather than to challenge it as its foe.

The large bulk of a nation's laws has thus its origin

in customs which have, as it were, spontaneously come into existence and been maintained in force, partly by the mere facility of obeying the promptings of habit, partly by the influence of public opinion exerted in favour of what is familiar and consecrated by long use, and partly by the felt convenience of having settled rules, institutions, and practices, to which the mass of the community may be expected at all times to conform. But though these customary rules and usages not only contain the germ of all future law but are identical in spirit and matter with the most important portions of that law, yet it is convenient to confine the use of the term *law* to those rules which attain commanding validity only when the State can be looked upon as fully developed in all its essential departments. Before this epoch of the complete evolution of the State it may, indeed, happen that many of the phenomena of law are present, as though by anticipation, in an unmistakable guise.

For instance, a regular practice of recurring to Courts of Arbitration, more or less adequately and permanently organised, may subsist, and the award of the Court may be carried out by the exertion of some amount of social force. There may also be a skilled class of professional men, usually belonging to a priestly caste, who will be held possessed of exclusive competency to decide disputed points in the detailed application of recognised rules, or to draw out of some mysterious repository a hitherto unrecognised or forgotten rule or custom believed to be appropriate to a new case in hand, or to determine the equitable claims of rival disputants who each rely on some admitted custom as telling in their favour. But in such a condition of society, there is, as yet, no central authority, supreme over all the community, which, in however imperfect and inchoate a form, may be said to wield the forces of the whole community and to represent its will. In other words, there is no Government in the political sense, no State, and no true Law. Law is, in fact, the detailed expression of the will of the State published through its originator, the Government,—that is, the Supreme Political Authority of the day. Thus, however closely related is early law to highly developed custom, yet they must not be confused together, and cannot be so confused without loss of distinctness in political thought.

It is possible that, owing to foreign conquest, internal discord or revolution, or mere weakness in the political institutions, an assemblage of laws may, at a particular moment, be imposed on a people who are unprepared for them by preceding customs, or who are, on other grounds, persistently averse to them. In such a case there will be a more or less conscious and open struggle maintained between the genius, spirit, and mental and moral necessities, of the people, and the mere physical power, expressing itself by law, of the ruler. If no compromise is arrived at by a gradual process of mutual concessions, the only two alternative solutions are, either that the State is dissolved into lasting anarchy and barbarism, or else a certain amount of civic order is maintained,—possibly through the influence of a continuing religious unity,—while an enduring opposition is kept up between the people and the Government which is incompatible with all political and social progress and constantly threatens revolutions and spasmodic changes in the personality of the rulers.

Instances of all these classes of consequences, which follow from attempting to impose laws out of harmony with the previous usages and the temperament of the people, are abundantly supplied by history, though the influence of religion and of priestly castes or functionaries has often gone far to counteract or modify purely political causes and to enhance the difficulty of an exact analysis.

It is impossible to exaggerate the mediating influence of the early Christian Church in promoting at once national distinctness and international unity among the new States which arose from the settlement of the Teutonic invading tribes in the provinces of the Roman Empire. This was effectual not only through the hierarchical and territorial organisation of the Church but through the body of common rules, ordinances, practices, and ritual, which laid hold of the bulk of the people at the most susceptible part of their being, and in an incredibly short space of time took the place of all purely secular rules and customs, however ancient and fervently cherished by the popular imagination.

It was the good fortune of the Arab conquerors that religious proselytism went hand in hand with military conquest; and the permanence of these consequences may largely be accounted for in this way. The victories of the Ottoman Turks further illustrate the force which a military adventurer possesses when he carries with him a religious law either already professed in the invaded countries or which he is prepared to impose as paramount over all other law. Similar illustrations might be found in the history of the Thirty-years' war in Germany.

It may be feared that, while the religious impartiality of the English in India has won them a character for toleration and justice, the process of governing and civilising the whole country has been impeded and delayed by the want of a more open, if not more intolerant, profession of the religious creed, and observance of the religious law, prevalent among the English people at home.

When once it is settled that Law, in the true sense, can only be found in the perfected, or at least fully created, State, and that Law and Government imply each other, it is obvious that it is of no consequence whether Law be written or unwritten, so far as its essential nature is concerned. It necessarily happens, indeed, that the spontaneous customs of which early law consists, or out of which it is generated, do not admit of being written down even in an unsystematic form. This may be due to the absence of literary methods and habits, to the unsymmetrical and irregular form of the rules themselves, or to conscious reticence on the part of a learned or priestly class who, in pursuit of some end or other,—beneficent or the reverse,—deem it to be inexpedient to communicate to the public more of the customs than from time to time are called for by the exigencies of pending controversies. Primitive codes, such as the XII Tables at Rome, the Laws of Moses, the Capitularies and Codes of Charlemagne and his successors in different countries, by no means mark only a stage of insurrection against the assumptions of a priestly caste. They may indeed denote such a stage, but only as a part of a broader phenomenon.

The essential features of fully developed law, as contrasted with primitive custom, are that it should for the most part be uniform for all the members of the State; that it should be certain, that is, not susceptible of ambiguous and variable interpretations according to the caprice of irresponsible persons; and that its administration should be public, or at least conducted in a method which shall bear searching and even unfriendly public criticism. To substitute such uniform, certain, and generally intelligible, rules for fragmentary and doubtful customs is the obvious interest of every independent ruler who has a clear view of the task of Government which lies before him; and it is a policy which must recommend itself to all statesmen in the nascent community who are bent on bringing about as speedily as possible that national unity and consolidation on which the hopes of order and of progress repose.

It may happen that, even in a highly advanced State, a large portion of the law may for ages continue unwritten; and this may proceed from very opposite causes. Thus there are no indications of a systematised written law in Ancient Egypt, from the earliest times known to us till it became a Roman province; but there are plenty of indications from early papyri and inscriptions that even before the time of Rameses II., in (say) the fifteenth century B.C., the land laws, the laws of inheritance, family law, criminal law and constitutional law, and even the rudiments of a law of Nations, had reached a high degree of development. In Greece, besides the legendary legislation of such statesmen as Lycurgus, Draco and Solon, and the Utopia of Plato's 'Laws,' there are no signs, amidst all the exuberant intellectual activity, of any attempt to recast the national laws and express them in an exact and systematic form. So, in all the feudal States of modern Europe, even in England, it is only within the last century or century and a half that any determined attempts have been made to republish the customary law in a written and clearly intelligible form.

The reasons which delay the reduction of laws to writing are different in different countries, as is manifest from the very opposite circumstances of the countries in which the laws have been left for ages uncodified and unwritten. Among the reasons for maintaining the law in an oral and unsystematic shape was, undoubtedly, the dominant influence of a professional or priestly class, the conservators and interpreters of the national customs, who alone possessed an amount of leisure and education sufficient for the purpose of mastering the whole of the treasured rules and practices and for deliberately determining where and how they apply, in detail, to new and particular cases of fact.

The influence of the priestly colleges in Egypt; of the Parliaments in France, especially that of Paris; of the Judges in England,—who were a direct emanation of the Norman King's feudal court, and were supported at an early stage by a compactly organised legal profession,—was of this overbearing kind; and while, in each case, it tended to keep the law stable and uniform, and perhaps rendered it plastic in its application to individual cases, it made it difficult of reform in compliance with the public needs.

In England as distinguished from other countries the mischief of legal immobility was corrected, partly by the growth of a secondary system of supplementary law known as 'Equity,' and partly by the early development of positive written law.

In Rome the delay in reducing the laws to writing was due, at all events after the date of the XII Tables, to a different cause from that explained above; and the absence of any body of written laws in Greece may probably be explained in the same way as the like phenomenon at Rome.

Both in Rome and in Greece, in their best days, from a political point of view, the national intellect only laid hold of law on the side of procedure. It was in the actual contests of the Forum and of the Dicasteries that the main public interest was aroused, and on these that the broadest amount of scientific zeal was concentrated. In Rome, indeed, in the latter days of the Republic, though the interpretation and application of well settled rules of law in the interest of friends, clients, and pupils, had become the refined pursuit of the wealthy man of culture, yet this implied no widely extended and enlightened care for legal knowledge. The public appetite for acquaintance with the law, even if excited, was constantly appeased by the fortunate device,—afterwards to some extent reproduced in the Court of Chancery in England,—of an assiduous modification of the written and unwritten law through the medium of the Prætor's Edict. By his Edict and his peremptory remedies, the Prætor always presented law before the minds of the people as stable and yet not inflexible from age to age; and by supplementing unwritten traditions with tentative written rules he withdrew attention from the composite and unsystematic character of the whole body of law.

Simultaneously the political activity of the hour in

Rome, as also in Greece, habituated the people to look to persons, and to pressing political measures and exigencies, rather than to abstract logical principles and to the conclusions to be drawn from them. There is an essential incompatibility between a legal and a political age, as between an individual legal and political mind. It was not until the overpowering pressure of the Empire at Rome, and of the Macedonian ascendency in Greece, had paralysed all genuine political activity in both States that the popular and the scientific mind was at leisure to follow purely logical and speculative pursuits. The appearance of such a treatise as the 'Institutes' of Gaius,—which is only a specimen accidentally preserved of countless other similar productions dealing, after a logically arranged method, with the whole or parts of the law,—and of systematic compilations of Imperial enactments, marks the advent of an era of codification which reached its culmination in Justinian's time. In Greece the liberated scientific— and indeed the popular—thought betook itself rather to philosophy than to law, though, in the Logic of Aristotle, which was the last and not the least precious fruit of the Greek mind, that identical tendency is conspicuous which in Rome and Constantinople took the form of legal reasoning and systematisation.

Apart, however, from the consideration of the circumstances which favour the conservation of long established unwritten law generated by primeval custom, the task of re-casting the whole body of national law, written and unwritten, in the systematic shape of a formulated series of positive enactments, without injuriously innovating on fixed rules and institutions, is so difficult that it is no wonder that it has, in fact, never been proceeded with except under some extraordinary and powerful impulse. For a long time, indeed, the whole body of law is so small,—that is, in its express rules and comprehensive principles,—that there is no sufficient reason for undertaking a difficult, hazardous, and thankless task. As the law grows in quantity through the internal development which comes from fresh incrustations of industrial and mercantile customs, and from successive interpretative decisions of Courts of Justice, and through direct legislation, the task of systematic reconstruction becomes at once increasingly difficult and increasingly necessary.

But the minds of lawyers are trained in the law in the form in which it came to them, and therefore they naturally shrink from encountering a change which must be most favourable to the young, who have least to unlearn. They are also abundantly occupied in solving the practical questions which hourly present themselves, and so cannot be expected to afford much time to engage in projects which seem to them speculative and idealistic. On all these accounts, nothing short of urgent political necessity has hitherto produced a total transcription of unwritten into written law. The pressure may proceed from a despotic sovereign, or from a resolute people, or from statesmen acting in the face of circumstances which cannot be evaded.

Thus Justinian only brought to a head a process of comprehensive codification which the distribution and re-combination of the provinces of the Empire between Diocletian's time and his own, the decomposing influence of the ecclesiastical institutions as they became constantly more dominant, and the judicial re-organisation of the Empire effected by himself rendered inevitable. Julius Cæsar seems to have contemplated a like task, though his aims were probably no other than those of Frederick the Great, namely those of making the internal order and unity reflect the external harmony achieved by his arms and policy.

Napoleon I., by Codification, only carried out what had been recognised among the earliest projects of the Revolutionary leaders as one of the most pressing requirements of the Republic. The abolition of the relics of feudalism,—especially in the land laws,—the total reconstruction on a humane and rational basis of the criminal law, and the amalgamating into a common system the usages prevalent in the two classes of provinces governed respectively by Feudal usage and by Roman Law, were all considerations which, in the eyes even of a superficial statesman, made the task of Codification a necessary sequel of the Revolution. Napoleon may have the credit of recognising this to the full, and no doubt his military and organising habits of mind disposed him to follow the same course as those congenial to Julius Cæsar and Frederick the Great of Prussia. That Napoleon used the opportunity of comprehensive legislation to introduce such enactments on Divorce and Succession as would favour the dynastic interests of himself and his family detracts from his moral honesty, but it is no disparagement to his intellectual credit that he perceived one of the most urgent political wants of the day and did his utmost to supply it.

The circumstances of the English in India have been such as to make an entire reconstruction of the prevalent legal systems an ever increasing political necessity in proportion as new States were incorporated and central Courts of Justice were from time to time instituted. The local village customs, the dominant influence of Mahommedan and Brahminic law, especially in matters of inheritance and succession, the so-called 'Regulations' issued by the officials of the English Government, and the occasional legislation of a comprehensive kind by the British Indian Government or by the British Parliament, formed a congeries of laws which rendered the administration of Justice by central Courts, especially of Appeal, a matter of almost insuperable difficulty, and yet which only reflected the alternative anarchy or tyranny that confusion of laws must entail among the population.

It has taken a long time, amid political and military distractions, to reduce even special departments of the law into an organised form not inharmonious with the principles of reason and humanity believed to characterise English Law at home. But the task is rapidly being accomplished. Anyway the Anglo-Indian experience is a good illustration of the bearing of political exigencies on the question of converting unwritten into written law.

Codification has of late years progressed with great rapidity in Canada and the United States of America. It might have been anticipated that fewer obstacles to radical legal change would be encountered among a people whose ancestors had, within very recent times, migrated as colonists from another country and brought their law with them in the detached and insulated form of Royal Charters, and such maxims of the English unwritten law or statutes as were, in the language of Courts of Justice, alone held applicable to them in their new circumstances.

So violent a change of attitude towards the bulk of the national law in use at home could not but prepare the colonists and their descendants for legal and constitutional modifications according as public convenience might from time to time suggest. Similar agencies in the Spanish and French Settlements, which ultimately gravitated, by the force of pacific arrangements or conquest, to the side either of the United States or of the Dominion of Canada, produced like results, manifesting themselves in an easy disposition to amend the law and even to reconstruct its form from the foundation.

The excellent Codes of Louisiana, the partly adopted and partly projected Codes of the State of New York, and the Canadian Codes, incorporating in some cases the old pre-revolution French Law with the modern English and Colonial legislative enactments, are specimens of the superior facility for legal reconstruction which is likely to be found in Colonial settlements as contrasted with the obstacles encountered in long established societies.

As to the employment of the term *Law*, it has been debated whether it should be extended so as to include all commands whatever, express or implied, proceeding, at a given time, from the supreme Political Authority then dominant, and, therefore, to all intents and purposes representing and personating the State; or whether it should be restricted to such of these commands as are designed to meet something more than a merely temporary emergency, and have some generality in their character, as being addressed to classes of persons or as relating to classes of acts commanded or forbidden, or concerned with classes of occasions which are generically described in the terms of the law. It has been said that in the case of a mere single act commanded or forbidden by a Legislature, there lacks the permanence, generality, and in some way the dignity, which are of the essence of a true law.

The real distinction is probably to be sought between the enacting Legislative Authority all whose commands of all sorts are true laws, and the Executive Authority which, though acting in accordance with law, does not make law, but only carries out the will of the Legislature by doing acts of practical Government. Some of these acts often include the issuing of bodies of rules which are not distinguishable from partial Codes of Law. Such are the by-laws of Railway Companies in England as approved by the Privy Council,—which, for some purposes, is a portion of the Executive Government,—and Police or Municipal regulations made by the Chief of the Police or a Mayor and Corporation in accordance with special Acts of Parliament. But though these by-laws, rules, and regulations have all the aspect of true laws, and by virtue of the subordinate legislative powers under which they are made have all the effect and operation of true laws, they are, from the point of view of the authority immediately enacting them, merely Executive Acts.

When a portion of the Legislature, such as the English House of Commons, has customary powers conceded to it for making rules in defence of its own rights, dignity, and authority, and for enforcing compliance by punishing offenders, either within or outside of its own body, by fine and imprisonment, its regulations are true laws in respect of their form and cogency, and in virtue of the delegated authority by means of which they are made. But, from the point of view of the actual enacting authority, they are merely Executive acts, and the House of Commons is, for these purposes, treated as a branch of the Executive Authority, and is endowed with powers appropriate to the due exercise of its functions.

In those cases in which, by the Constitution of the United States, the Senate is empowered, in concert with the President, to do certain purely executive acts,—as to conclude a treaty of peace, or to appoint a foreign ambassador,—the form of these acts may include issuing bodies of rules and regulations binding on all American citizens. But they are only true laws because they are made by a delegated and subordinate Authority dependent on the Legislature,—that is, on Congress as a whole. On the face of them, however much they may bear the semblance of law and have all the effect and operation of law, they are only executive acts.

The opposite phenomenon is manifested so often as the whole Legislature, acting in its corporate capacity, and with the use of the same solemn forms which are observed when it enacts laws, does isolated acts of an executive kind having none of the generality and permanence usually associated with the term *law*. This takes place when a gift of houses or lands is made to a successful general as an heirloom in his family, or when a public ceremonial is decreed, or a grant of money in relief of some private or public disaster awarded, out of the public funds. To the same class of acts would belong the sudden suspension of the common law, or of some general statute, to prevent the crew and cargo of some particular ship believed to carry infection being disembarked at a certain port, or at any port, for a certain time. Here again, a state of things converse to that adverted to above exists. In outward form all these acts are of an executive nature. They are occasional, temporary, almost spasmodic, and seem to have none of the sort of relation to the permanent consciousness of the people, and to their natural expectations, which is the usual characteristic of unmistakable law.

Nevertheless these acts are all true laws, and nothing is gained by not calling them so. They formally emanate from a genuine, and the only genuine, legislative authority. They are commands addressed not only to the persons directly within the purview of the policy resorted to, but to all persons whatever on whom they impose fresh duties. Such persons are not only those whose rights are restricted by the enlargement of the rights of the other person in whose favour the command is issued, but all those judicial and lower executive officials who are bound to take cognisance of the command and to secure general obedience to it exactly as to the most unquestionable legal enactments. Thus, in distinguishing between a law and an executive act, it is rather the ordaining authority than the purport, contents, or form, of the rule that has to be kept in view. This leads at once to a consideration of the terms *Legislative* and *Executive*.

4. *Legislative* and *Executive*.

In early times there is Law and there is an Executive Authority; but either (to put it one way) there is no Legislative Authority, or (to put it another way) the Legislative and Executive Authority are indistinguishable. A Legislative Authority is an Authority engaged in making or altering or repealing laws. But in the earliest form of national society the laws, or recognised usages, of the people are either so immovable that none but a rash and suicidal conqueror ventures to innovate upon them; or else are so uncertain, confused, heterogeneous, and disordered, that the despotic will of that conqueror supplies the only approaches to any settled rule or order. It may be, indeed,—especially as society advances,—that a sort of fixed condition of compromise is attained, and a steady line of demarcation drawn, between the laws which shall be regarded as unalterable and those which may be changed or abolished at the ruler's will. Of this state of things in which the germs of a true political constitution are manifested, specimens were exhibited during the era of the earlier Feudal Monarchies of Europe, and, still more remarkably, in the relations of the Secular Head of the Holy Roman Empire towards his ecclesiastical subjects.

The natural rise of a true Legislative Authority may be not improperly illustrated by the mode in which the English Feudal sovereignty,—with purely executive powers, controlled by the vassals and territorial magnates, and in the presence of a fixed body of customary law,—step by step bifurcated into a legislative and an executive authority, of one of which authorities the monarch was a component portion, and of the other of which he was the chief representative. It was notorious that the change was brought about by the incidental dependence of the monarch, for military services and supplies, first, on his immediate vassals, and afterwards on chosen representatives of town and rural interests throughout the country.

RISE OF A LEGISLATIVE AUTHORITY. 89

The feudal vassals, and subsequently the deputies of the people, made the redress of practical grievances the *conditio sine quâ non* of submitting to taxation for the king's foreign enterprises. But the form which the petition for the redress of these grievances took was the better observance, by the king and his officials, of the terms of some long standing and well recognised compact appertaining to popular or feudal rights; or else of some charter granted by the king or his predecessors; or of some ancient laws,—possibly mythical in their origin, and, at any rate, of uncertain but vaguely beneficial import,—such as the 'Laws of Edward the Confessor.' When the king granted petitions of this sort, there was no true legislation in the fullest sense because there was no intentional or actual change of the law. But the effect undoubtedly was not only to give fresh securities for the recognition of the law by the king and his officials, but, by bringing some of the terms of a partly forgotten and neglected law into fresh prominence, to re-enact the law, and thereby, in fact, to inaugurate a true process of legislation. This process was sometimes carried one stage further, in the case of obstinate abuses,—as in the reign of Richard II.,—by appointing a Commission charged with the function of administering the Government, and, within limits more or less clearly defined, of superintending the execution of the laws hitherto violated.

This act of creating an executive authority is a true legislative act, inasmuch as it imposes new duties, confers new rights, and introduces new rules or ordinances. The Legislative Authority progressively continues to assume its true functions, and it is not long before it begins to criticise the whole existing legal system, and boldly to abolish laws which seem bad, to reform those which are inadequate to their end, and to enact new laws intended to meet the wants of the day.

In this course of inchoate legislation it may happen that a king, like Edward I., may co-operate with the reforming spirit or even take the initiative in broaching novelties. And it is probable enough that in early essays in Legislation, as in the times of Edward III., Richard II., Henry VIII., and even of Elizabeth, serious economical, ethical, and political misadventures may be encountered in entering on yet untried paths. But the important point is that the Legislative Authority thus becomes conscious of its own powers, responsibilities, and distinctness from the Executive Authority as personated by the King.

Where an energetic and independent Legislative Authority in an extreme political emergency goes the length of abolishing the monarch, or the monarchy, as in the case of Charles I. and James II.,—to take no earlier instances,—the Legislative Authority, divorced momentarily even from the monarch himself, becomes conscious of a still more exceptional amount of independence and responsibility. Exerting a new-found capacity of action it takes upon itself to re-cast, within limits defined only by the popular sentiment of the hour, the legal outlines of the Constitution itself, and to emphasise laws and distinct rules of Governmental action in relation to the people, for which only a friendly imagination can find a precedent in the past. Such a legal reconstruction was effectually achieved by the Long Parliament, by the first Parliaments after the Restoration, and by the later Parliaments of William III.

The above account might be regarded as only the

accidental historical development of the Legislative Authority, in relation to the Executive, in one particular country, and therefore as containing no materials, or only casually suggestive ones for the establishment of scientific truths. But a closer examination will show that, just as Feudalism itself is only an illustrative exhibition of a normal and recurrent stage of social and political growth,—in which the military leader establishes definite terms of relationship and of reciprocal service between himself and his companions in arms, and of which the occupation of conquered territory is at once the medium and, as it were, the Sacramental register,—so the escape from Feudalism proved in England by the growth of a genuine Legislative Authority, in opposition to the Executive still represented by the monarch, is a world-wide phenomenon simply made more conspicuous in England by the slow, steady, and uninterrupted manifestation of every one of the links in the chain of development.

In other countries the process has only been accomplished after hundreds of years of political stagnation, or after periods of anarchy or after the social chaos produced by religious corruption. Revolutions have at such times vindicated the popular claim not to be left behind in the political race, and have not only wrought definite constitutional and legal reforms but have called into being a Legislative Authority after the fashion of countries fortunate enough to have had a more tranquil career of internal progress.

Such has been eminently the case of France, where, for ages, the only protests in favour of a constitutional Legislative Authority were the often ineffectual refusals to register the king's decrees on the part of the Parliament of Paris, which had degenerated into a mere professional body of advocates. The king might indeed, by appearing in person and holding a *lit de justice*, contrive to supersede this popular or, at least, professional interference. But it was an advantage to public liberty that legislation proper was, presumptively, and according to the vulgar apprehension, shared between the feudal monarch and other Constitutional authorities, although by an act of apparent and exceptional usurpation the monarch might for the occasion re absorb the legislative power and rule alone. As in early England, so in France on the verge of her great Revolution, it was the urgent want of money that precipitated a recurrence to the people by summoning their representatives as Estates of the Realm; and the first stage of the Revolution was nothing more than a somewhat violent transfer of the Legislative Authority, from the king alone to the king and his constitutional partners.

The history of the growth of a Legislative Authority in Germany is somewhat different; but this difference is mainly due to the peculiar federal constitution of the German Empire and not to any dissimilarity in the principles involved.

It must be remembered that the Councils and Synods of the Church were visible examples of quasi-representative Assemblies co-operating with a spiritual potentate who was recognised, for many purposes, as supreme and absolute, yet they held themselves entitled to modify, repeal, or enact rules for the government of the Church as an organised society: as a judicial body they pronounced sentence on alleged infringers of existing rules as well as determined the meaning or application of ambiguous rules: and, more generally, they mediated between what was believed to be the eternal framework and constitution of the Church and the imperative demands of a progressive secular society which surrounded, and yet was included in, the Church. These Councils and Synods were not only habitually regarded with almost superstitious veneration even at the very time when their decrees were dissented from and their authority practically repudiated, but their acts were accomplished in the sight of all men, and the effect of these acts was to bring them incessantly into collision with the Civil Power.

The result was that throughout the Holy Roman Empire, including the large mass of what are now the leading States of Northern and Central Europe, the civil constitution of the several States tended to imitate and reproduce the type of Government which was not only familiar but obviously reasonable and convenient. The Emperor came through perpetual contact to be the correlative of the Pope even rather than the typical semblance of the Roman Emperor of old. The Diet of the Empire similarly reproduced the Ecclesiastical Assemblies; while the Electors of the Empire in appointing the head of the Executive enacted in the corresponding sphere the part of the chief Ecclesiastical officials. In these functions of the Diet and of the Electors the conception of true legislative tasks was included; though, from the essential infirmity of the Federal constitution, the performance of these tasks was restricted to the choice and limited control of the Executive Authority; to making a few desultory provisions for the peace of the Empire; and to maintaining a sufficient friendly accord between the secular and religious authorities. The actual amendment of the customary private law prevalent in the different States was either entirely neglected or left to the local legislative authorities which were contemporaneously growing up, slowly enough, on all sides.

And here it may be noted that, even in England, it is only within the present century that the private civil law and the criminal law have been boldly grappled with by the Legislative Authority. Before this period all the energy of that Authority was addressed to those parts of the law which directly or indirectly affected the political rights of the people. The old feudal land law, in its essential character, the law governing industrial and mercantile contracts, the law of personal relationships, and the bulk of the criminal law, were only reformed within living memory by the slow action of popular custom and judicial interpretation,—not to say by judicial collusions.

In contrast to the process of the rise of a Legislative, as distinguished from an Executive, Authority on the dissolution of Feudalism, may be taken the case of the establishment of a Legislative Authority in the Roman Republic and Empire. In the earliest strictly historical times the consuls, prætors, quæstors, ædiles, and the rest, including afterwards the tribunes, represent a strong and all but omnipotent Executive. The only checks on absolutism were the constitution itself, so far as there was one, and the Civil Law. The Senate and the various Comitia were, at the outset and for ages afterwards, only a machinery for electing the different members of the Executive, for deciding matters relating to Foreign affairs, and for passing measures of comprehensive legislation only in respect of political rights or, what was nearly akin to them,

THE LEGISLATIVE AUTHORITY IN ROME. 95

of claims to share in the occupation of the national soil. When the Comitia were really and effectively called upon to engage in the task of radical legal reform of a comprehensive nature, it was always at some crisis of the national fortunes when some influential citizen came to the head of affairs and, by the weight of his character or even of his political power, overcame the inertness of the unwieldy masses and the scruples of oligarchical coteries.

Such were the circumstances of the legislation of the Gracchi, of Sulla, and of Julius Cæsar. The vigorous and independent legislation of Augustus, still confined within the formal precincts of republican ideas, was a medium between the legislative efforts of republican reformers and the despotic constitutions, decrees, rescripts, mandates, and pragmatic sanctions of his Imperial successors a few generations later. The full legislative effect given to resolutions of the Senate marks an intermediate stage in the process of Imperial absorption of legislative powers.

The only correction to this abuse and usurpation lay in the necessary constitution of the Empire itself, in which the complicated organisation of the civil service required by the enormous area of Government led to such a natural distribution of powers that the Emperor's legislative, judicial, and administrative functions were, in fact, severally exercised by tolerably independent, though bureaucratic officials. The secrecy and consequent absence of all responsibility to public opinion was only one of the glaring defects of such a political constitution.

Thus the instance of Rome, like that of France in the course of the political vicissitudes she has undergone since the first Revolution, exhibits not only the natural process of elaborating a Legislative Authority by the side of the Executive, but the reverse process of re-absorption of the Legislative by the Executive Authority,—a danger to which would-be democratic Governments are notoriously exposed, at the hands often of the military officials of the State. The ordinary legislative machinery of Athens was succumbing to one Executive chief or cabal after another before Philip of Macedon took upon him to personate all the powers of the State; while Sparta is a memorable instance of a State which successfully held on its own narrow course, and maintained its parsimonious existence, by ignoring from first to last the functions of Legislation, and throwing all the weight of Government on the shoulders of a captiously watched Executive.

Here and there, indeed, there are to be found instances of what at first sight seems to be an even and steady process of growth, from the first, of an Executive and Legislative Authority, side by side, with ascertained relations to each other, and with vigilantly guarded principles of apportionment. Such may be taken to be the primitive rural cantons of Uri and Appenzell in Switzerland in which the whole population, to the amount (says a recent traveller[1]) of 8000 people in the last mentioned canton, meet on a certain day of the year, and choose the Executive officers for the year, and do acts of legislation, by adopting or rejecting any proposal for legal reform which may be brought before them.

In cases such as this there is undoubtedly witnessed a fine and, no doubt, primitive balance between the

[1] *The Shores and Cities of the Boden-See*, by S. J. Capper.

Legislative and the Executive which only accidental circumstances of an exceptionally favourable kind could have made possible. But even there it would be found on closer inspection that the very roughness of the constitutional mechanism, and the multitudinousness of the legislative body, excludes (as was the case with the popular *comitia* in the last days of the Roman Republic) the consideration of any proposal which cannot be formulated in such a way as to admit only of two alternative courses, adoption or rejection, simple and entire. This necessity is a consequence not only of the numbers, but of the heterogeneousness, inconstancy, and political unfamiliarity of a mass of people of all ranks and conditions, meeting together no oftener than once a year. This of itself excludes the bulk of the Legislation required by an advancing country for prescribing rules to the Executive, for supervising and checking its course, for correcting accidental abuses in the current execution of the Law, and for applying amendments to Laws which are either becoming obsolete, or which, from one cause or another, no longer approve themselves to the public mind or conscience.

When it is remembered how unsuitable are the primitive democratic assemblies alluded to for even moderate legislative tasks like these, it is evident that they are Legislative Authorities in little more than name, though, inasmuch as they choose the Executive, and can potentially alter the whole law, they do truly constitute such Authorities. In modern Switzerland the paramount authority of the Federal Government renders these local institutions mainly interesting as historical fossils and as political illustrations.

In what has been said, at some length, of the nature and growth of the Legislative Authority, there has been incidentally disclosed the meaning of the term *Executive* and the scope of the conception which the term is used to express. The Executive Authority and the Legislative Authority together compose the whole Supreme Political Authority which in any State always has, theoretically, absolute power over all members of the State for all purposes whatsoever, and which in fact also has it except in case of Revolution, of approximate Revolution, or of serious civic discord. There is, at any given moment, no theoretical limit to the powers latent in this Authority. The only practical limit is set by the chances of Revolution or of a supercession of the existing Supreme Authority by a new one in case of popular disaffection.

This Supreme Authority may consist of one person or of several; and if of several, they may either be precisely determined and have definite relations to each other,—as in the case of the English King or Queen, the members of the House of Lords in their corporate capacity, and the members of the House of Commons, similarly in their corporate capacity; or the Supreme Authority may consist of an indefinite number of persons accurately, but not precisely, determined,—as in the case of that number of persons in the United States of America, who throughout the several States are required to co-operate in order to effect a change in a constitutional Law.

It has already been seen that the Supreme Authority at the first is of simple and homogeneous structure, and exerts its powers of Government solely by a series of executive Acts. A Legislative Authority concerned with prescribing rules of action for the Government, and amending the customary usages in force among the people, slowly grows up within the precincts of the Supreme Authority, and the result is a sort of distribution of organs and of functions recalling the gradual composition and internal differentiation of the higher classes of organised bodies.

What shall be the final relationship between the Legislative Authority so developed and the Executive Authority which it vigilantly watches, and on which it has encroached, is one of the most arduous problems of constitutional Statesmanship, and one to which modern ingenuity,—as will be seen hereafter in discussing the Constitution of a State,—is mainly directed.

At the time of founding the Constitution of the United States, there was no question on which more able and acute speculation was expended than the relationship between the Legislative and the Executive Authority;[1] and the final solution adopted of a Supreme Court of Justice, independent of the Legislative Authority, and a President elected by the people independently of Congress, absolute for Executive purposes during a four years' term of office, is an experiment as to the success of which well-founded doubts have in the course of time suggested themselves, as will be seen later on.

Sometimes the term *Executive*, which strictly means an Authority which puts the laws in force, is opposed to the term *Administrative*, which implies the performance of every other sort of immediate Governmental act, such as collecting taxes, organising and directing the Army, Navy, and Police, supervising trade, locomotion, postal communication, and carrying out in

[1] See the writers in the *Federalist* generally

detail legislative measures for promoting public health, education, morality, and general contentment; such as in Imperial Rome demanded public shows and a distribution of food on cheap terms to large classes of the population.

But the term *Administrative* is, — especially in scientific and constitutional treatises,—less used than *Executive*; and the distinction is not very convenient, inasmuch as there is a large class of subordinate officials,—such as the English 'policemen,'—who have an assemblage of multifarious duties cast upon them connected with the revenue, and with the preservation of public order and decorum, which are almost as important as their task of apprehending offenders and facilitating the administration of Justice. In the same way the functions of certain of the higher English Judges,—who co-operate with the Crown in the Exchequer to appoint Sheriffs of Counties,—are administrative rather than, according to the distinction in question, executive. On the whole it is best to use one term, *Executive*, to express the portion of the Supreme Authority which is not Legislative in the full and true sense, and only to oppose *Executive* to *Administrative*, when, for a special purpose, it is necessary to consider apart from all other functions the function of ensuring obedience, in detail, to the Law as it is.

5. *Right. Prerogative.*

Jurists have often attempted to analyse the ideas which enter into the notion designated by the term *Right*. Some such term appears in the political terminology of all advanced States. The term usually connotes, in one country and period, some idea or ideas which do not elsewhere present themselves. Thus in the Egyptian language, as commemorated by the hieroglyphical writing of the earliest dynasties, the same syllabic group of signs indicates the notions of justice, truth, moral righteousness, and political law, though one and another of these distinct notions are also expressed by special groups. In Greece the terms δίκη and νόμος share between them the notions expressed in Rome, according to a slightly different distribution, by *jus* and *lex*. The Greek νόμος covers the meaning of positive enactment chiefly conveyed by *lex*, but it also covers some of the meaning of settled constitutional morality conveyed by *jus*. But in the Latin *jus* there is an element of abstract morality which is only to be found in νόμος in its sense of primitive distribution.

The German *recht* and the French *droit* are nearly coextensive in signification with each other and with the Latin *jus*. The English word *right* does not include the technical legal meaning of *recht*, *droit*, and *jus*, that is, it does not mean a body of purely legal rules; and the English term is far more loose and unsettled on its ethical side. It is, in fact, only in the sense of a claim recognisable either by the State, by abstract morality, or by conventional sentiment that it squares pretty exactly with one of the meanings of the corresponding term in the Latin, German, and French languages.

From this terminological enquiry it appears that the best consolidated States have found the need of appropriate terms for the several distinct notions, first, of settled and generally binding law, whether as based on positive legislation or on judicially enforced custom; secondly, of long established usage, binding on the legislative and executive Authorities, and even on the indefinite mass of persons to whom those Authorities are responsible and owe their existence ; thirdly, of individual claims founded upon such law or such established usage. The English term *right*, so far as it has a definite meaning for political purposes, expresses the third of these notions, that is, the claim of a private person or an assemblage of private persons, accorded either by law or by well-understood usage, which, whether grounded on absolute morality or on conventional public sentiment, has all the force of law, and even more than this force, being anterior and superior to it, though it may need the intervention or even the enactment of positive law to give it practical effect.

When the claim expressed by the term *right* is based on strict law, the purport and limits of the claim share that precise exactness which belongs strictly only to law. A claim being accorded to one person at the expense of another or others, one of the most prominent functions of Courts of Justice is that of ascertaining what is the measure of concession which the law has granted in favour of one litigant in derogation of the general claims to unrestricted action enjoyed by another. Thus the claim in question may be described as a 'power,' but as exercisable only through the use of certain definite instruments. It is thus only analogical, at the most, to a physical force or to material machinery. It matters not whether it can or cannot be described as existing for the benefit of the person exercising the claim. If it is not for his benefit, directly or indirectly, he can forbear to exercise it. Thus even a trustee or guardian has rights, the direct advantage of the exercise of which is wholly restricted to other persons; but, inasmuch as the rights may have to be exercised by the trustee or guardian in order to fulfil his personal responsibility to a Court of Justice, the existence of the rights might be described as being indirectly advantageous to him.

The more politically important signification of the term *right* is that which attaches to it when the claim indicated by it is based on what in England is known as constitutional usage. But the term is undoubtedly used, for political purposes, in a wider and less exact sense than this. It has, on some memorable historical occasions, been employed as co-extensive with a claim based on abstract morality, that is, on such notions of morality as prevail at the day. It is also used in current political controversy in an intermediate sense, as indicating a claim more precise and more readily ascertained than any that merely ethical considerations could suggest, and yet less distinctly formulated than a claim founded on the actual or traditional constitution of the country.

The American 'Declaration of Independence,' and the French 'Declaration of the Rights of Man,' abound in ethical assumptions purporting to be the foundation of political claims which,—whether justifiable or not as scientific propositions,—are (as Bentham pointed out in detail,) far too vague and undefined to form part of the constitutional morality of any State whatever. The English 'Bill of Rights,' containing as it did a series of propositions in the closest relation to actual historical facts and documents, may be contrasted favourably with the corresponding French and American proclamations. Not indeed that these latter served their immediate purpose less effectually because of their vague and unrestricted language. On the contrary, as Coleridge pointed out, nothing is so popular, and, therefore, at some periods so perilous, as comprehensive doctrines conveyed in the briefest of phrases. They often, nevertheless, have a truth of their own, and correspond to some true and irrepressible instinct or aspiration which they rouse into energy, however impotent they may be to direct or restrain it. This subject, however, more properly belongs to the theory of Revolutions.

Much ambiguity in the conduct of political controversy ensues from the common confusion of the various uses of the term *right*. Thus it was for some time a question in the English Courts to what extent, if any, the status of slavery was recognised by the Law of England. It was, after careful judicial reasoning, decided towards the end of the eighteenth century (in Sommersett's case) that a slave, if brought to an English port, had a *right* to recover and maintain his freedom. At the same time no such *right* was admitted as to the port of an English Colony. But in the first quarter of the nineteenth century it was argued on all sides that slaves in British Colonies had a *right* to their freedom, in the sense of a *right* to have freedom conferred upon them by law. In the third quarter of the same century it became a matter of burning political controversy in America how far the *right* of a slave to his freedom was a legal *right*; or, if it were not so, whether it had only ceased to be so through an initial violence to the constitution, and so was still a *constitutional* though not a legal right; or if it were neither a legal nor a constitutional right, whether it were not an abstract *moral* right, which no law nor constitution could outrage consistently with the continued welfare, stability, or even existence of the State.

Similar ambiguities in the use of the term *right* have notably presented themselves in controversies on the suffrage, on the tenure of land, and in respect of some of the finer shades of exemption from any personal degradation used as a mode of criminal punishment. Questions as to what are a person's rights,—human, constitutional, legal, or merely conventional,—have, of late, entered largely into discussions on claims to appropriate the soil of a country, on claims to vote at parliamentary or municipal elections, and on claims to absolute immunity from cruel or so-called derogatory punishments.

The term *prerogative* is closely parallel to *right* as being based on established constitutional usage; though, in England at least, its employment as a political term is restricted to expressing the constitutional claims of the Sovereign. But, owing to the course of development of the English Constitution by which the limitation of the personal authority of the Sovereign has been only gradually achieved by slow marches from point to point, the term *prerogative* covers, at present, the constitutional rights of the Sovereign as one of the Estates of the Realm and as the chief executive Authority,—which rights are exercisable only in certain definite channels, by the aid of ministerial agents responsible to Parliament,—and also those indefinite and dignified personal claims of the Sovereign which the progress of Constitutional Government has not yet invaded. To this last class, of purely personal claims, belongs the important one of deciding in the last resort between one candidate and another for the post of Prime Minister, when each candidate has, presumably, equal chances of commanding the confidence of the Legislature. A similar, but more disputable, claim is that of dismissing, without cause assigned, a Minister who renders himself personally obnoxious, though probably a capricious use of this prerogative would lead to its limitation. The prerogatives concerned with precedents of all sorts are, in a political sense, too trivial to need being further particularised, even for the sake of terminological illustration.

CHAPTER III.

POLITICAL REASONING.

IN the course of the investigation into the scientific claims of Political enquiries, it appeared that one obstacle to the successful assertion of those claims was the necessity for immediate action, by which even the most speculative statesman is beset on every side. A critical opportunity arrives, and the statesman must act promptly or annihilate himself altogether. There may be only a limited number of directions in which action is possible; and one of these directions must be chosen; and yet it may be one which is very far from good in itself. The utmost that a sagacious statesman can do is to anticipate such moments of hurried action by giving a beneficial direction to the general course of his conduct, and by persisting in it at times when no passions are aroused, when no strong prejudices or antipathies have had time to consolidate themselves, when no interests prejudicial to the general good have become vested. The statesman's own personal influence may also do much to awaken feelings favourable to his own preconceptions of a rational course of policy, and, at the worst, he can bend into judicious and modified lines determinate resolves which he cannot break.

In this way it comes about that, provided political

phenomena admit of scientific arrangement and treatment at all, the logically-disposed statesman will always find opportunities for a course of action dictated by purely scientific considerations. Nor is it true that the democratic constitution of modern States, if more favourable to rhetoric than to logic, is inimical to scientific government. Mr. Grote was at great pains, in his 'History of Greece,' to establish that, in spite of the enormous play which rhetoric and oratory, undoubtedly, had with an Athenian audience, yet, on the whole, a disposition was manifested on momentous occasions to act on purely logical grounds, to reconsider again and again hasty decisions, and to give a hearing to all sides impartially before drawing a conclusion. If, notwithstanding these instances, the Athenian people were lacking often enough in practical wisdom, this was only one among many proofs of the insufficiency of their political constitution and the backwardness of political science.

In the case of modern democratic Assemblies, it would seem that the tendency of popular education, the influence of the Press, and the pressure exercised by the free right of public meeting and association, all conduce to restrict increasingly the power exercised by rhetoricians and demagogues. If the English House of Commons is taken as the most aristocratic type of a democratically constituted assembly, and the Lower House of a British Colony, however denominated, as the most democratic type of the same, it would be found that, in both the one and the other, the most convincing of all arguments are those drawn on the spot from statistical considerations, or from evidence sifted by commissions or from the reports of recognised authorities on the subject under discussion. Mere rhetoric, volubility, declamation, even passion and party spirit, make a more and more feeble stand against antagonists armed with such purely logical weapons as these; or, if a momentary victory is won, the fruits of it are worthless, for it is inevitably reversed at an early day, so soon as the outside public has had time to master the issues and deliver its judgment.

The place that pure reasoning is thus found to be taking in the conduct of Government leads the way to consider whether inductive or deductive methods of reasoning are likely to be most prominent in this department of thought, and whether there are any peculiarities in the extension of common logical processes to the field of Politics which need special notice. Sir George Cornewall Lewis, in his invaluable treatise on 'Methods of Observation and Reasoning in Politics,' has given an exhaustive statement of all that can be said on this subject, and has illustrated it with the wealth of his rare erudition. But the very completeness of this work renders it unsuitable for incorporation in a treatise which, like this, professes to cover the whole ground of scientific Politics; while, on the other hand, it would be unjust to the learned critic to sever his conclusions from his arguments and illustrations in order to give a compendious enunciation of their general results.

The distinction drawn between inductive and deductive methods is rather of psychological than of practical importance. There is hardly any department of scientific investigation, which has progressed beyond its initial stages, where both methods are not incessantly and alternately resorted to. In those sciences which, by their nature, are the least stationary, it is impossible to say, at any particular moment, which is the most characteristic and prominent organ of search. On the face of it, it would appear that the framing of general or universal propositions is peculiarly alien to the scientific temper in Politics. It might be said with truth that here if anywhere *dolus latet in generalibus*. The most erroneous theories and destructive fallacies have, undoubtedly, proceeded from an attempt to include in some sweeping generalisations all the varied conditions due to differences of time, place, and accident. But, because a logical method has been used wrongly or inappropriately, this is no sufficient argument against its being used at all. Nor does the mere difficulty of using it rightly justify its neglect, or even disentitle it to its rank as a primary instrument of thought.

Nor, indeed, are the facts, when fairly examined, adverse to the claims of deductive reasoning in Political studies. The progressive advance of these studies, as in the case of the physical sciences, has led to the framing of an increasing number of general propositions of incontrovertible cogency. It is only necessary to cite the broad doctrines that the end of Government is the highest attainable good of the largest number of people present and to come; that, by way of corollary, Government and Governmental institutions exist for the advantage of the whole people, and not of the rulers only or of any other limited section of the whole people; that the interference of Government with prices, wages, contracts, or with the operations of industry generally, is presumptively less conducive to national wealth than the permission of unrestricted freedom, and,—if resorted to at all,—can only be justified by some considerations of an entirely different kind; that stringent constitutional precautions are needed against abuses by the Executive Authority; that criminal punishments must not be cruel, vindictive, or only retaliatory, but should be devised and imposed with the main end in view of preventing the recurrence of offences, and be rendered, as far as may be, compatible with the secondary end, of promoting the personal amendment of the criminal; and that (by way of a final example) the chief Judicial Authority should be rendered independent of the other departments of the Executive Authority.

It may be said that the truth of these and such like propositions is very far from being everywhere accepted,—still less acted upon. It might be added that, as to some of the propositions themselves, their application must be restricted to certain countries and conditions of society, that what may be true in Western communities is only true under certain limitations in the East, and that the propositions are even reversed in different stages of the growth of the same society. In fact the propositions themselves, it might be argued in disparagement, are only valuable when accompanied by all sorts of limiting qualifications and hypothetical additions; or in other words, they are true only so far as they cease to be propounded as universal or even general.

But while to recal such imperfections in the generality of the propositions of Political Science is an indispensable key to their true use, yet it is easy, for rhetorical purposes, to exaggerate the real significance of all such limitations. The generality of many political propositions, of the kind above cited in illustration, is found to increase with every advance in political improvement and with every extension of all the best elements of what is known as civilisation. It is not so much that the propositions are generally true, as that they tend to become more and more indisputably accepted as true. The limitations, on the other hand, are becoming more and more partial and insignificant, and are driven further and further into the background of the argument. In fact, the conduct of political controversy at present, whether in formally assembled Chambers, in public but informal discussions, or in private and select conversation, exhibits the increasing prevalence of a growing series of general propositions the truth of which is, for serious argumentative purposes, held by disputants, on both or all sides, to be beyond the reach of doubt.

It is an interesting exhibition of this fact to notice the process at work on all sides, by which the general premises of political syllogisms are being gradually fashioned by a joint use of inductive and deductive methods. Thus, by way of illustration, it is still a most unsettled point in this country whether an income tax is or is not a wise or justifiable source of national income; whether direct taxation has any conclusive advantage over all kinds of indirect taxation; whether the land of a country can or cannot be appropriated by private owners in the same way as money, the fruits of the soil, and manufactured products; whether central or local control, or a combination of both, is most applicable to such topics as police, poor relief, sanitary improvements, and expenditure for economical objects; and, lastly, whether the care of such works as irrigation, locomotion, and postal and telegraphic communication, belongs most fitly to the State or to such private persons or associations as may choose to undertake them.

Some of these problems are more nearly approaching solution and final settlement than others. In respect of all of them, the primary instrument of research is the observation of the results of actual experiments in a variety of countries, whether these experiments were intentionally conducted among more or less rigorously superintended surroundings, or were only the outcome of fortuitous social conditions. The proper use of this instrument implies the usual attention to the 'infirmatory' circumstances which physical science has rendered so familiar as impairing the value of observed facts.

Mr. John Stuart Mill pointed out, in his 'Logic,' the impossibility of conducting any real experiment in Politics. For the conduct of any true experiment, not only must all relevant circumstances be fully and accurately known, but the elements of the enquiry must admit of being altered, modified, multiplied, reduced, and readjusted at will. It is obvious that, owing to the element of human personality which is the leading fact in all political problems, and to the extraordinary influence of the past, however recent, on the future, no combination of circumstances can ever be repeated even once, let alone often. And apart from the possibility of repetition, with exactly estimated variations at will, a true experiment is impossible. What is often called an experiment in Politics,—as for instance the imposition of a novel tax, or the introduction of a constitutional change in the Government of a Dependency,—is, in fact, nothing but a slight and special extension of the field of purely historical enquiry, and is liable to many of its characteristic defects. Even the use of statistical results is only a peculiarly precise and formal mode of conducting the methods of search implied in reference to History and to the reports of travellers in other countries. In all their forms, History and Travels are the chief sources for the facts to which observation must be directed for the purpose of founding general political propositions.

In a remarkable chapter of the book already alluded to, Sir G. C. Lewis has carefully scrutinised the claims of History to serve as a source for the ascertainment of Political truth; and his remarks should be well studied as, at the least, a complete statement of the perils attending the mis-reading of History, and the common sophistical arguments founded on distorted historical facts. It is probably rather in the broader, than in the narrower, survey of the historical field that political truth is to be discovered; and the comprehensive view of the whole past, taken by such political philosophers as Auguste Comte, is less liable to generate political error than the examination of the working of any single institution or group of institutions, in a particular country.

The wider causes of the political deterioration of Rome,—such as the inadequacy of the aristocratic Senate to represent, to control, or to resist, the ever growing multitude of the Commons, and the operation of the system of land tenure and of slaveholding, as well as the concentration of wealth in the hands of a few,—are unmistakable indications of permanent tendencies in human affairs, and, when cautiously stated, afford safe general premises for political reasoning.

But causes of the above nature,—while they are only ascertained and understood and distinctly formulated after a patient study of all the accessible authorities, and, as matter of fact, are by no means beyond the reach of controversy yet,—existed during some centuries, and were, some of them, at last co-extensive in their action with the Roman Empire.

The general truth that a constitutional structure which is defective for purposes of confederation and the want of a spirit of cohesion are fatal to the political existence of a number of small States, inhabited by the same race, and having common interests and even sympathies, is certainly illustrated and enforced by the broad facts of the History of Greece and of the British Colonies in America.

Similarly, the history of modern France may fairly be held to establish the fact that, in proportion as civilisation and education become equally diffused, a purely selfish system of Government, in the interests of a narrow class, becomes impossible, and if a change is not brought about by timely reform, revolutionary violence will attend the first social pressure or disaster, whether occasioned by famine, by war, or by casual excitement. The same truth has been abundantly driven home by the recent history of other European countries; and England has enjoyed of late a fortunate pre-eminence in illustrating the same truth, by showing that revolution can be prevented by anticipating too loud a popular cry for reform, and by making concessions just in time to save the appearance of their being extorted by force.

Such broad historical lessons go far to encourage and direct the statesman, as well as to support him in the advocacy of principles of action which may, at the moment, be unpopular in the particular region in which he has to work. But they are of too indefinite and extensive a kind to be the basis of specific courses of action, and therefore can hardly be abused for a dangerous purpose. It is otherwise with those minute historical parallels which often furnish the food of adroit rhetoricians, and against which an imperfectly informed audience cannot always be on its guard.

Because the Senate of Rome was, at one period, one of the ablest administrative assemblies ever known, it is argued that a narrow aristocratic Assembly (however composed) is the indispensable complement of every sound political constitution, and even has certain transparent advantages over every other form of Assembly. Again, because the same Senate of Rome became oligarchical, despotic, and corrupt, therefore every other second Chamber of an aristocratical kind, has, and must ever have, identically the same characteristics. Because it was proved to be impolitic to tax in a certain way the thirteen American Colonies, therefore, it is argued, no English dependencies, to the end of time, ought to be required to bear their share of the expenditure incurred for their defence. Or, on the other hand, because the American colonies have prospered through their separation, therefore no effort is to be made by suitable economic settlements,—as between the Australian or South African Colonies and the mother country,—to retain the loyal adhesion of Colonies. It is obvious, at once, that arguments such as these are superficial and worthless in the extreme. Nevertheless they constantly appear and reappear, not only on platforms and in newspapers, but in the most serious debates in Legislative Assemblies.

The spurious reasoning based on the reports of travellers is almost more familiar than the perverse misreading of History. In the latter part of the last century, Montesquieu and Rousseau gave popularity to all sorts of political theories, some true and most of them false, by adducing alleged practices adopted in imperfectly known communities. Rousseau, indeed, enforced this line of argument by his panegyrics on a State of Nature, in virtue of which he held social and political conditions to be commendable in proportion as they receded backward from the prevalent habits of the civilised States of the West.

Such vagaries of the imagination, indeed, have no place in the political reasoning of the present day. But, in their place, a true comparative science, based on attention to the rude usages of uncivilised communities, has attained inordinate proportions as supplying a wholly satisfactory clue to the nature of man and of human society. The modern reports of travellers differ from the old in being exact, full, diversified, multiplied, and exposed to every mode of critical test. They are prepared with the help of all the acumen and statistical completeness habitual in purely physical investigations.

The result is that what have been long regarded as fundamental institutions of society are felt to have their authority shaken, and their permanence endangered. Monogamic marriage, the domestic affections, the spiritual equality of man and woman, the advantages of free institutions, and even of personal liberty, which have been long treated as axioms in christianised States, are felt to be in a state of solution, and to possess only a temporary and relative,—in place of an eternal and absolute—value. Polygamic societies, instead of being neglected as *data* of political thoughts or condemned as merely retrograde anomalies, are patiently investigated as important political experiments, and even indulgently nurtured in order to prolong the process of social vivisection. Wide-spread religious systems, confessedly false and corrupting, are not only protected, but encouraged and stimulated, on the ground of their possibly having some permanent affinity for certain races of mankind. Even cruel and obviously barbarous rites are witnessed with toleration, and are repressed with timidity, for fear of their concealing some yet unrecognised elements of humanity which, if left alone, will one day be appreciated and tabulated.

All this speaks of a primary and transitory phase in the true use for political purposes of the information supplied by travellers. No doubt the practices of races yet in their infancy, and uninfluenced by contact with people more advanced than themselves, may throw much light on the general nature of man in the earlier stages of the transition from all but animalism to a genuine humanity. The fault in the reasoning arises when it is attempted to draw from any number of such observations, however varied and scrutinised, conclusions as to the nature and requirements of man in a social and political condition. It may be that even yet civilisation has not advanced far enough for any universal propositions to be laid down as to man's essential nature and possibilities. But, because these are still unknown, that is no sufficient reason for resorting to a wholly fictitious process in order to put on the appearance of scientific inquiry. It is, of course, helpful, in prosecuting a research into the indispensable conditions of man in society and under Government, to know as much as possible about him under all other conditions. But the most complete knowledge of him, under these other conditions, must be used with the greatest caution and self-restraint, in the course of converting truths applicable to man in his closest alliance with the animal, into truths applicable to him in that state of which the main characteristic is that the physical and animal nature of the individual man is wholly and finally subordinated to the spiritual nature of man as a member of a political society.

Besides the difficulty of framing general political propositions arising from the obscurity and the complexity of the subject-matter, whether past or present, to which alone observation can extend,—there is another logical difficulty, appertaining to the scientific treatment of Politics, which is peculiar to the present age, and is closely connected with some of the peculiar advantages for the prosecution of rigorous political thought which this age pre-eminently possesses. This difficulty relates to the due use and co-ordination of general propositions borrowed from other, but cognate, departments of thought and research, such as Economics, Statistics, Ethics, and Law. While, as has been more than once observed already, it is a pledge of the growing completeness of political studies that these increasingly exact topics are being imported into all serious political controversies, it is none the less essential for their due use, and for the purpose of saving them from early obloquy and distrust, that the syllogistic reasoning based upon the propositions to which they severally give rise should be fairly and strictly conducted. To the disproportionate and extravagant prominence, from time to time given to one and another economic or ethical proposition,—of undoubted truth within its own limits,—may be traced some of the strangest vagaries of modern politics, and some prevalent delusions which, when once they have obtained a hold, can hardly be dislodged.

To give a casual illustration of the danger here adverted to, it is sufficient to notice the extraordinary influence in the political world exercised by Malthus' very moderate and temperately stated argument to the effect that population tends to increase at a greater ratio than the means of subsistence. This was a mixed social, economic, and physical, fact, which might be used in all sorts of ways by political reasoners. As it happened, it has been almost exclusively used to enforce the opinion that it should be the object of all legislators, in all European countries at the least, to repress, and not to encourage, the growth of population.

It is a recognised economical truth that the substitution of machinery for hand labour tends to increase national wealth, to promote a rise in wages, to multiply employments, and to benefit the labouring class. But it is also true that the sudden introduction of machinery on a large scale, into an industry conducted by hand labour, is usually attended, at first, by wide-spread distress and poverty. To build a national policy—so far as policy is concerned—on the first of these propositions, to the neglect of the second, must lead to disastrous consequences, and often has led to them during the present century, especially through the administrative action of Government itself, operating as an employer on the largest scale.

In an important chapter of his 'Treatise on Morals and Legislation,' Bentham discusses the element of 'Time and Place' in Legislation; and it is just in neglecting this element that the most abusive employment of newly-fledged ethical and economical propositions takes place. The customary arguments for and against 'Capital Punishment' illustrate this class of logical perils. Thus it is admitted as a proposition of legislative science that there are certain advantages and certain disadvantages in retaliatory punishments. One class of disputants dwell exclusively on the advantages, and recommend capital punishment. Another class dwell only on the disadvantages, and object to it. In formal reasoning, the advantages and the disadvantages ought to be stated together, and set over against each other.

But even when this is done, there is still the question of time and place. It may be well to teach savages what death means, by a public instruction of the most open and ceremonious kind. It may also be well to teach a generally civilised people what a reverence for life is, by abstaining from judicial homicide. The introduction of private executions in England shows that this last argument is acquiring force in the present age. The argument against retaliatory punishments, in an advanced state of society, is used against the resort to flogging for any offences whatever, even of the most brutal description. An argument in favour of such punishments, as applied to the same offences, is urged on the ground that the criminals and their associates in such cases are tarrying behind the rest of society and can only be affected by the ocular demonstration of the connexion of wrongdoing with physical pain.

In all these and like cases, a certain amount of attention to the several propositions affirmed is due; but too much is often made of them through their being isolated from other important rival propositions, through their being stated in too unqualified a shape, or through too much or too little credit being given to the actual results of empirical experience under certain well-ascertained conditions.

A pernicious example of delusive reasoning of this sort is supplied in all those cases in which ignorant credulity assumes the aspect of a modest deference to superior scientific attainments, believed to be possessed by a limited class of specialists, in certain lines of enquiry calling for an exceptional amount of protracted study and mental absorption. This is particularly the case in the various departments of the medical profession. And yet, the greater the amount of studious absorption and undeviating devotion which medical specialists are required to bestow on their occupations, the greater are the time, thought, and energy which they must withdraw from social and political pursuits.

It is, then, no disparagement of medical practitioners to assert that, *primâ facie*, they are less likely, --though analogous cautions are needed in the case of religious ministers, military and naval officers, philosophical students, and the devotees of the physical sciences generally,—to be wise political advisers than persons more conversant with the broader fields of human affairs. Nevertheless, in practice it is found that a notorious logical confusion prevails, by which the value of a purely physiological, medical, or sanitary, fact is imported into an entirely different field, and made the basis of instantaneous and reckless legislation. The fact in question may, in itself, be of great importance, but it needs to be laid patiently side by side with other facts, relating to such matters as public liberty, police administration, centralised or localised authority, espionage, Government interference, and perhaps public morality, before legislation can wisely take place. The authority, however, of the specialist in his own department is not discriminated from his authority, or want of authority, as a political adviser, and, in a moment of public apathy, facile legislation takes place, which it may take years of effort to undo.

It would be useless to attempt even to indicate all the kinds of false and abusive reasoning which creep into political arguments and often lead to dangerous practical consequences. Indeed it is the custom with writers on Logic to draw some of their most effective illustrations of fallacies and sophistries from the field of Politics. Owing to the extraordinary but, at the moment, unrecognised dominion which custom and tradition exercise over the minds of each generation, at any given time there are usually found to prevail a number of unconsciously held political beliefs and premises having a wide-spread operation, the real force of which can only with difficulty be estimated at another time and under different circumstances.

Thus, towards the close of the English Civil War, and at the Restoration, much attention was drawn to idealised political communities such as those portrayed by Harrington, Hobbes, Algernon Sydney, and, less distinctly, by Milton. It was generally felt that there was some type of excellence in political construction which could be followed with advantage by all States, and from which the best organised States only deflected.

Sir Henry Maine, in his 'Ancient Law,' pointed out how, similarly, the fiction of a 'Social Contract' became a dominant idea in England and France from the middle of the seventeenth to the end of the eighteenth century, and was only displaced at last by the rise of the modern Historical School. The earlier prevalence of the Patriarchal and 'Divine Right' theories of Government is equally notorious. In Greece and Rome the existence of slavery was taken as a political premise, as in the later Roman Empire the duty of supporting the establishment of Christianity.

Burke's antipathy to the constitutional proceedings of the early leaders of the French Revolution was mainly based on a foregone conclusion that the English constitution, as re-settled on the accession of William of Orange, was the only admissible pattern for all States whatever, in all times, and that the modes of conducting the English Revolution of 1688, were the only tolerable methods of political renovation, whatever were the social circumstances, or however peculiar were the obstacles to be encountered.

There are still plenty of examples, on all sides, of the extraordinary hold taken on those who should be self-possessed statesmen by theories antagonistic (if exclusively applied) to all Government, to order and to public liberty. These theories are seldom quite destitute of truth, and, where they are used as standards of revolt against tyrannical injustice and oppression, the elements of truth in them are of service as rallying points to a scattered and usually indifferent population. But when applied to political construction, they are valueless or pernicious. They are even found, owing to the one-sided exaggeration which accompanies them, to be self-destructive.

The aspirant for a newly wrought material and artificial equality annihilates the sources of production by withdrawing the stimulus to accumulate capital, and only substitutes general poverty for unevenly but widely distributed wealth. The advocate of over-Government only succeeds in his ends by sacrificing personal freedom, by weakening private and public energy, and by substituting machinery for life. The advocate of doctrines which would restrict Government to the mere functions of defending property and order must account it a success when the convenience, the health, the morality, and the prosperity, of the innumerable weak and poor are placed under the irresponsible control of the limited number of strong and rich.

The absolute or divine claims of Kings, of special Dynasties, of the People, of Majorities, of Constitutions, and even of mobs, whether rich or poor, have all been asserted, and are some of them still being asserted on many sides with unhesitating assurance, and not without practical and most unequivocal effect. The only remedy or preventive is to be found in applying sound logical methods to the subject in hand, with as much caution, patience, perseverance, and breadth as well as depth of insight, as is now habitually used in the pursuit of the physical sciences.

CHAPTER IV.

THE GEOGRAPHICAL AREA OF MODERN POLITICS.

WHEN principles of Government are to be laid down, it is requisite to put some limit to the number of countries which, at a particular moment, are to be considered. Of course, if Politics is a science, its principles are universal and permanent in their applicability; and, for the purpose of drawing inductive conclusions, no *data* supplied from observations conducted anywhere can be shut out. But, though the truths of the science are invariable and irreversible, and must be collected from experience gathered in the greatest possible variety of situations, it is a misleading attempt at generalisation to hold all political communities of equal relevancy at a given moment for the purpose of political investigation either theoretical or practical.

There is a certain normal condition of a State which renders it a hopeful object of sound political manipulation, and which fits it in a peculiar degree for the function of imparting political lessons. No doubt the weakest, the youngest, the most senile, the most decrepit, State has its momentary lessons on Government to convey, and will benefit from the application to it of wise rather than unwise constitutional adjustment and legislative methods. But, considering the enormous width of the field if it be not limited, and the impediments to exact observation, it is important, in proportion to the difficulties of disentangling what are relevant facts from what are irrelevant ones, to select the most remunerative spots and to concentrate attention on them, while temporarily neglecting those societies which satisfy curiosity and afford bases for purely ethnological researches rather than shed any broad light on politics.

Such a selection is always unconsciously made in practice, though the grounds of it are neither acknowledged nor apprehended. The progressive societies of the Western World usually arrest political attention at the expense of the whole of those of the Eastern, with a few noticeable exceptions, such as Japan. Some countries, such as India and (to some extent) even the Australian Colonies and China, are regarded with political concern, less for their own sakes than for the sake of their indirect influence on the Governmental action pursued in European countries. Some countries attract attention for the sake of some special social experiment conducted within their limits; and when the experiment is believed to be completed they cease to interest till some new emergencies or vicissitudes again force them into prominence. Such was the case of Russia during the recent emancipation of the serfs; of the several Australian colonies again and again, on the successive occasions of their trying fresh constitutions; and of the United States, in respect of one and another permanent or provisional institution, such as of polygamy in Utah, of slavery, of Federalism in its successive forms, and of a series of constitutional variations from time to time introduced or practised.

A State may either be too young and immature, or too effete, or too much subjected to special arresting influences, to be counted as a relevant subject of direct political action. In the course of development from the condition of a mere congeries of tribes, with only occasional and most imperfect organisation, to the condition of a true State, a number of social changes take place which all tend one way, though the rate and modes of progress admit of all sorts of variations. The character of these metamorphic manifestations is of course of the greatest interest to the social philosopher, the psychologist, and the general historical student; and the revelations of the facts of man's nature obtained by such investigations, after being properly sifted and systematised, can often be turned to direct account by the political enquirer. But, as concerned in the movements of the political world, or as affording direct political instruction, immature States have no place.

Where immaturity ceases and a true political life begins cannot always be decisively determined. But the recognition of such a boundary to the field of profitable enquiry goes some way to help in drawing the line with practical accuracy in the particular cases to which alone doubt can extend. The most perplexing cases are those of colonial societies or other novel settlements founded by politically advanced races. The shock of change of place, the experience of new and often arduous economical conditions, and the absence of all familiar moral guidance and sanctions, place such societies and settlements in something of the same position as wholly immature tribal communities. Nevertheless, hereditary acquirements, active intellectual advancement and imported constitutional traditions distinguish an immigrant race, in some essential political features, from an aboriginal people, spontaneously making a tentative progress towards civilisation.

The political interest attaching to the Australian colonies and to the newly settled districts in the Western States of America is partly related to the peculiar and transitory experiments in Government or Sociology that are being conducted within their limits, and partly to their importance as subordinate parts of the whole political systems of England and the United States. It satisfies something more than political curiosity to ascertain from actual experiments (using this term in the loose way against which a caution has already been interposed) whether two legislative chambers or one are most favourable to the free and secure working of Colonial institutions; whether a purely representative, or a conjoint representative and nominative system of legislative organisation is most appropriate for the like ends; whether internal Federation among groups of colonies, or territories geographically connected, is favourable to their own advantage or the advantage of the rest of the world.

But such questions, important as they are in their own degree and time and place, are of quite secondary moment when compared with such a consideration as whether England should follow a policy of binding the colonies more closely to herself by some, perhaps yet untried, constitutional machinery or should do her utmost to precipitate their entire political independence; or with such another consideration as whether the Federal system of the United States can resist the strain of distance and of vast diversity of local interest which threatens its self-defensive policy of centralisation.

Thus, in estimating the geographical area of modern Politics, it is necessary and expedient to exclude from consideration the internal political manifestations of all Colonies, dependencies, and remote settlements, in professed subordination to an independent State. This result further excludes the internal Government of British India from direct political cognisance as a matter of scientific reflection.

Owing either to some essential political institutions being as yet unformed or interrupted by immigration, a State may be in such a condition of stagnation as not to figure at all as an integer in the political world. This condition of stagnation may be due to mere immobility of temperament superinduced by continuously operating moral or religious causes, or to long-protracted oppression by an alien Government, or to illiberal institutions which fetter the intellect of the people and hamper the growth of national energy.

It is scarcely necessary to cite in illustration of such conditions China even at the present moment; Japan up to the middle of this century; the countries of Middle-Age Europe when crushed beneath the military domination of Rome and then when confined within the tight leading-strings of the Feudal system. In such cases, as before, the political situation is of the highest importance, as supplying scientific instruction; but to countries so circumstanced no further direct political interest extends.

It is of great importance to notice the earliest unmistakable symptoms of independent political life. Such symptoms have disclosed themselves of late years even in China; and the waking up of Russia from a long dormant condition marks another recent extension of the field of scientific politics. The suppression of public liberty and of true political energy in the Asiatic States of native India, and in the Asiatic States intervening between the Ottoman, the Russian, and the British, dominions, in the same way removes all those States from the purview of Politics strictly so called.

A State may not only be immature and stagnant, but may have reached a condition, which, by a metaphor borrowed from the analogous region of individual human life, is often designated as senile. There is a sort of exhaustion of faculty, of invention, of national feeling, of purpose, which certainly seems to represent the stage of life in an individual man at which the body has ceased to be an adequate instrument of the spirit's activity,— even if that activity itself is not rendered temporarily torpid by disuse. History is full of instances of such a failure of national energies after a brilliant promise of lengthened vitality; and some modern States present instances scarcely less unequivocal, though, as the drama is not yet closed, it may be premature to distinguish between the symptoms of disease and those of old age.

The historical cases of senile failure of States are especially valuable as explaining some of the causes of this decadence.

It is well known that Rome, during the last two hundred years of the Republic, was suffering from three political evils which all co-operated to arrest her growth, and which, but for the corrective sequence of events which resulted in the Empire, must have precipitated her ruin, or rather antedated it by some hundreds of years. These evils were the prevalence of slave labour, with its attendant social, industrial, and economical paralysis; the misgovernment of the remoter provinces constantly in course of being annexed; and the inefficient governmental institutions for preserving the balance of powers in the State and for adequately representing the actual distribution of the political forces.

These several cancers in the State conduced to the gradual substitution of an aristocratic plutocracy for all the organs of Government which had sufficed for the earlier Republican period before the acquisition of territory outside Italy, but which were becoming more and more unsuitable to the strain put upon them. Nothing but bold and even audacious reform, such as the Gracchi conceived but were, by themselves, unable to carry into permanent operation, could have revived the expiring energies of the State. It was only through paroxysms of civic violence that a series of leaders with broad political views and the capacity of giving practical effect to them were ultimately brought to the top.

Marius, Sulla, Julius Cæsar, and Augustus represented an order of men suited to the times, but wholly different from the heroes of the older Republic. With all their several shortcomings and vices, private and public, they probably all co-operated to galvanise into life a State that had, by military successes, acquired an Empire which, at that stage of the world, it was only just possible to administer with justice or safety.

The conspicuous parallel to the later stages of degradation in the Roman Empire is the present state of the Ottoman Empire. This Empire, indeed, has behind it none of the peculiar and exhilarating antecedents of the early Roman Republic. But it had,—in common with the later Republic and the earlier Empire,—the faculty of conquest and the taste for indefinite territorial annexation. Unlike Rome, however, Turkey never had institutions of which the memorial and typical reproductions might throw a beneficial shadow. The unrelieved picture of its past is that of aggression, massacre, fanaticism, and licentiousness. The only foundation of Empire was physical courage. The result is that wherever the Ottoman power could effectually extend itself, the provinces have been unfitted for self-government. The only art in which they are accomplished students is that of revolution.

The prolongation of political vitality in the central Government was a dream of some sanguine English statesmen, of whom Lord Palmerston was the most conspicuous and the most influential, at the time of the Crimean War. This visionary hope is now dispelled. The rapid decadence of Turkey is found to be due to senility and not transient disease. The only relevant political questions affecting her are as to the future Government of the provinces in course of separation from her one by one, and, in the interval while the process of disintegration is yet uncompleted, as to the amount and quality of the pressure from without which can be brought to bear, in order to vindicate, in the provinces still submitted to her, the barest claims of humanity. The special cases of Egypt and of the Turkish provinces in North Africa have a political interest, not because they form, technically, part of the Ottoman dominions, but either as affecting the mutual relations of European States, or as disclosing some of the phenomena of nascent States, acquiring a true political character for the first time.

By this process of selection of States politically important at the present time—either because they exhibit real and independent manifestations of genuine political activity or because they afford political instruction of a complete kind,—the area of thought and observation is reduced to countries and populations of a comparatively limited extent. Of course in any such demarcation as is here attempted, where such subtle grounds of distinction are admitted as alleged immaturity, torpidity, and final exhaustion, there must be something arbitrary and inconclusive in drawing a precise line. But, if once it is admitted that some such line exists, and that its direction can be ascertained by reference to established political principles, the dispute as to whether a given State, of doubtful pretensions, lies on one side or another of the line, is of very small moment. When the occasion is presented, by a current controversy or a pressing problem, for including that State within the area of relevantly important political communities, its claims are sure to be argued *ab initio*, and no theoretical preconceptions as to its exclusion from consideration would be allowed to prevail.

Nevertheless, it may be worth while to distribute the politically relevant States into those of primary importance, those of secondary importance, and those of only occasional or hypothetical importance.

To the first of these classes belong, according to the above mentioned principles of selection and distribution, all the Independent States of Europe, only excepting the very recently emancipated Provinces of Turkey, which are so far under European control and protection that their destinies are determined in a great measure by the mutual relations and policy of other States over which they directly exercise a very insignificant influence. But, as to this exception, the line can only be drawn uncertainly, and while Greece is clearly on the political side of the line, Servia, Roumania, and the other provinces which have attained a practical release from, or modification of, their vassalage to the Ottoman Empire, are on the non-political side of the same line.

The United States is a prominent member of the class of States of primary political importance, and Japan is effectually asserting her claims to a like position. It might be a matter of indeterminable controversy how far China,—overborne as her Government is by Russian, French, and English influences, and internally oppressed by the immobility and decentralisation of her political system,—is becoming on a par with Japan as a matter of political concern. China is both old and young, progressive and stagnant. Probably a few years will decide the true place of China in the political world. Its manifestations are too recent, too confused, and too equivocal, to enable it at present to rank side by side with the equably and freely developed State of Japan, and still less with the States of Europe and the United States.

To the class of States of secondary political importance belong all newly-formed but independent States; all mature, but quasi-dependent States; and all States, which, though (perhaps) in process of degradation and dissolution, are not yet advanced far enough in the course of decline to cease to be objects of political regard. The first of these groups contains such of the recently emancipated provinces of the Ottoman Empire as are not included, according to the above mentioned tests, in the class of States of primary importance; and States recently emerged from barbarism, such as certain islands in the Pacific Ocean, especially the Hawaiian or Sandwich Islands, and also some of the organised political communities in the interior of Africa. The second group,—that of mature but quasi-dependent States,—includes Egypt and the provinces of the Ottoman Empire on the Northern Coast of Africa; the native States of India; and such States as Affghanistan and Persia, which owe their significance mainly to the neighbourhood of more important States. The third group, of effete States, not yet quite exhausted, includes some of the political communities in South America with a Spanish or Portuguese origin, and the Ottoman Empire.

To the class of States of occasional or hypothetical importance belong those political communities which may or may not be true 'States' in the strict meaning of the term given by International law, but which, any way, from time to time exhibit such marked political manifestations of an interesting kind, on so large or so prominent a scale, that they cannot be left out of account in defining the area of significant politics as presented at any particular moment. The internal Government of British India, though on one side of it only a phase of English Politics, is, on another side of it, rife with political problems and experiments, with which England and the rest of the world generally have only a very indirect concern. The same is true of the political manifestations of the Australian Colonies, in respect of constitutional adjustments, the occupation of land, taxation, commercial tariffs, and immigration. The United States of America, again, disclose, in the internal and local Government of the component members of the Union, a quantity of political experience which is none the less instructive and morally impressive, as well as urgent, because the 'States' of the Union are, in one aspect of them, only subordinate portions of a comprehensive whole.

On the same principle the constitutions accorded from time to time by the Western Powers to special provinces of the Ottoman Empire, such as Syria, Eastern Bulgaria, and Crete, have attracted to themselves an amount of political attention wholly out of proportion to the relations of the countries themselves to the decrepit central Government on which they are technically dependent. In the same way it has happened that the Government of Dutch colonial settlements, whether in Java or in the Indian Ocean or in South Africa, has presented distinct political problems of a general interest which has far exceeded the concern that would have been bestowed upon them in their relations to the kingdom of Holland.

The object of these observations is to show that, while it is necessary to classify the existing political communities of the world, in order to ascertain their relative political significance at any given moment, yet that the line between States which are more and those which are less important can only be drawn with hesitation and difficulty, and never in such a way as to exclude the possibility of controversy at all points. Furthermore, the line is constantly shifting, and must be incessantly retraced afresh. Sometimes the line is violently displaced; and the issue of a battle, the sequel of a pestilence or famine, or even a mistake in diplomacy, may have the effect of reducing to protracted political insignificance a State lately the 'observed of all observers.'

CHAPTER V

THE PRIMARY ELEMENTS OF POLITICAL LIFE AND ACTION.

IT is not the mere suggestion of historical considerations which enforces the notion that there is in every political community a group of elements or factors which are presupposed in the very existence of Government, and on the due manipulation of which successful Government depends.

A true State only comes into being when these primordial components have attained a certain stage of development; and its vitality, at all stages of its growth, is threatened whenever these components have their integrity impaired, or are badly adjusted, or when they spontaneously decay. That there are such indispensable elements in the compositions of every State is admitted in every political controversy that does not deal with a purely ideal world, or Utopia, where the ingredients and conditions can be created as well as handled at the controversialists' will. But an attempt to enumerate such elements for all conditions of society in all time would give a delusive appearance of absoluteness to a Science which must always continue relative to the changing conditions of humanity and of social development.

In Aristotle's time, and even in the beginning of

this century in America, slavery was treated, consciously or unconsciously, as a necessary and invariable concomitant sentiment of all political society, or of political society in certain parts of the world. The mere lapse of time, changes in ethical sentiment, and the shock of events, have rendered this mode of thought at the present day, even in America, an anachronism. Slavery is universally denounced as, at the best, an accidental and transitory institution which, instead of being an essential constituent of human society, is, in all its forms, its most formidable foe.

Another fact, which up to late into this century has worn the appearance of an immutable institution, is the political subordination of women to men. Though ancient polities differed much from one another in the freedom allowed to women, and such characteristic societies as those of Athens, Sparta, and Rome, —let alone the earlier ones of Egypt and Palestine,— distributed the functions of men and women each according to its own customary prepossessions, yet they one and all, it would seem (leaving, for the moment, the still unsettled problem of Egyptian civilisation, at certain stages, out of account), concurred in giving an enormous political, legal, and social preponderance to men over women. Mr. John Stuart Mill, following the rational divination of Bentham, was the first, in his 'Subjection of Women,' to explain this universal preference,—not to say injustice,—by reference to the historical advantage enjoyed by men through their possession of that special sort of physical strength which, in the earlier stages of society, is most conspicuously in demand. Travellers among incipient communities have one and all substantiated this view, and have shown that, although there are not wanting examples of communities in which women have a social preponderance over men, yet in these cases it is the women and not the men who, from superior muscular strength, courage, agility, endurance, or numbers, bear the main brunt of the conflict with nature and with competing races.

Mr. Mill's argument derives illustration and force from the notorious fact that the less militant, feudal, and physically contentious society becomes, the larger is the space found for women's activity, and the more it encroaches on the occupations traditionally reserved to men. It also is admitted with less and less reluctance, that even in estimating and comparing degrees of physical strength, nervous energy; and elasticity or adaptability, capacity for endurance, susceptibility to the claims of unforeseen emergencies, are not only of more importance in an advanced community than the mere muscular strength which resists mechanical obstacles, but that these qualities are found in average women more abundantly than in average men. This is found to be the case in spite of all the disparagement which women have suffered owing to the dominating tradition in favour of the superiority of the claims of men. It can only be seen by gradually equalising, on a large scale, the political condition and the general occupations of men and women, to what diverse social functions they are respectively most adapted by nature.

However this question may be ultimately decided, it is now only relevant to notice that it is recognised, as it never was recognised up to the beginning of this century, as an open one. Not, indeed, that premature efforts have not already been made to close it, by various

PRIMARY ELEMENTS OF POLITICAL LIFE AND ACTION. 141

kinds of solutions more or less different from the old and almost obsolete one. M. Comte's system has elevated women to a higher intellectual position in a social constitution than has that of any other thinker, and if it withdraws them from the task of practical administration, it depresses lower than other political constructions the position of all those conversant only with practical arts,—including the art of Government. M. Comte, however, emphasises far more than any other reformer in this direction the final opposition in faculty of men and women. Mr. Mill hardly admits any permanent or essential opposition at all.

It is not necessary to give further illustrations of the truth that while there are undoubtedly, in any given State, at any given time, certain facts and institutions which must be looked upon as primary and indispensable, and as forming the material on which the statesman is called to work, yet there are very few facts, indeed, even of those bound up with the constitution of man himself, which must be treated as unalterable and irreversible.

For the purpose, however, of Political science as capable of being studied at the present day and as coextensive in its application, in different degrees, to the geographical area already limited, it is possible to assign certain main facts, conditions, or relationships, which may be treated as permanent and as calling for recognition by the statesman.

Without, perhaps, being exhaustive, the following list certainly includes a large number of the facts, conditions, and relationships, which, either independently of each other, or in their combination, are at the very root of political society.

PERSONS.
   Age.
   Sex.
   Physical conditions and liabilities.
   Mental and emotional conditions (including religious proclivities).
   Heredity.
   Capacity for association.
THINGS.
   Land.
   Movables.
   Sea, and Water generally.
RELATIONSHIPS.
   Domestic.
   Social.
   Economical.
   National.

Though, for strictly juridical, or even for some philosophical, purposes each of these political elements must be investigated separately, there would be a falsity in applying the same method of research when the object is purely political. There is hardly a single one of these elements which the politician can isolate, even for a moment, from the rest and can contemplate alone, and it is in a due combination of them, and in a sort of perspective adjustment, that he exhibits his skill and scientific attainments to most advantage.

The original, as well as the permanent, function of Government is the exercise of such a control over the relations of persons to one another in a State as may bring those relations into accord with the requirements of pure reason, may protect majorities and minorities from aggressive interruptions on the part of each other, and may, by the help of the best economic organisation, facilitate the mere mechanism of society in the presumed interest of all its members.

Of course, it is scarcely necessary to recur to history and to current facts in order to demonstrate that Governments have seldom confined themselves, even in outward profession, to these limited functions, and that even where they do so in outward show, the inherent vagueness of any attempted detailed description of these functions renders all sorts of extravagant pretensions admissible and even plausible. But, it being assumed that the functions of Government are, for scientific purposes, of the broad nature above described, it appears at once that it is with the relationships of persons to each that Government is alone concerned. These relationships are of various kinds; and are either *absolute*, in so far as they terminate in the persons themselves who are the subjects of them, or are *relative*, in so far as they are concerned with objects, that is, with material things, immovable and movable, outside the persons themselves who are the subjects of the relationship.

A leading fact to be noticed is that the relationships controlled and formulated or even stimulated by Government must be, in themselves, natural,—that is, in accordance with the physical, moral, and mental constitution of man as a social being. This constitution is determined (as Aristotle put it) not by what man is, at any given time or in any given place, but by what he is capable of becoming, and that in the most favourable circumstances; that is what, in the absence of obstacles, he tends to become. It is difficult to speak of a 'natural' constitution or 'natural' order without committing a *petitio principii*. It is so easy in speech to confuse what is customary and perhaps in the highest degree artificial, or what is the result of mere neglèct and immaturity, with what is 'natural' and necessary, that the utmost precautions can hardly guard any statement on the subject sufficiently to avoid fallacious error.

Nevertheless, the researches of physical and psychological science seem to prove that man's physical constitution is governed by definite and unalterable laws, although the discovery of those laws is difficult in the extreme, and the laws themselves are found to differ within certain narrow limits in different times and countries. What is true of man's purely physical constitution seems to be proved more and more convincingly to be true of man's moral constitution as a member of society. The problem, indeed, of ascertaining the laws which govern this normal condition becomes increasingly difficult with every step upward in the scale of social complexity and ethical obscurity. But the arduousness of finding out and stating a law must be clearly distinguished from any doubt attaching to the fact that there is or is not such a law.

It is of practical quite as much as of speculative importance to recognise that human relationships, such as daily experience on every side and the whole current of past history shows them to be, are the independent framework on which the politician works, and not due to his own creative activity. In all affairs, human as well as mechanical, it is easiest to work in the direction of least resistance. The resistance is least where the common appetites, the sentiments, the desires, the passions, of mankind rather co-operate than oppose. Government, indeed, is found, historically, to grow out of some preponderant impulse in favour of supporting existing facts and institutions. But these very facts and institutions themselves are only the aggregate expression of instincts, habits, propensities, operating through long periods of time and by means of the intensifying force of concert and of associations of all kinds hardened into grooves. At the time that true Government of a permanent kind has come into being, society is becoming self-reflective. Not indeed that Government itself is a creation of deliberate reason, and still less that its reason is always in excess of the reason to be found elsewhere in the society. All that can be said is that it is from the very first the expression of the best and most orderly dispositions to be found in the average mass of the community. If it were not so, it could only persevere for a time by virtue of physical force exercised either by a foreign power or by the few over the many. It could not live and still less grow and develope.

The case is, however, otherwise. Though a primitive Government is weak in the extreme, yet it subsists and progresses only because, on the whole, it is the embodiment of the new capacity and desires of the bulk of the people for national organisation. Hence, not only is it inexpedient for a Government to trifle with the fixed and spontaneous practices and dispositions of the people, but it is impossible for it to do so for long together without committing an act of suicide. In very early society, there is only the choice, but there is the choice, between Government and a return to barbarism. In a later stage, as in that of early Greece, political inventiveness has multiplied the number of alternatives. Thus Constitutions take their rise, and a limited number of possible forms of Government,—that is, the rule of one, of a few, of many,—are admitted as alternative ways of escape from a recurrence to anarchy.

It is the great gain of the modern world that the number of constitutional forms seems almost inexhaustible, the possible modes of combination of Chambers and schemes for representation being as large as human ingenuity itself. Therefore the question now never is nor can be whether the alternative of anarchy is to be selected, on any failure of Government to do the work expected of it, but only what modification in the existing form of Government is most urgently called for.

Not, indeed, that changes in the form of Government are not still often enough revolutionary and attended by a social catastrophe. But if the State has any vitality anywhere in it, such phenomena are only transient. An instant competition takes place between the advocates or personal representatives of the various forms of Government between which, at the place and time, a choice is seen to lie, and very little time is lost before, at all events, an experimental Government is in full exercise of supreme power.

It will thus be noted that from first to last, in spite of all divergencies from its true end and aim, and of all personal errors and crimes, every Government which has lasted in any State has done so in virtue of its aptly recognising and co-operating with the spontaneous dispositions of the great mass of the people. It becomes, then, of the utmost importance for a legislator who, in conformity with the constitution of his State, is bent on adapting to circumstances and needs the general rules which bind the people to inform himself what are the institutions and tendencies which, at the moment, must be treated as essentially immutable. These institutions and tendencies may admit of indefinite adjustment and improvement, and the necessity for this may, by proper measures for diffusing information, be made intelligible and even popular. But to modify is not to abrogate, and any untimely attempt to do the latter, will absorb, in a hopeless effort, all the energy needed for the former.

A prominent instance of the function of Government in controlling and developing, without ignoring, an institution is supplied by the history, in all countries, of the Tenure of Land. It is only when a race or aggregation of tribes becomes settled on a definite territory that all the conditions can be satisfied on which national life, in the true sense, depends. No doubt there have been vast assemblages of races, such as the Teutonic races, that in the fourth and fifth centuries overran the territories of the Roman Empire, which have possessed a considerable amount of true national organisation. But the want of fixity in their occupation of the soil was a defect in their political structure which could not be made up by the presence of other elements, such as monarchy, public order, and even national self-consciousness and cohesiveness. The want of fixity interfered with the steady development of family life, and of economical relationships and enterprise, and with the treasuring up from one age to another of the hereditary associations supplied by place, scenery, and neighbourhood, on which so many of the ingredients of national existence rely for their proper nutriment. The growth of towns was also rendered impossible; and this might be taken as, in itself, a fatal obstacle to national life and expansiveness.

Assuming then, that the occupation of a definite territory is an inseparable factor in true political existence, the question is presented, at the earliest moment of national existence,—and has to be answered again and again at successive crises in the later history of the State,—upon what principles the distribution of the soil is to take place.

The question of the distribution of land is, in fact, only a part of the larger question relating to the general distribution and use of all material things whatsoever. Long before the true State is formed, and when first the instincts of order and property are beginning to assert themselves, rough rules and customs are evolved for the use, acquisition, transfer, and even inheritance or forfeiture, of such physical objects as are appreciated at an early stage of society, but are not supplied in proportion to an indefinite demand. But the regulations existing for such purposes, interesting as they are as an exhibition of primitive social usage and as illustrating the primordial stages of law, have little political significance.

It is only when society becomes in a measure settled, and when agriculture and the growth of towns become characteristic phases of a fully formed, though yet elementary, national life, that the rules for the appropriation of physical objects,—and most of all of the national soil,—become of ever increasing moment as purely political factors. So soon as merely predatory and pastoral habits are relinquished, the competition for land begins. It is instantly perceived that even if, in one sense, there is enough land for the real wants of each and all, yet that one piece of land differs from another in its propinquity to the centre of the national life, in its capacity for being cultivated and improved, and in its possession of facilities for the conveyance of its produce to markets. Its quality, and, at a little later stage, its scenic attractions, and hereditary or other like sentimental associations, introduce new grounds of distinction between one portion of land and another.

Various social and legal incidents of a familiar sort follow in the wake of these facts. Of these there have been conspicuous illustrations in the emphatic enforcement of class and plutocratic distinctions, brought about through the medium of the enormous slave-worked farms (*latifundia*), which so heavily weighted the later Roman Republic; the military ascendency and minutely regulated gradation of classes which characterised the Feudal system throughout Western Europe; and the phenomenon of rent which, with the attendant institution of the relationship of landlord and tenant, has had so profound an influence on the distribution of classes in many countries of Europe, and most of all in Great Britain and Ireland.

The occupation of land has, up to the present century, proceeded very much by hazard, and has been determined far more by specious considerations of immediate justice, and of the commanding claims of public order from day to day, than by any deliberately conceived policy. There have, however, during the last two centuries, been causes at work which have gradually changed the land question from one of law and administration into one of a purely political order.

Such causes are the vast emigration movement which, through the colonisation of the American Continent and Australasia, has been proceeding at a constantly accelerated rate of activity. The effect of this occupation of temporarily unlimited territory on a vast scale has set free the statesmen of the countries primarily concerned to treat the question of land-appropriation from a wholly new point of view. No doubt the actual tenure of land in the United States of America, in Canada, and in the Australasian Colonies, has been determined very much by the accidental circumstances in which the original settlement took place. Sometimes,—as in the case of South Australia, —a deliberate attempt was made from the first to distribute the soil in such a way as to prevent too rapid a dispersion of the holders of it, and to favour rather than to impede the development of towns. In other cases, as with some of the early American Colonies, the purpose of a grant of land to a chartered body of Colonists was the cultivation of some special product for the home market. In some of these Colonies the land was acquired by pacific arrangement with the aboriginal inhabitants, for the purpose of supplying the wants of a community already possessing a religious and quasi-political organisation.

What distinguishes all these cases of the occupation on an extended scale of the soil of new countries, is that the problem is felt from the first to be a large political one, and not a mere narrow legal one. No doubt in most of the actual cases, all sorts of mistakes, selfishness, false policy, and reckless neglect of priceless opportunities, have played their part. But still the relationships of citizens to each other, in respect of land, were not determined by the accidental course of a slowly developing civilisation, but by views entertained by numbers of persons consorting with each other, having consciously in view ulterior as well as present interests, and having a practically unrestricted territory to deal with. The question thus assumed political proportions.

To a similar, though not identical, class of causes of the recent development of the political aspects of land tenure belongs the process of acquisition by England of British India.

The result of the British acquisitions in India has been (speaking generally) the displacement of the older land-tenure system, as based on an organisation of Village Communities, and the substitution, partly of the landlord and tenant system existing in England, partly of systems of peasant proprietorships, guaranteed by settlement for a long but definite period, partly of new and peculiar tenures, proved to be specially advantageous to the cultivator of the land, and introduced for the first time in compliance with the Reports of Commissions.

The policy of all these land systems has been abundantly criticised; and Sir H. S. Maine, especially in his 'Village Communities,' after pointing out the modes in which the British Government has anticipated the natural decay of antiquated institutions, expresses alarm at the social disintegration likely to be brought about by the premature substitution of individual for corporate ownership. Other objections have been founded on the alleged interference with the rights of private contract, with the rights engendered by previous Government settlements, and with such secondary rights of money lenders and mortgagees as, through the long operation of pauperising systems of tenure, had grown up in profusion. Nevertheless the Government has persisted in its course ; and land legislation in India is now, as heretofore, conducted solely in deference to broad political, and scarcely at all in deference to narrow legal, considerations.

A similar state of things is just being witnessed in Ireland, though the immediate causes which have wakened up the British Government to a political view of the whole situation are different from what they were in India. Both in India and in Ireland the proximate pauperisation of the bulk of a population mainly agricultural supplied the needful impetus to a political change of attitude. In Ireland, however, a long series of acts of misgovernment had generated disaffection of a serious kind, while the neighbourhood of England rendered a change in the Irish land-tenure system an evil omen to proprietors of land on the other side of a narrow channel. In India, on the other hand, the obstacles to reform due to prejudice, fixity of ideas, race antipathies, and vested interests, though by no means absent, yet were too scattered and intangible to compete with the urgent necessity for developing the country and for putting a stop to the recurrent famines. In both countries one and the same result has been brought about,—that of treating the tenure of land from a political, and no longer only from a purely legal and administrative, standpoint.

Events on the Continent of Europe, from the beginning of this century, have tended in the same direction. In Germany the system of land tenure, credited with the name of Stein (though the proportions of his reform have been exaggerated), was introduced as a political cure for widespread evils, the relics of expiring feudalism and of the social devastation caused first by the Thirty Years' War and then by the military aggressiveness of Prussia. In France, the sudden break-up of feudal and aristocratic institutions which had long been an anachronism threw the great mass of the soil of the country into the market, and made it share in the purely political reformation by which, at the time of the Revolution and since, all the institutions of the country have been recast. In Russia, within still more recent times, by the abolition of villenage a most far-reaching reconstruction of land tenure has been brought about, the effects of which on the purely political destinies of the country, while they must be extensive, cannot yet be evaluated.

It is, then, admitted on all hands, and has been authenticated in one country after another in the most distinct language, that the relations of citizens to one another in respect of land is one of the most prominent departments of Political Science. When once so much is confessed, it becomes necessary to examine how different modes of distributing the soil of a country and of providing for its acquisition, use, and transfer, bear upon the political well-being of a country. A number of problems are thus originated which can only be solved in precise detail for each country, age, and class of circumstances to which it is intended to apply them. Certain leading principles are, however, already ascertained, on a due apprehension of which must depend any satisfactory solution of the problems which may occur.

The principle of first importance is that the soil of a country belongs to the whole population, present and to come, and not to any limited part of it. Stated in this way, the proposition is either a truism or is likely to be denounced as flagrantly or absurdly untrue. And, indeed, it is one of those propositions both the direct affirmative and the direct negative of which are equally untrue, and which can best be stated in an abbreviated form, solely in order to call attention to the appendant qualifications. The best explanation of the proposition is an historical one.

In the earlier stages of society the quantity of land is, except in very rare circumstances, far out of proportion to the simple wants of the population of which the State is composed. By one method and another, —of an accidental kind so far as political intention goes, —the whole soil is gradually appropriated. Through the continuous operation of customary usages, originating in convenience or in common sentiments, of judicial decisions made in compliance with current notions of abstract justice, and of occasional legislation taking place from time to time in order to supply the shortcomings of Courts of Justice, rules are laid down for the acquisition, use, and transfer, of the national soil. But while this goes on, the population or its wants, and generally both together, increase indefinitely, while the land remains the same in quantity, and its capacity of use only increases at a wholly disproportionate rate.

If this process were to go on without limit, or without being arbitrarily arrested, the portion of the population which, through the competition for wealth, had been worsted in the social struggle, would be excluded from the territory altogether. In countries where excessive emigration is going on, this process is already at work. It is however almost always impeded at a much earlier stage. Gross apparent inequality of fortune, widespread pauperism, unsatisfied 'hunger for land,' and competition for a share in agricultural profits, awaken the attention of the statesman to the fact that land is a political instrument, which cannot be treated like other physical things,—as capable of being indefinitely created or reproduced through birth, growth, or manufacture.

On further consideration, it is found that it is only by an historical accident or series of accidents that the national soil has been exclusively appropriated by a comparatively minute fraction of the population; and that it would be irrational and unjust to jeopardise the whole future fortunes of the general community by conforming, in deference to merely sentimental considerations or to self-interested appeals from private persons, to a state of things which, when analysed, is found to be ethically indefensible. At the same time, the requirements of internal locomotion, the demand for public works and structures, the increasingly recognised interests of public health, recreation, education, and even refinement, combine to press upon Government the necessity of putting in, on behalf of the people as an integral whole, novel and preponderating claims to a share in the land already absorbed.

Still further reflection and observation teach that the State has other ulterior interests, in respect of the land, which far outvie the historical claims of the actual proprietors. Some modes of tenure are found more conducive than others to good agriculture, to the creation of an interest in public affairs, to the formation of stability and continuity in common political thought, and to the simplification of Local Government. It must be the object of a judicious statesman to seize every opportunity which may offer, to change the worse for the better system of tenure, and the more broadly statesmanlike habits of mind are diffused, the more such changes are likely to be facilitated.

The way this characteristic modern view of the conflicting interests of the whole community, and of private proprietors, in respect of land formulates itself is by asserting that the land is, or ought to be, national property and not susceptible of being finally absorbed by private persons and their hereditary representatives from one generation to another. To maintain this doctrine, and still more to enforce it by practical legislation, naturally excites the strongest antipathies in a variety of quarters, on the ground of its being redolent of 'confiscation,' and of its implying an alleged national breach of faith with existing proprietors.

The Feudal system, which was at the root of the land tenure in the most important countries of Western Europe, reserved the dominant claims of the Feudal monarch, who personified the State as paramount over all derived estates, and 'allodial' property became in the highest degree exceptional. The progress of that system, however, was first to transmute service into the payment of rent, so far as the subordinate and derived estates went; and, at the same time, through aristocratic encroachments on the Crown,—or rather, through a fresh division of functions between the Crown on the one hand and its high Councillors and officers on the other,—to reduce the significance, or abolish the memory, of services due to the Crown.

It thus came about that the larger landed proprietors stepped into the place of the Crown, so far as its paramount ownership of the national land went, while they have not inherited from the Crown, together with their estates, the corresponding political obligations. Hence, in the countries where the Feudal system has taken the deepest root and for the longest time,—such as England and France,—the laws as made by the nobility, or as being the surviving relics of the system itself, especially favoured the larger proprietors, and conduced to the accumulation of estates in a very limited number of hands. At the same time the moral claims of the cultivator, and of the actual resident on the soil, had a far worse chance of being effectually asserted or borne in mind than might have been the case had the tenure of land been left to follow the more spontaneous development which took place in territories which were longer under the shadow of customary institutions protected by the waning force of the Roman Empire,—such as Italy, Switzerland, and the South of France.

Of course, when the charge of 'confiscation' is made against any contemplated re-assertion of national against private claims, it must be remembered that such a charge would only be justified if the perpetual policy of a State in favour of deferring to the claims of abstract Justice were really infringed. These claims, undoubtedly, demand that reasonable expectations, called into being by the State itself, should be satisfied to the utmost extent possible, and, at least, never left out of serious account.

But when a question of abstract Justice presents itself, a solution cannot be obtained by taking account of the claims on one side and no account at all of those on the other. If, through a series of political accidents during a long period of time, any important class of the community professes to have enjoyed privileges or exclusive advantages, from which other equally important classes have thereby been shut out, the absolute claims of Justice itself demand that a re-adjustment be effected with as little delay as possible, though, also, with the least possible economical or moral loss to either of the competing classes of claimants. In respect of new land-legislation, pecuniary compensation can usually go some length in avoiding needless economical loss; though it may be that the loss to certain sentiments of ownership may be irreparable.

If it seems harsh that the burden of sudden reforms should all fall on a single generation, it is also harsh, in another way, that a single generation of taxpayers should have to pay the price of compensation to the vested interests violated. This inequality of pressure in national burdens between one generation and another is a necessary, though often vexatious, consequence, of the continuity of State life, and it will always be the aim of the wise and just statesman, by loans and payment of loans and other financial devices, to distribute, as equally as may be, the burdens of the State between one generation and others.

Besides the characteristics of the individual man and woman, the fact of which is assumed in the organisation of the State, there are relationships into which persons of both sexes and all ages equally enter, which, through their internal coherence and external links with each other form the material out of which the State is moulded and consolidated. The groups so constituted are Families having their foundation in Marriage.

The history of Marriage, as a political factor, is the history of the gradual training of mankind out of a condition in which a purely animal propensity predominates over a dormant social and moral instinct, into a condition in which that propensity is completely subordinated to complex human sentiments capable of attaining the richest kinds of development. It is not true that, even in the most primitive savagery, marriage is wholly non-existent. History and the reports of travellers lend no support to such a view, which is, otherwise, opposed to the known constitution of man as a gregarious being. But the mere witness for marriage as something more than promiscuous cohabitation is compatible, it would seem, with any amount of degradation attending its early manifestations; with any number of varieties in the forms of conjugal combinations of men and women; with rites, ceremonies, and usages of the most grotesque and often of the most apparently irrational kind, and with every kind of confusion and intermixture in the families which spring from marriage relationships. The progress of society, and of the State which is based on this progress and on the institutions which it implies, is marked by nothing more distinct than the gradual evolution of a strict form of monogamic marriage out of all its antecedent and anticipatory manifestations.

It is still denied in some quarters, not wholly undeserving of attention, that monogamic marriage is to be always and everywhere the final form which the marriage relationship will assume in the perfectly developed State. It would be unscientific, as has already been repeatedly indicated, to lay down any absolute propositions about states of society indefinitely remote and on which past experience of any sort could only throw an uncertain light. But, inasmuch as the art of Government calls for prevision before all else, and therefore must rest upon Scientific experience and observation conducted within appropriate limits, it is necessary, as it is possible, to draw conclusions of some sort from the past as to a future not indefinitely remote.

The result of the teaching of the past is to show that though polygamic marriage is, in certain undeveloped stages of society, compatible with the existence of a true State, yet that it is not compatible with the existence of an advanced State. There are only two noticeable instances in which it might be claimed that polygamous institutions are compatible with a high degree of political progress. One is that of Judaism, which the habitual study of the Bible has rendered the most familiar and cherished of all historical precedents. The other is that of Mohammedanism.

If the late Dr. Deutsch's theory be correct,—that Mohammedanism is only Judaism adapted to the conditions of Arabian life,—these two instances really amount only to one. But, on a closer scrutiny, the value of these instances of apparently successful polygamy is largely reduced. Neither Judaism at its best, nor Mohammedanism in its richest political and military manifestations, has exhibited any but the most immature forms of true political life and organisation. The monotheistic beliefs, the priestly institutions, and the military necessities of Judaism, placed as it was, geographically, between Egypt, Syria, and Assyria, combined to impart to it, at its highest moments under the early kings, political qualifications of a high but precocious kind.

The weakness of the constitutional basis, however, on which the political order rested is manifest from the extraordinary influence exerted on the national fortunes by the personal character of the king, and from the mode in which, in spite of the political sagacity and importunities of a memorable line of statesmanlike prophets or prophetical statesmen, the policy of the State vacillated with every oscillation in the diplomacy of surrounding States. It succumbed to all its rivals and neighbours in succession, instead of holding,—as a small State so situated well could, and at rare times did,— the balance between them, and so securing the amount of regulated independence which the Egyptians, in the lowest depths of their fortunes, under the same Assyrian oppression which bore so heavily on the kingdoms of Israel and Judah, succeeded in vindicating.

The order of the Jewish State was built up on a traditional national instinct, on common ceremonial usages, on a religious unity, on far-sighted hierarchical arrangements, on tribal sympathies or antipathies,— but not on family life. Of course marriage of some sort and the integrity of the family were recognised abstractly in their institutions, and were enforced by teachers and prophets in the clearest and loudest tones. Otherwise the State could never have lived as it did, nor have so lived that, being dead, it yet speaketh. But the very prominence of the teaching and reproofs, and the notorious examples of the eminent persons whose biography has been preserved, point to the lowness of the common standard of conjugal fidelity and the absence of monogamy as a theory or a practice. The want of this unit of family life could not but tell with weakening and isolating effect on every part of the political organisation, till, at the summit, it touched external politics, and hastened the time long foreseen when the nation went forth one way to meet its enemies and fled seven ways before them.

The history of Mohammedanism, when adduced as a favourable instance of the working of polygamic institutions from a political point of view, affords, if possible, a still more decisive proof on the other side. It may, first, be noticed by the way that polygamy was no original or essential institution of Mohammedanism, and that Mohammed was enlightened and keen-sighted enough to perceive that for the purpose of creating an organised nation out of the wild and undisciplined Arabs who supplied the material for him to work upon, the first thing to do was to regulate family life, and to restrict the prevalent looseness of relationship which prevailed between men and women. This he achieved by binding his followers to content themselves with a definite number of wives, (that is four,) though he subsequently allowed himself and his successors in his office an unlimited number. Considering that Mohammed seems to have been perfectly faithful for years together to his first wife Hedijah, and only after her death to have allowed himself more than one wife, and that his whole policy became simultaneously more warlike and less religious, in an ethical sense, there can be little doubt that he underwent a personal degradation of sentiment in this matter.

The results were impressed on the history of the Mohammedan movement. The principle of importing regulation of some sort into marriage and family life has, in spite of the libertinism of thought and aspiration which so much of the system inspires, admitted of some few of the nations penetrated by Mohammedanism attaining a very considerable amount of political prosperity. But the allowance of more wives than one, the facilities for divorce, the recognition of concubinage and of slavery have prevented any Mohammedan nation passing on to the higher forms of political life. All these higher forms presuppose first, the equality, before the law and in the State, of all its members,—men and women alike; and, secondly, their settled distribution into the natural but strictly organised family groups, in and through which alone social and political life can be trained, concentrated, animated, and rendered subservient to other broader forms of association. The combination of these two conditions,—the equality of men and women and the distribution of all members of the State into distinct families,—can only be achieved by monogamic marriage.

It is, perhaps, scarcely worth while to notice the eccentric reversion to polygamic marriage which has been attempted in the Mormon Society settled in the territory of Utah in the United States of America. It is not likely that the experience of the so-called 'Saints' of Salt Lake City and the adjacent districts will be cited as favourable to the general re-introduction of polygamic institutions.

The subject of Mormonism, as a political scheme, is a complex one, since it combines the elements of socialism, colonisation, religious superstition, and only as an accidental, and historically later, clement, polygamy. It is sufficient to notice that the fortunes of the society have practically been more weighted by that abnegation of true family life which polygamy has involved than by any other of its peculiarities. The abnormally numerous progeny claiming one man as their father throws the burden of supporting the different groups on the mothers of each, and encourages the common father in indolence and neglect of all parental duties; while the natural rivalries of the different wives and the inane frivolity resulting,—as in Eastern harems,—from habits of life absorbingly preoccupied by conjugal and puerperal solicitudes, keep the women at a depressed level of cultivation—possibly even as compared with the men.

The general consequences are being every day more clearly seen in the gradual dissolution from within of the cohesiveness of the old organisation, which is further precipitated by the intrusion, for purposes of commerce, of an active and healthy 'Gentile' element, and by the decay of the early religious faith consequent on the removal by death, one by one, of the original Apostles and leaders. The instance is mainly noteworthy, in a political sense, from its establishing that, even if an Oriental community which has stagnated at a polygamic stage can long retain its political organisation and some moral health, yet no community which has once passed that stage can revert to it without soon encountering moral degradation of the deepest sort. Not even religious fanaticism, colonising zeal, nor a communistic spirit of co-operation, can save it or long delay its destruction.

The essence of marriage is not only that it should be monogamic, but that the association it contemplates should be life-long. It is this second characteristic,— the necessary life-long tenacity of the marriage tie,— which has suffered most assault at the hands of modern civilisation, or which, more correctly speaking, has the greatest difficulty in establishing itself in the face of dislocating and corrupting influences, themselves the product of civilisation.

There is no doubt that the march of civilisation has been signalised in a considerable degree by the substitution, in large departments of relationship, of voluntary contract for *status*, that is, for involuntary conditions. Slavery and Vassalage have given place to domestic service and free engagements between workmen and capitalists; while even Government itself is held to be based on determinate and reciprocal advantages, reaped simultaneously by the Governors and the governed respectively, and not on mysterious irresponsible claims of privilege on one side or on inevitable submission on the other. By a not unnatural analogy it has been attempted to extend the reign of contract everywhere, even to regions in which it is wholly inapplicable. There is a still greater disposition to do this when, as in the case of marriage, some of the incidents,—such as those involving pecuniary arrangements,—may properly become subjects of true contracts.

But though marriage involves, for its inception, the highest exercise of unbiassed volition, the existence of the state of marriage after its creation excludes, with equal peremptoriness, the notion of its dissolubility at the bidding of licence or caprice on either side, or even on both sides. So soon as once the state of marriage is created, the parties to it are no longer in a condition of responsibility only to one another. Beside them and above them is the community to which they belong.

The community not only represents the claims of possible children and relations of all sorts, deeply concerned in the fixity and permanence of bonds which control their own lives, but has an interest peculiarly its own. It is of the utmost concern to the community that the family groups which compose it, in the last analysis, should be definite and unmutilated; that the utmost opportunity should be afforded for the quiet and orderly development of the affections, and of the sentiments of mutual trust and dependence which are only brought to maturity in the life-long home; that the family should be a school for the restraint of passion, for self-discipline and for conciliatory self-surrender, not an arena for the practice of irresponsible self-indulgence; that, in fine, in the family the social capacities should gain predominance over the centrifugal individualism of savagery, and the State itself should be at once reflected and anticipated in its most ubiquitous and natural type.

All these requirements enforce the notion that for marriage to be dissoluble at will, or dissoluble at all, except in the most limited class of circumstances, as regulated by judicial circumspection of the most stringent and delicate kind, is suicidal to the true conception of marriage itself. In all political constitutions, and in all legislation which depends upon them, there is a place found for the remedy of a condition of things which the State is bound to regard as exceptional. The recognition of judicial divorce belongs to this remedial department of State provisions, and it may, undoubtedly, be admitted in such a way as to co-exist with the most strenuous support of the life-long permanence of marriage. In the same way a bankruptcy law implies no political patronage of recklessness as to the payment of debts.

Though, in the way above indicated, marriage and the family relationships which spring from it must be treated as essential and primordial elements in State life, it is also obvious that the final and best result of that life, and not only the initial condition of it, is to impart to them their highest development, dignity, and stability. In the laws of every State which has advanced beyond an embryonic condition, personal relationships form the subjects of the most prominent chapters. They are usually the products of older and more deeply rooted customs than even laws of property, while, on the other hand, the necessity of determining questions of succession and inheritance, of guardianship and of the claims of women, implicate those customs in every part of these laws.

Before quitting the subject of the Family as an essential and primary element of political existence, it seems desirable to pause for the purpose of recapitulating and emphasising the points in which the recognition of family life is of importance to the statesman. The secure limits which are placed on the tastes and affections afford the repose and opportunity demanded for the even development of the less animal functions and for the gradual attainment of complete supremacy by the spiritual nature. In this way, the best possible field is opened out and guarded for the nurture of children, their unconscious and conscious education and their future separation under the most favourable auspices from the parents' home. From this separation new families take their rise without the tender links with the old ones being broken, and rather with the result of increasing than of diminishing the aggregate effectiveness and felicity.

It is needless to say how profoundly concerned is the statesman in movements and connexions such as these. Not only is it historically true that from the union and multiplication of families springs the tribe, and from the union and multiplication of tribes springs the State, but even in the advanced State domestic disorganisation is a sure augury of early political disaster. The natural duty incumbent on parents, of providing for their children, has in all civilised though immature States had a marked effect on the law of succession to property. The helplessness and yet the value of the young life has called forth, everywhere, laborious provisions for guardianship and protection. The mutual responsibilities, physical and moral, of husbands and wives, of parents and children, and even of remote relatives by consanguinity and affinity, have been, from the earliest dawn of political society, matter of concern to the nascent legislature. Not indeed, that, at first, regulations in respect of such matters are consciously formulated or even dimly contemplated. But they grow up with the State itself and are but one expression of its growth.

It may be long before the conscious statesman arises and ascertains the value of the laws and institutions which have come down to him with the stream of generations and are ready to his hand. He may have to prune here, to add there, to abolish elsewhere, and to amend and reform everywhere. But the materials and elements which are bound up in family life are none of his making, and while they will survive him, not the longest line of his successors will survive them.

But the family, essential and momentous as it is, as an element in State life, needs supplementary elements to maintain it in health and to prevent it becoming a mere centre of an individualism not less selfish than the isolated member of the race. The very sentiments to which family life gives preponderance, the exclusive and concentrated affections, the absorbing cares, the desperate solicitudes, the heated passions,— strong through confinement in a narrow area and aggravated by sympathy,—have an evil as well as a good side, from a political stand-point. Indeed from the stand-point of its own well-being and happiness, family life cannot afford to be wholly self-contained. Its affections and interests must be driven outward; and it must learn the meaning of corporate magnanimity as well as that of individual sacrifice.

Historically speaking, it is the tribal and village organisation which first healthily extends the sympathies and interests of family life. In the more advanced State, when the tribe has become the nation, and the village has become the town, the rush of economical necessities, as well as the impulse of social fellowships, operate to lead families out of themselves and to blend them in a great and common life. The State, itself, is from the first moments of its growth, reacting upon these spontaneous tendencies and fostering their influence. In the advanced State there are endless forms of association which intervene between the family and the political community as a whole, and it is the due control or use of these associations which often supply to the Statesman his most arduous problems.

A distinction, however, has to be made between the associated groups of persons which, as the State advances, owe their existence to mere economical progress, and those of a more complex and varied kind which are the product of the organisation of the State itself, though they are also of the number of its elements and powerfully react upon it.

To the first or more primitive class of purely economical relationships belong the trade and commercial connexions which spring from a constantly increasing division of labour. Such are the connexions between the shopkeeper and his customers, the landlord and his tenant, the employer and the employed, the farmer and the farm-labourer, the capitalist and the workman, the master and the servant. In this economic and social bifurcation of society there are generated great pairs of classes of persons, of which each pair represents two sets of mutually opposed interests. It may be that circumstances favour the concentration of these interests in the form of guilds, corporations, companies, clubs and trades-unions. The formation of such communities is a matter of the keenest interest to the Statesman, and he has to determine how far he shall recognise, control, encourage, or disallow it.

Apart from any intervention of the State, the influence of these associated interests must be always of a dubious nature, and it must depend on a number of concurrent social circumstances whether on the whole it is good or bad. Thus, in the case of artisans' guilds, such as grew up side by side with the great City companies in Plantagenet England, one of their effects was to stimulate artistic workmanship by guaranteeing privileges and monopolies, and by promoting apprenticeships. Another class of effects was to prevent competition, to restrict invention, and to sustain prices at a point higher than that determined both by the cost of production and by the law of supply and demand. The community was thus the loser in some ways and the gainer in others.

It would depend on the particular condition of the Society at the time whether more was likely to be gained by the encouragement given to special artisans or lost by the artificially high prices and the limitation of the field of labour.

It is a well-recognised principle of modern politics to abstain as far as possible from actively fostering trades and occupations by according privileges and monopolies. But when associations of persons are created by voluntary contract, and the associations are potent and extensive enough to succeed in confining to themselves special kinds of work, it becomes a serious consideration for the Statesman how far, if at all, the contract ought to be recognised as valid.

The most modern form in which the problem presents itself is that of Trades Unions. The moral use of certain forms of these Unions to the workmen themselves is recognised as great. They tend to train the workman out of a merely selfish and individualistic spirit of reckless competition, and to accustom him to blend the interests of himself and of his family with those of his fellow-workmen. Their actual result has been to raise the character of the working-man, to make him more prudent, as being under a sense of communistic responsibility, and yet less anxious and more self-respectful, because less exposed to suffer from the mere irresponsible caprice or selfishness of his employers.

But, on the other hand, the danger inherent in all such associations is that the special advantages they enjoy are purchased at the cost of the general community, in the increase of prices, the limitation of the labour market, and the expulsion of capital to foreign countries. It will afterwards be seen, in connexion with the subject of the Province of Government, that the only function left to the State in this matter is the protective one, of guarding both those within and those without the Union against certain inevitable influences of combination which, alone, they might be powerless to resist. How far this protection is to go, is a question of time, place, and circumstances. It only needs here to notice that these associative tendencies, and the sentiments of attraction and repulsion they call up, form some of the most important constitutive elements with which the State has to deal.

In the most advanced condition of the State, association becomes the natural form into which all commercial, social, philanthropic, religious, and political, energy throws itself; and the State is constantly confronted with the question how far it is to recognise, or to restrict, the more or less formal organisations which spring up in consequence. In whatever terms the answer may be made,—and there is no topic on which States and

Statesmen have committed, and continue to commit, more serious mistakes,—it is well to remember that the associative principle is the natural and necessary schoolmaster to bring the citizen to the perfection of State existence.

It is in the subordinate connexions and relationships of a social and economic kind with his fellows that man learns to look outside himself and his own petty life and even outside the life of his family,—dear as that is and properly supreme to him as are its claims,—and to venture forth his emotions and powers into a wider field. He becomes used to multiplied and endlessly varied relationships, and is transmuted into a fuller being himself. He acquires, as on an exercise ground, the instinctive art of weighing the competing claims of each against all and of all against each. He learns something of what it is to give and to serve, to hope and to wait, as well as to receive and to have. He dives deeper and deeper into the mine of human feeling and into the possibilities of reciprocal sacrifice. He finds himself hourly animated by countless examples, —often of the humblest kind,—and knows himself to be ever surrounded by a long-familiar cloud of witnesses. He is braced up to adjust his every action to the standard of duty incumbent on a citizen of what his life-long training has taught him to regard as 'no mean city.'

CHAPTER VI.

CONSTITUTIONS.

IT has already been noticed that, in one sense, the conception of a Constitution is wholly of modern growth. It is true that in the best times of Greece, if not earlier, the question as to the best form of Government in the abstract, and for particular States, had already attracted attention; and the general subject was regarded as of theoretical as well as of practical importance. But it was not till the human race had become universally enfranchised in men's minds, and the depth of root which political rights have in morality had been recognised, that the full extension of the term *constitution* could be reached.

The Christian Church, indeed, by its organisation, its notion of the essential spiritual equality of all men, and its competition, at some points, with the secular power, prepared the way for the supposition of there being some settled condition of human society in which each member would have his appropriate place; in which each would contribute to the efficiency of all, and all to that of each; and in which no act of violence, whether proceeding from a monarch or a mob, could suddenly introduce fatal change.

In the time of the English Commonwealth, religious zeal and political activity co-operated in the direction both of practical change and of favouring the construction of ideal forms of social organisation on a basis of equal rights for all. Based as these schemes were on the rude and weather-beaten materials which the form of English Government in the seventeenth century supplied, they could, at the best, be but rough sketches of an ideal polity. They are mainly important as marking the rapid advances which the notion of a political Constitution,—as distinguished, on the one hand, from a mere body of constitutional laws and, on the other, from a description of a form of Government,— was making in England and in the world at large.

Montesquieu's panegyric on the English Constitution, in his *Esprit des lois*, tended to popularise the true conception of a Constitution as belonging to universal politics, though France was hardly ripe for the idea till the flames of the Revolution had fully awakened the national spirit and conscience, or rather witnessed to their awakening.

In England Hobbes, and after him Swift, kept alive the political imagery which owed its creation to Puritan times and with which the days of the Restoration and of the Whig Revolution were little in harmony.

In the meantime, however, the British Colonies in America were upholding the conception of a true Constitution in a multitude of somewhat varying forms, and laying the foundation of the first actual Constitution which should be constructed on the lines of theoretical science and yet should, after a hundred years' trial, hold out promise of eternal duration and growth. In the written Constitutions of the Thirteen Colonies, the English reader will find for the first time transferred to systematic writing what are held to be the inalienable rights, privileges, or prerogatives of an Englishman, but the title deeds of which in England are only to be found expressed tacitly in institutions or scattered up and down in archives and antiquated records.

The right to Trial by Jury, the security against despotic Treason trials, the principles of the Habeas Corpus Acts, the exemption of an Englishman's person from outrage and contumely even in the name of the law, the independence of the Judges, and the most valuable clauses of the Bill of Rights, will be found expressed in clear and concise language and ranged in distinct propositions on the face of the written Constitutions of the several Colonies. These documents are of the highest interest in many ways, inasmuch as they establish the conception of the constitutional position of Englishmen held at home at the time the Charters were granted to the several bodies of Emigrants; and also because, indisputably, they supplied the type, and much of the language, of the constitutional laws of the Union, when these came to be framed.

The word 'Constitution' in some of its familiar modern uses, testifies to the new and profounder meaning it has in modern times. Thus a distinction is sometimes drawn between a British Colony which has a Constitution and one which has not. Here *Constitution* does not mean a form of Government, because what is known as a 'Crown Colony,'—which is opposed to a Colony with a Constitution,—has a very precisely described form of Government, including a Legislative and Executive Authority,—subject, of course, as the Government of all Colonies is, to the Government at home.

A Colony with a Constitution means a Colony which has Parliamentary institutions and is no longer governed by a small legislative body or Council every member of which is directly nominated by the Executive Authority, that is the Crown, at home. Thus the word Constitution is made co-extensive with the expression 'having Parliamentary institutions.' These institutions may include a Chamber, nominated,—as now in New South Wales,—by the Governor, who himself is appointed by the Government at home. But the recognition of a general right, in all male members of the community, under fitting precautions and conditions of uncertain but not unmeasured limits, to take part in the Government by themselves or by their proxies, supplies the foundation of a true Constitution. Similarly, when the numerous revolutions took place in Europe in 1848, the result was said to be, in many cases, the granting of a Constitution, which meant the introduction, revival, or reformation, of Parliamentary and representative Government on a tolerably broad basis of electoral rights.

In all these conceptions of a Constitution, there enter the ideas of universality, of widely or rather indefinitely, diffused personal rights, and of popular intervention in Government. These ideas are compatible with a great range of variety in the actual form and composition of Government, and, obviously, also with a great variety of degrees of completeness with which the essential notion of a Constitution is embodied in a political organisation.

Constitutions may be good or bad, weak or strong, lasting or transient, even popular or aristocratic. In fact it may come about, at certain moments, that the

Constitution exists in idea and sentiment only, and that, owing to accidental events, the people of a country have no political rights at all. In such a case, as to some extent in France under the third Empire, and even in Russia and in Egypt now, the Constitution is in suspense. It is a matter of hope, regret, and perhaps of expectation, and soon of revolutionary zeal. But a country which has once imbibed the notion of a Constitution differs wholly from one in which that notion has never been framed or could never be framed, as in China, and the Native States of India, and in large portions of the Ottoman dominions and the uncivilised States of Africa.

In all the countries which, according to the principles already enunciated, are at present the proper subjects of Political Science, the idea of a Constitution has made considerable advance; and, in some of them, an actual Constitution has been wrought out into shape with no small amount of elaborateness in the execution of the details.

In respect of the practical task of planning a Constitution, an initial question presents itself on the threshold as to whether the terms of the Constitution can be completely or satisfactorily expressed in writing. During recent years,—beginning with the Constitution of the United States,—a large number of Constitutions have been translated into the terms of written law; and even in Constitutions, such as that of England, in which the quantity of unwritten law and usage is the greatest, there is still a large and growing proportion of the whole which takes the form of Statute Law.

The question, however, is not whether it is within the wit of man to write a Constitution down and to describe in precise terms and phrases the rights and duties of all public officials and all members of the community in respect of Government, but whether, when this is done ever so skilfully and providently, there must not still remain, outside any constitutional Code, the most important part of all, which is too indefinite, too subtle, too fluctuating within imperceptible spaces of time, to admit of compression within the limits of exact language.

In the United States, after all the provisions of the existing Constitution are described with as much exactness as could be attained, there is still contemplated the possibility of a change in the Constitution being desirable, and an elaborate electoral and representative machinery has been devised in view of the necessity of bringing about a change. As a matter of fact a number of more or less important changes have been brought about in this way, and no insuperable difficulty has been experienced in working the machinery. But, supposing that the change desired was at once considerable and yet not such as to commend itself to the large majority requisite for giving legal effect to it, the only result must be the alternative of social disruption or revolution.

Such a state of things did come at the time of the Secession war; and it was found that no mere written language could bind the fealty of the whole people. The Constitution, as it stood, was only acceptable to the Southern States so long as a series of favourable accidents gave them the political influence they desired. When the Constitution legally operated in a direction less favourable to their interests, they resisted the execution of the law and claimed to dissolve the Union.

Thus in times of real emergency, when interests and

passions are divided, it matters little whether a Constitution is written or unwritten. There are felt to be forces and instincts stronger than the law, as they are the basis of all law. It is in the hereditary and habitual training of these forces and instincts, perhaps continued for centuries, that what may be called a true constitutional temper really exists. Where such a training is found, anarchy is impossible, and revolution is shortlived. Where it is not found, a permanent condition of order is hardly attainable and revolutions are incessant.

The recent history of France illustrates the state of a country undergoing a rapid constitutional training through the vicissitudes of a single century. The condition of the Ottoman Empire shows how easy it is to frame written constitutions and to enact them, but how impossible it is to impose them where no advance has been made in the ethical preparation of the people and of the ruling class.

There is, however, no doubt that it is for the interests of order and of regular Government to have as many parts as possible of the Constitution reduced to writing. Not indeed that discussion is thereby prevented, as may be seen by studying the volumes of law written on the 'Constitutional Limitations' of the Government of the United States, and on the operation of the written Constitutions of the English Colonies. But in times of ardent differences of opinion, not to say of discord and sedition, it is a great advantage on the side of order to have a plain course of proceeding mapped out by written law. Action proceeds while people's minds are still being made up, and, before they have finally chosen their side, an act performed has acquired the pretensions of prescription.

The French nation experienced in 1878 the advantage of their written Constitution when, in precise accordance with its terms, they elected a successor to President McMahon without delay or hesitation; and at various epochs in English history the advantage of a written rule or even of a well remembered precedent stored up in the archives of written history, however imperfectly applicable, has suggested and determined a course of action which has commended itself to the bulk of the community by its show of formality, and has thereby arrested revolution. Instances of this are supplied by the operation of the Act of Settlement in facilitating the accession of the House of Hanover, and of the Regency Acts of the Reign of George III., each of which smoothed the way for the passing of its successor.

The first question which has to be settled by a Constitution is as to the number of persons who are to take part in the Government, and the share in it which each person is to have. Mr. Austin, in his celebrated Lectures on the 'Province of Jurisprudence,' pointed out with inimitable clearness the fact, which is not so much contested as neglected, that, at any given period in the existence of a political community, there is some person or assemblage of persons who are habitually obeyed by the bulk of that community.

In the Greek communities, as investigated by Aristotle, the absorbing question was as to the number of persons who formed this sovereign authority; and even in modern times the mere breadth of the legislative Assembly or Assemblies, and the numerical extension of the electoral surface, are points of considerable relevancy in the comparison of the merits of Constitutions. But there are many reasons which now conspire to reduce the significance of the mere quantitative estimates which, to the minds of Montesquieu and even of De Tocqueville, were the basis of the distinction between a Monarchy, an Aristocracy, and a Democracy.

The deeper notion of human rights which is acquiring the dignity and the fixity of an ethical maxim changes the question as to how many, and who, ought to be admitted to share in the Government, into the converse question as to whether any, and who, can be legitimately excluded from sharing at all. The victory which was obtained for the emancipated slaves in America by their admission to the electoral Franchise was as much a gain to the human race, regarded as capable of political organisation, as to the immediate objects of the enfranchising Amendment to the Constitution of the United States. In the same way the movement which promises an early success in favour of Women's Suffrage in England, by removing an obstacle, based only on tradition and prejudice, and confessed to be of no practical value,—even if not economically detrimental,—goes far to fortify the notion that, apart from special and clearly established personal disqualifications, the right of taking part in Government belongs, as an essential part of the heritage of civilised humanity, to all alike.

Even in the times of Hobbes and of Locke, the two theories,—in the somewhat cumbrous legal forms of the Divine Right and the Social Contract,—were being brought face to face. Both these conceptions have,— after a brilliant history well sketched out by Sir H. S. Maine in his 'Ancient Law,'—dissolved away before the analytical solvents of History and Logic. But there still remain sternly antithetical to each other two inconsistent views of the true basis on which a constitution ought to be founded: namely, that of procuring the absolutely best law and administration, and that of procuring law and administration which, if perhaps not the best, yet is the best expression of the clearly ascertained will of the people, or of the preponderant majority of the people at the time.

These two views either appear on the surface or are covertly implied on every occasion of electoral change. It is usually attempted to make a compromise between them, and disputants who recognise the value of each view, when isolated from the other, do not always perceive the extent to which they are, or may be, incompatible.

It is surprising how many affiliated questions are connected with this primary discrepancy. Such questions are, whether a representative system ought to succeed in reproducing in the legislative assembly all important phases of political opinion or only the dominant phase, or a few dominant and ostensibly competing phases; whether representation in any sense can be looked at as a satisfactory and permanent instrument of Government, or whether (as some English followers of Auguste Comte hold) it marks only a transitory and immature condition, for the needs of which it provides at best but a rough and cumbrous machinery; what are the mutual claims of local and of central Government; and to what extent the Executive Authority should be subjected to popular checks and control.

With the view of ascertaining the true principles

which, for the purpose of a Science of Politics, must be held to underlie all profitable discussion of this class of subjects, a few broad premises have been, in modern times, clearly established, and must henceforward be taken as starting points in the argument.

One premise is that the Art of Government tends increasingly to become, in quite a different sense from anything known before, a specialised art, needing peculiar training, concentrated attention, and long and appropriate study. The internal administration and the conduct of the Foreign relations of a Modern State are, with every advance in the arts of life and in economical and social organisation, becoming matters of special knowledge.

In Ancient times, and in the Middle Ages, the governing class no doubt were far in advance of the community, and possessed acquirements and diplomatic accomplishments for which there is less opening now. But the financial, the moral, the religious, and the sanitary,—let alone the judicial and military,—functions of a modern State, even of the youngest and smallest, are complicated and embarrassing to an extent for which there could be no precedent in the older world.

It is not now, however, the fact that the classes habitually called upon to take part in the Government are better informed than other classes of the Community. Indeed the opposite is usually the case; and the persons best informed in their several trades, occupations, and professions, are content to devolve the charge of Government on persons less specially instructed in any peculiar branches of knowledge but, otherwise, generally competent and trustworthy.

The result is that the art of Government is becoming

a new and special one, quite distinguishable from every other art, and yet involving some cognisance or, at least, some recognition of the claims and province of every other art and human interest. So far from this becoming less true as time goes on, it will become more true with each step of social advance as expressed in a new division or subdivision of occupations, and the danger rather is that the art of Government may need such an amount of distribution into departments as may seriously impair the due co-ordination and supervision of the whole.

The question, then, is presented, how far the premise which propounds this specialisation of the art of Government can be reconciled with another premise to the effect that, with the growth of civilisation, the claims to intervene in the Government of the country are increasingly recognised as inherent attributes of humanity.

The only solutions which have been attempted of this problem have been found in the devices, firstly, of Representation and, secondly, of Party Government.

The result of all the investigations of M. Guizot, of Mr. Hallam, and of later writers, into the history of the modern institution of Representation is that this institution is rooted partly in the representative Councils of the Christian Church,—which themselves as time went on reproduced the administrative and judicial usages of the centralised Roman Empire,—and in the nature of Feudalism, involving as it did the substitution of man for man as its essence, and a representative system in the Courts as its inseparable working machinery.

The later development of representative ideas and facts in the modern political world, beginning in the history of the English Parliament and recalled to life on the Continent of Europe by the first French Revolution, is only a chain of direct consequences from notions which had been deeply instilled into the consciousness of the Teutonic and Romaic races. The necessities of confederation which had been felt and acted on in America a hundred years before the War of Independence, and the operation of the Federal systems of Switzerland and the United Netherlands, had further familiarised men's minds with the practical convenience attending the conscious delegation, by the many to the few, of the forces of Government.

In the course of this evolution a still unsettled question has been mooted which is involved in the term *delegation*, and which contains in itself the gist of the theoretical embarrassment which is inherent in representation. It may be asked to what extent is there implied in representation, or in political delegacy, identity of opinion and of resolution, between the representative and those whom, to some extent or other, he is held to personate. There is room, here, obviously, for a great variety of degrees of conformity of sentiment between the two. The representative may be the merest mouthpiece and echo of conclusions reached elsewhere. Or he may be left to say and do as he likes, according to the dictation of new circumstances,—those who depute him being either indifferent to the matters in issue or content to leave ulterior courses and decisions in the hands of one in whom they confide more than in any other person at the moment available. Or he may receive,—like an ambassador,—general instructions, but retain the capacity to diverge from them if unforeseen emergencies suggest a new course.

Upon this characteristically modern difficulty attending representation little light is thrown by recourse to the history of representation in the past. In Feudal times, the one question which absorbed or overshadowed all others was that of money, or in place of money, of personal service; and the mutual economical dependence of class upon class was so close that no feudal lord could grant to his superior an extraordinary levy, or aid, or burden, without himself incurring proportional loss or deprivation. Thus the identity of interest was complete and manifest, though it extended over a narrow range.

In ecclesiastical matters, again, the subjects discussed at Church Councils ranged over an enormous area, doctrinal and practical,—yet the Bishops in attendance, who personated the lower clergy and the congregations, were, no doubt, sufficiently in advance, in point of learning and of familiarity with the questions at issue, to demand at their hands an amount of personal confidence which the coarser interests of politics, better understood by the mass of the community, could hardly have secured.

It is in very recent times, since legislation, instead of being exceptional, has become continuous and all-embracing, and when the members of a Legislature can claim every day less and less of a monopoly of instruction, that a decision has to be come to as to the amount of identity which is to prevail between a political deputy and his constituents. The subject is naturally complicated by the fact that the same causes which promote an endless discrepancy of opinion and of sentiment between the deputy and the most sympathetic of his constituents tend likewise to promote the discrepancy between one of those constituents and another.

The device, accidental invention, or casual existence of government by Party has gone some way to prevent the essential difficulty which attends representation from being obtruded as it otherwise must have been. In fact, even now the imperfection of representative Government is more felt in those places, such as the British Colonies, in which parties are not strongly organised and the spirit of party does not mount high, than in such a country as England, in which many circumstances concur to sustain this form of manifestation of political activity.

In spite of the ever growing assimilation of opinion, among all intelligent persons, on those large classes of questions, dynastical and economical, which,—partly owing to sentimental prepossessions and partly to the unequal spread of knowledge,—once divided them, there appears no sign of an absence of fervour for political combination; and in the House of Commons, as well as in the country at large, it is still possible to distribute into two distinct camps the vast mass of political combatants.

The important point to consider is whether this phenomenon is to be regarded as permanent, or as a mere cinder-heap, artificially kept alight. Some lessons may be learnt in respect of the future of Party from glancing at popular government as conducted in other countries in which the play of new social conditions has been less controlled than in England by traditional institutions having a strong local hold on the imagination, by the firm tenure of an Aristocratic

Assembly, and by the pertinacious retention of a religious Establishment.

In America, the history of Party since the foundation of the Union would of itself be a valuable contribution to the study of Political Science. Professor Van Holst's Historical treatise on the Constitution of the United States, which has been translated from the original German into English, and which is founded on a minute investigation of all State papers to be found in America or in England, as well as on observations conducted in America, will be found to contain all the materials for such a history. It is only not such a history, because it is so much more.

On the whole it may be said that, soon after the Union was constituted, the only question which broke up all persons taking part in Politics into two opposite factions was that of States-rights; one faction inclining to the notion that the basis of the Constitution was the inherent independence of the several States; the other faction being more favourable to the Federal Constitution, and holding that the several States only retained so much independence as had been expressly left them when the Union was constituted.

Of course the forms and grounds of opposition were not formulated so distinctly and concisely as this. It was only by experience, and especially by the different policy which, owing in some measure to different geographical conditions, emerged on the question of Slavery, that the organisation into the 'democratic' and 'republican' parties became complete.

What is most remarkable about this history is that while, on the face of it, there would seem to be no connexion between these American parties and the old

English parties (which prevailed in America at one period, and in name are scarcely yet extinct) of Whig and Tory, yet the supporters of absolute State Rights became the advocates of slavery and the opponents of the party of Progress. They were, in fact, the party of the landed proprietors and planters of the South, as opposed to that of the commercial world and petty agriculturists of the North. Thus it was brought about that the most celebrated, and still momentous, of party divisions in America was, and is, based on an opposition of interest far more than,—as was the case with the old English parties,—on an opposition of sentiment, of religious belief, or of personal loyalty. It is, however, true that the seeds of the opposition between the two leading American parties will be found in the different circumstances of the early colonists and in the personal differences of the various classes of these colonists themselves.

The history of Party in the United States has been affected, during the present century, by various waves of political interest and agitation which have temporarily occupied or obscured the whole horizon. Thus the expediency of extending by any modes the territorial area of the Union; the advisability of liquidating, in one form or another, the financial obligations of the Union; the policy of reconstructing the Union after the War of Secession in one fashion or in another; and the more personal questions raised by the recognised necessity of taking measures of one sort or another to repress official corruption; are all topics which have proved, in their time, weighty and stirring enough to bind together strong political parties in the firm ties of mutual loyalty, for the purpose of severally carrying out their own ends even at the sacrifice of the independent proclivities of masses of individual persons. The capacity and habit of free and spontaneous organisation, which exist in the United States more than anywhere else, and for which the mechanical working of the Constitution of each State and of the Union itself is an incessant training, favour the rapid generation, as well as the early generation, of political parties. Thus it is difficult for a foreigner ever to learn and understand the quickly coined phrases of party-warfare. They are often out of use before they have had time to be absorbed by literature or translated even into the English spoken at the other side of the Atlantic.

The political experience of the Colonies of Australasia since New South Wales and Victoria obtained, in 1855, from the British Parliament, complete Parliamentary Constitutions, differs instructively from the experience of the United States in respect of Government by Party. In the Colonies of New South Wales and Victoria, the circumstances of political life have not succeeded in calling into being any deep and widespread and strongly marked oppositions of opinion and of sentiment analogous to those represented by the terms *Whig* and *Tory*, *Liberal* and *Conservative*, in England, or by the terms *Democrat* and *Republican* in the United States.

The parties in those Colonies have hitherto rather resembled the secondary and transitory parties already alluded to as fitfully crossing the stage of American politics without leaving any permanent memorial or even influence. They have usually centred round some prominent personage, and been connected with some strongly felt and clearly expressed interest.

It is true that the political life of these colonies is not yet of thirty years' growth. But their institutions were framed, formally, after the model of English institutions, so far as was possible, and there has been no break of revolution or anarchy to interfere with a rapid unfolding of all natural political products.

The most notable exhibition of a true party organisation, as distinguished from mere accidental personal loyalty to a leader, has taken place in Victoria, in which colony the supporters of a policy favourable to the aggrandisement of large landed proprietors on the one hand, and, on the other, those of a policy favourable to an equalisation of fortunes and to the diminution of the influence of wealth have, for years past, ranged themselves in camps of increasingly menacing proportions and dispositions. The battle has been mainly fought round the constitution of the lesser House or Legislative Council, which has been from the first a plutocratic representative Assembly. As it will be a long time before the absorption by agriculture of the plains now employed by wealthy pastoral occupiers, and the exhaustion of the mines, have reduced the opposition between the few rich and the many with only moderate means, this ground of party feud will probably be long-lived. The place will, probably, be taken, by newly evolved oppositions of interest which will be of a fleeting kind, and scarcely deserving the name of party differences.

The lesson taught by these Colonies,—as by the history of the United States,—is that in the democratic organisation of the future the opposition of conflicting interests will be found a more solid basis of political organisation than personal moral differences or sentimental ties. These will have their weight as between one person and another, but they will be shifted from a primary to a secondary place. The main hope is that the progress of education and the diffusion of knowledge will lead to more enlightened views of what people's best interests really are; and, although it must always be expected that, in the competition of economical forces, one man's loss will be another's gain, yet it makes a great difference whether a fair and just balance is preserved, on the whole, between the losses and the gains of all, or whether, as in the old world, the gain is exclusively for the few and the loss for the many.

Party organisation is invaluable so far as it is confined to maintaining a wisely adjusted balance of political and economical forces. It is mischievous and an anachronism if, by resting on spurious sentiments and unmeaning or hypocritically-professed beliefs, it arrests, from time to time, real improvement, and becomes a hindrance instead of a help to national development.

From the time of the Restoration in France till now, the history of Party in that country has passed through various phases which illustrate these remarks. The best marked distinctions have been based upon dynastical ties or preferences; the Buonapartists, the Orleanists, and the Bourbons each commanding a following just sufficient to interfere with a Government conducted by either of the other parties, which yet could not themselves solidly combine.

The Empire of Napoleon III. was mainly serviceable to France by interposing a lengthened period of prescription against the Orleanists and both branches of the

Bourbons; by securing peremptory order and unquestioned submission; and by affording time and opportunity for the exhaustion of the Napoleonic allegiance already owned by none but a few Parisian veterans, and which a newly grown population hardly remembered. Under this Empire, however, the party of the Buonapartists naturally received an enormous impulse and extension, and a new party, which the Revolution settlement had called into existence,—that of the conservative peasant-proprietors,—became an important factor in politics.

The result of the fall of the Empire by the event of Sédan was an early reconstruction of political parties. The peasant-proprietor could no longer see in Buonapartism a security for order, or for peace, or for escape from the proscription, or for regulated taxation. The financial basis of the Empire at Paris was shaken to the ground by the siege of Paris, and by the financial embarrassment caused by the German debt. There survived only two possible grounds for the construction of new Parties wide and influential enough to govern France. These were the party who were in favour of order and peace, at any sacrifice of dynastic allegiance or antecedent sentiment, and those who saw in some reconstitution of the Republic,—which two Napoleons had first turned to their own account and then overthrown,—a meeting point, and the only meeting point, to which all France would sooner or later rally.

A coalition of the Republicans and of the party of peace and order produced the Thiers Government, and then a change in the balance of the coalitionists produced the Government of Marshal McMahon. The decisive development of pure Republicanism expressed itself in the French Constitution of 1875, and the working out of this Constitution has witnessed the growth of parties founded on little else than mere degrees of democratic conviction, expressing themselves in demands for a more or less popular system of representation and for a more or less radical reform of the conservative Senate. The attitude of France towards Germany, and in respect of Foreign policy generally, has introduced a special element into party warfare which must be regarded as of purely accidental significance.

The history of Party in France during the first half of the present century recals the vicissitudes of the political parties in England during the fifty years after the accession of William III.; but England has no parallel,—unless it be found in the parental home-policy of George III.'s reign,—to the operation of the empire of Napoleon. In England the Hanoverian dynasty became more and more consolidated and associated with unbroken successes abroad, and, at no late date, with legislative improvements and with accessions of public liberty at home. Thus, at this day, party in England is undergoing a slow and steady transformation in which it is almost by forced subterfuges and suppressed convictions that political organisation is maintained.

In France the various shades of Republicanism will, no doubt, as political activity becomes diffused throughout the country, connect themselves with real and clearly understood interests. The proper appreciation of these interests, and the intelligent support of them, will afford a sound basis of political activity, and statesmen will find that they can hold power only by introducing real and substantial reforms, and not by appealing to shadowy and superficial sentiments, however momentarily popular.

The general result of this inquiry into the place likely to be occupied by party organisation, as political communities become more democratically constituted, is that real practical interests will, as grounds of party divisions, more and more succeed to the place of sentimental predilections; that these interests will become increasingly intelligible and even laudable, instead of being secret and sinister; and that while the economical and industrial organisation of society will always bring large classes of persons into polar opposition to each other, on certain points of legislation and administration, yet the competition between these classes will proceed more and more on grounds admitting of logical statement and discussion and not maintained, on either side, without professed subordination to the common welfare of the community as a whole.

In fact party will become the political expression of the real and necessary distinctions of interests which are implied in the division of labour and of social functions. Thus, instead of being superseded, it is likely to grow and develope. It will serve to maintain unity and continuity in government and to secure the preference of what is most important at a particular moment to what is least so. It will continue to train the community in habits of loyalty to worthy leaders, and in the practice of making sacrifices for sufficient ends. On the other hand, it may be expected and hoped that more and more of what is still, and has long been, most immoral in party combinations, that is, the artificial adhesion to opinions long obsolete, the prevalent indifference to truth, and the unscrupulous support of unworthy champions, who are good for nothing but to comply formally with a party test, will pass away and give place to influences already, in the most advanced countries, making themselves distinctly felt.

Assuming, then, that the practice of party combination must be taken as a permanent and essential portion of political organisation, the question returns as to how the practice must be regarded as necessarily affecting the novel relations of the governors and the governed.

It has been seen that the modern problem of political organisation presupposes two *data*,—one, that the art of Government has become special, difficult, and absorbing, in a way it never could have been before; and the other, that the great mass of the population of a modern State has unprecedented opportunities and capacities for intervening in governmental acts,— whether they do so by freely choosing their governors, by ousting and changing them, by free criticism, or by anarchical revolutions. The problem can only be solved by the use of such political constructions as can, first, secure the utmost amount of trained skill and knowledge for the service of Government; as can, secondly, obtain for the Government the fullest measure of support and acquiescence; can, thirdly, turn to the largest account the peculiar ability possessed by the people at large to pronounce clear moral judgments and to correct the bureaucratic and despotic disposition which experience proves the mere continuous exercise of the art of Government to bring with it invariably; and can, fourthly, prevent the need or desire for Revolution.

Any political machinery or proposed reform of existing machinery must be judged by the contribution it makes, not to the attainment of any one of those ends alone, but to the attainment of all of them without the sacrifice of one. It has been more by historical accident than by political ingenuity that experiments towards the attainment of some or all of these ends have been hitherto witnessed in different countries. But in different countries in ancient and in modern times a sufficient number of devices have been employed to indicate the lines of the directions which political constructiveness can alone take in the future. For the sake of brevity of expression, the rallying points of controversy in this matter may be designated as (1) the extension and distribution of the Electoral Franchise, including the questions of the rights of Minorities, and of the machinery of Representation; (2) the duration of Parliaments; (3) the expediency of having one or more Chambers, their composition, and their mutual relations, if more than one; (4) the relation of the Executive to the Legislative Authority and to the people.

(1.) *The Extension and Distribution of the Electoral Franchise.*

The positions which have already been assumed as starting points for modern political construction, and, therefore, as already belonging to Political science, are, first, that the object of political organisation is not the attainment of good laws and administration as abstracted from all consideration of the sentiments of the people and of the relations between the governors and the governed; and, secondly, that a presumption exists against the exclusion of any person or class of persons from all right of control over the Government.

Admitting these positions, which are rapidly, though unconsciously acquiring the force of axioms, and which each new revolution and constitutional change tends to reinforce, it is not necessary to travel over ground which has been thoroughly explored and occupied by facts rather than by *à priori* reasoning. It may be laid down as an indispensable basis of Government in all States which look to a future, instead of merely clinging to a past, that the political franchise is presumably co-extensive with the physical, moral, and mental capacity to do any legal act whatever; and that, to adopt a concise though hackneyed phrase, Government is to be conducted in some measure by the people as well as for the people.

The real difficulty arises when it is attempted to ascertain what shall be the proportions in which different classes of persons, all in the possession of the franchise, shall share their control over the Government, and what shall be the amount of that control. In other words, the Constitution of the State has to determine both the relations of different classes of electors to each other and the relations of electors generally,—that is the governed,—to the elected,— that is (speaking broadly) the governors.

The extreme theory in respect of the mutual relations of classes of electors is to recognise no classes or distinctions of persons at all, but to give every person, of sufficient understanding to know what they are doing, and not disqualified by taint of crime, an equal electoral right. This democratical constitution, in order to be complete and logically consistent, must be reproduced in the composition of all the constituent parts of the Legislature, if more than one, and must be secured against an undue preponderance of the Legislature or the Executive by short Parliaments and by effective control, at every point, of the Executive by the Legislative Authority.

Such a condition of things is often pictured as the consummation of Democracy, and is the ideal of numerous classes of Reformers. There has probably never been any State which has satisfied all the requirements here indicated; and there is none which approximately satisfies them now.

Such States as present the nearest approximation to a purely democratic constitution, such as the United States of America, the Swiss Confederation, and the British Colonies in Australia, will all be found, even on a superficial view, to fail in some essential characteristic. In all these States the Executive Authority, or, it may be, the Federal Legislature, or,— in the British Colonies,—a nominated or plutocratic Upper House, has a disproportionate share in the control of the government; and that, not only at particular moments, which may be incidental to their character, but permanently and by an inevitable process of encroachment on the purely popular organs of Government.

It would seem, indeed, that the more purely democratic is the constitution of the State in its prominent structure, the more urgent necessity is felt for a forcible Executive to balance, control, and direct the popular energies. History is full of examples of the tyrant succeeding to the organised mob, and (as Aristotle and Montesquieu pointed out) it requires superlative virtue to prevent a mass of equally enfranchised citizens degenerating, at least occasionally, from the highest to the lowest type of political authority. The opposition presented in the Constitution of the United States between the firm seat of the President for the period of four years together with his almost uncontrolled Executive authority in some of the most critical departments of government, and the popular mode and conception of his election, is felt by the best American statesmen themselves to be an anomaly for which a remedy must some time or other be found. Even in the British Colonies, so often as the popular will is really brought into conflict with the Upper House or the Governor, who represents the Parent State, the country is only saved from revolution by concessions and compromises, —that is, by repudiating the right of control and recognising the supreme dominion of the people themselves.

It appears then that an equal distribution of electoral power is no security for the maintenance of what, in the highest sense, may be called popular rights, and for the permanent dominion of the popular will. Except where, as in the limited world of ancient Athens, the space is confined enough to admit of rival orators and of demagogues disputing with each other the right of supreme control, that right will always be exercised in undue predominance by the person, or Council, or Assembly, in habitual possession of the organised forces of the State. He or they are constantly at the helm, and have the incommunicable advantage of unity of purpose, of concentrated knowledge of facts, and of acquired technical skill in rule. The people, on the other hand, are in danger of being satisfied, as under the Empire of Napoleon III. in France, with a mere show of reserved power testified by such a mockery of electoral forms as was exhibited in the *plébiscite*.

Even though, as in the Australian Colonies, strong divergencies of interest may be found among the people, yet these are either pitted one against the other in such a way as to enable the Executive Authority to re-assert and establish its power by arbitrating adroitly, and at critical moments between them; or one class of interests predominates over the rest, and becomes master of the Executive Authority, all other interests being thereby rendered subservient to the supreme class of interests. This state of things existed in the United States, when the Slave States dominated for years together over the Union and rebelled at the first symptom of a loss of power. The actual political equivalence of all citizens becomes the engine of a subtle and secret despotism, because the government is exercised in the name of the whole people, and all insurrection in pursuit of popular aims, as against a monarch or an aristocracy, is out of the question. Public liberty is not ignored or defied as in a State overtly governed by a despotic authority, but is rather silently eaten away under all the forms of a Government holding its mandate from nothing else than the popular will.

It is necessary to examine with some care the actual barriers which still exist in the best governed countries against such a perversion of democratical institutions, and to consider how far they can be treated as permanent elements of a political system, or how far they must give place to advantageous substitutes.

In England the existing obstacles to a complete equalisation of electoral rights are found, firstly, in the aristocratic constitution of the Second Chamber;

secondly, in the plutocratic basis of the county franchise; thirdly, in the unequal distribution of population throughout the electoral areas; and fourthly, in the balance maintained between the amount of representation respectively accorded to boroughs and to counties. The special representation of Universities in the House of Commons, of the Church, and now, in some measure, of the Law, in the House of Lords, is of less momentous, though of significant, account for the same purpose; and the indirect influence of Royalty cannot be wholly neglected, though the constitutional action of the Crown is almost wholly subordinated to the requirements of purely popular government. The influence and value of a second Chamber in itself form a separate topic, and may be treated quite independently of the consideration of the equal or unequal distribution of electoral power. The existence of such a Chamber, as in the United States and now in France, is found to be compatible with the perfect electoral equality of all citizens, though it may serve to obviate some of the natural consequences of this equality.

The actual obstacles to electoral equality above enumerated,—and they may be taken as fair specimens of all the classes of similar obstacles found in any other countries professing to be governed on popular principles,—are mainly due to historical causes, generally of an accidental nature. It is true that successive Reform Acts, following on long and anxious debates, have largely modified the electoral constitution of England as handed down to the present century. But the conservative spirit and the conservative forces of the country have been hitherto potent enough to preserve almost unimpaired the leading principles implied in the constitutional antithesis of town and country, in the structure of the House of Lords, and in the disregard to purely numerical considerations in the distribution of seats. At this day the notions of equal electoral districts based on population only, and of the equalisation of the town and county franchise, are held to be expedients scarcely less 'radical,'—in an offensive sense of the word, —than propositions for the reconstruction of the second Chamber on some other basis than that of hereditary descent.

The customary defence, indeed, of these institutions is not a sound one, and when keenly scrutinised, falls to the ground. It is that the House of Commons is pre-eminently an instrument for the representation in the Legislature of distinct interests; and that, on an equal distribution of electoral rights, the claims of property, and especially of landed property, would be insufficiently protected, there being always more poor than rich, and the richest members of the community being an exceedingly small and much scattered class. It might be replied to this that, in the most democratically organised communities, such as the United States and New South Wales, where wealth, as such, has little or none of the special constitutional protection accorded to it in England, the felt difficulty is how to restrict, and not how to guard, its proper influence. The rich always and everywhere possess opportunities of exercising an amount of direct and indirect, honest and corrupt, influence throughout the country, which, in their aggregate, form one of the most obdurate of the forces which Government has to bring under efficient control in the interests of all.

The power of economic combination is of itself a

weighty factor in politics, and the class of employers and of capitalists, especially when rightly organised for industrial co-operation, have, and can exercise, this power in a silent and unobserved fashion which more effectually protects their interests than any direct legislation could do.

As to the landholding class, their local weight must always preponderate out of all proportion to their numbers, and, in fact, what with the personal influence, the social authority, and the effectual power of this class in the economic hierarchy, the value of the direct votes of its individual members might be a matter of comparative insignificance. Nevertheless the unity of sentiment, of manners, and of pecuniary interest, which belongs to the ownership of land will always give an integral solidity to the votes of the proprietary class to which scarcely any other class can aspire; and this is the firmest of all guarantees for the due security of the interests of wealth.

The argument, then, that wealth needs special representation in the Legislature must not only be dismissed as founded on a perverse distortion of the facts of the case, but must be regarded as pernicious, inasmuch as it reverses the true reasoning applicable to the subject. If interests have to be directly represented in the Legislature, it is surely not that class of interests which are secure of the most uniform indirect and covert representation. It is not the socially and industrially organised classes who are in danger of being insufficiently heard and protected, but the vast masses of the population which—from their numbers, the variety of their occupations, their indigence, and their obscurity,—will never be heard at all, if special constitutional provision is not made for them,—except at such moments as those of the outbreak of the French Revolution and of the Revolutions of 1848.

But another error has crept into this reasoning in favour of specially and most effectually representing that which is always the strongest,—and indeed is strong without direct representation at all,—based upon a misapprehension of what is meant by an 'interest.'

Surely every member of the State, worthy of the name of man or woman, is concerned with the good government of the country for far other reasons than for the mere protection of his property or of his industrial or commercial gains. In the struggle between the classes severally personating the claims of capital and of labour, it is of importance to the parties on either side that the laws, and the execution of the laws, affecting their fortunes should be reasonable and just; and for this end the legislator must be thoroughly informed of the issues at stake and of the probable effect of any legislation he contemplates. The administrator of the law must likewise have opportunities of knowing intimately where the law presses and when, and where and to what extent its execution should be enforced or relaxed. But all these considerations rest upon plain and easily cognisable matters of fact.

There is no greater difficulty in finding out what are the precise rival interests affected by a Land Act, a Bank Charter Act, or a Currency Act than there is of discovering,—as is done by a Select Committee of the House of Commons,—what are the precise interests likely to be prejudiced by the construction of a new line of Railway or by the Amalgamation of two Railway Companies. To the extent that interests are real and definite,—and therefore as some say deserving of special representation,—they are likewise definite, and really, if not always numerically, computable, and can be thoroughly guarded without any direct representation at all.

If it be said that it may be true that these monetary interests may be understood through the machinery of oral witnesses and documentary proofs, but will only secure proper attention through the sort of political pressure exercised by special representatives, then the question arises as to the composition of the Legislative Chamber itself.

On this theory each class of distinct pecuniary interest must be adequately defended by special delegates, and the Chamber as a whole must reflect all the classes of interests which are forcible and conspicuous enough, and yet not too numerous and intricate, to secure a place. But, to revert to what was said above, these limited and ascertainable interests are, at the most, only a small, and by no means important, portion of the interests affected by legislation. They are more calculated to attract attention than other interests only because of the distinctness in which the outward incidents of property and of industrial intercourse stand out on the platform of human affairs. Every one can appreciate their value according (it may be) to a standard of his own, and the rivalries to which they give rise proceed in the eyes of all men, and without cessation or pause.

With respect to other interests, however, they are noticed by the mass of mankind only at such moments as novel questions arise having relation to them. They occupy, indeed, too large a space in individual and in political life to attract to themselves a special and concentrated attention which would be proportioned to their magnitude. They fill the canvas, and consequently the eye cannot estimate their real and comparative worth and significance.

It may be, indeed, that owing to a specific event, such as the threat of war, the tale of inhuman atrocities committed in a foreign land, a criminal trial, a gross administrative abuse, or a scandalous commercial fraud, public attention is roused, and the interests of public morality and of national right and duty are recognised as supreme. The public conscience is stirred to its depths, and (as happens from time to time especially in America and in France) a portion of the community usually reluctant to intervene in Politics comes to the front and determines to make itself heard. But the interval of such spasmodic zeal is shortlived, and when the evil has been redressed, the diplomatic course altered, the national character vindicated, the claims of the mighty interests for the time in jeopardy are forgotten or at least subordinated to the unresting calls presented by the clash of commonplace economical competition.

It may thus be expected that in what may be called quiet times,—that is, in ordinary times,—the claims of property, of commerce, and of fragmentary portions of the community will exercise an influence over elections wholly disproportionate both to their actual importance and to their effective weight at any momentary crisis when the community has its political sentiments strongly and deeply stirred.

It may be expected that the progress of the equalisation of electoral rights, as above described, will operate in favour of diffusing more broadly and evenly at all times the genuine political sentiments on the strength and correctness of which the State must rely at the most critical moments. The limited field of Athenian democracy, so far as the precedent is applicable in the modern world, certainly seems to prove that the equalisation of rights of intervention in government may elevate rather than depress the habitual character of political action.

It might be said, on a superficial view, that the experience of the United States is the opposite to this, and that the equal diffusion of electoral rights has been attended by a steady depreciation of political character and energy. But the truth is that the United States are only beginning to grapple practically and seriously with the very constitutional problem the elements of which it is the object of the present discussion to examine. The rapid political and constitutional movements, precipitated by economical and physical expansion, have forced the almost insuperable difficulties of the case into premature prominence.

So far as an indication of ultimate success in adapting the Constitution to the demands of a state of society based on an absolute equality of electoral power can be gathered from casual experience at critical epochs, the united energy of the nation in maintaining the Union, in re-organising the Slave States, in defraying the expenses of the Secession War, and in grappling with the scandals of administrative corruption, affords a rich promise for the future. The Republic of the United States can only be said to have failed when the bulk of the nation shall have indolently acquiesced in the vices and flaws of its government, when it has ceased to struggle, to reconstruct, to hope, and to believe.

P

It is plain then how superficial and inadequate is the view of a Legislative Chamber which supposes that the mere representation of a limited number of ascertainable material interests within its walls can ever be its final form. It is found, on reflection, that it only comes from national lethargy and inadvertence that these limited classes of interests are forced, in ordinary times, into political prominence; and that as soon as ever the public conscience and the educated instincts of the people are appealed to, those classes of interests become as nothing in the appreciating scale, and, in place of them, there instantly come to the surface considerations based on the claims of national right and obligation, of posterity, and of the more unprotected portions of the population, of religion (not of a purely denominational sort), of education, and of abstract morality.

It is to be remembered too that the tendency of free institutions and of the equalisation of political power is to impart substance and cohesiveness to this general order of ideas as dominating in the popular consciousness. An untrammelled press, security against police despotism, an unrestricted right of orderly public meeting, and ungrudged opportunities for the announcement of wishes and opinions in an organised form to the heads of Government Departments, all operate in one and the same direction of calling into mature existence political conceptions and instincts of the highest order, which, in default of these popular agencies, might remain embryonic or be starved out of life.

Yet it is just this order of ideas which, even though often false, uninformed, or imperfect, need to be brought into direct competition with the strong and purely material interests which are pretty sure to hold their own, whatever be the constitution of the Legislative Chamber. Industrial co-operation and the extension of centralised administrative work must be expected to increase rather than to diminish. But this involves the creation of compact political interests of a highly organised kind. The railway interest, the interest of large ship-owners, the interest of bankers, the interest of municipal corporations as such, the interest of the Army, of the Police, and, in many countries, of voluntary Churches, are likely to become more, and not less, effectually defended as time goes on. The only counterpoise to them will be found to be the general recognition of the truth that every member of the community has a concern in the development of its moral life far exceeding in magnitude and value that which he or another may chance to have in any enterprise capable of being counted, measured, or weighed.

The apprehension of this position is not here a subject of recommendation, which would be outside the purpose of this treatise. It is stated as about to become a political axiom which must be taken into account in all constitutional constructions based on the conditions of modern society. The direct representation of monetary interests must become less and less prominent or possible, while the representation of the class of ideas which are capable of commending themselves to innumerable persons at once will become more and more so.

Admitting, then, these conditions, the question returns as to what are the only possible modes of reproducing adequately in a Legislative Chamber the true spirit and will of the people in their various manifestations, consistently with maintaining a due amount of energy and continuity in the Executive Authority.

In England, at the present day, a considerable amount of variety in the composition of the Legislature, corresponding with broadly marked differences of opinion in the country, is secured by the distribution, on a definite principle, of the seats between the towns and the counties. This distribution is due at the outset to purely historical causes, though it has been, within recent years, consolidated and improved in pursuit of distinct political ends.

The permanence of the lines drawn between town and country representation cannot be relied upon as an essential factor in the constitution of a Modern State. The facilities of locomotion make the transit between town and country so rapid and easy that the town population is increasingly acquiring habits of working in the town and sleeping at several miles distance in the country. One portion of a family occupies the country house or villa or lodging and the other portion spends the working hours of the day in town and passes to and fro at night and morning. Thus the interests, sentiments and habits of town and country residents respectively become less and less separable.

In the meantime purely economical causes, such as the growth of population, the depreciation of agricultural profits, and the indispensable necessity of applying larger amounts of capital and on a more extended scale, if profitable cultivation is the object, are assimilating country labour to the highly organised labour hitherto only witnessed in large manufacturing towns. Furthermore, new towns, especially in America and the great British Colonies, keep springing into existence with unexampled rapidity, according as the discovery of a new mine, or the opening out by a railway of new markets, pastoral districts, or commercial centres, call for them.

The inhabitants of these new towns have none of the fixity of ideas, or traditional associations, or hereditary attachments, which go so far to give political coherence to the citizens of the older towns, while the migratory disposition which, in fact, gave birth to the new settlement, imparts to them a characteristic temper which distinguishes them alike from the dwellers in a rural village and from the freemen of an ancient borough.

Besides this, another compensating tendency is destroying civic life as a political factor altogether. The facilities for locomotion acting within a narrower range, and the more diffused and correct appreciation of the laws of health, as well as the improvement of towns from the point of view of artistic beauty and architectural convenience, combine to render the suburb of a town, as a political element, more important than the town itself. Even where the railway is not resorted to for the purpose of nocturnal flight into the country properly so called, the practice of sleeping and conducting family existence on the outskirts of the town, and not in its centre, is become more and more habitual. That, too, which is the luxury of the well-to-do clerk or tradesman is become the necessity of the skilled and unskilled artisan.

Every internal improvement which broadens streets, erects commodious warehouses, central railway stations, exchanges, town-halls, and places of amusement, and claims space for squares, public gardens and parks, drives the labourer and his family to find a home at an increasing distance from his work. The street-tramway and the early 'workman's' train adapt themselves to the new exigencies, and the result is that the outskirts of every great town are fringed with remote suburbs the reverse of 'fashionable,' which by the simplicity,— not to say the occasional squalor,—of the erections, merge into the common surroundings of the agricultural labourer.

It is evident then that every fresh economic impulse tends to obliterate that sharp distinction between town and country which could alone be a continuing basis of fixed differences in political representation. No doubt it will always be the case that the person whose life is most thrown with that of his fellows, who is best trained in habits of co-operation and in the culture of sympathetic emotions, who has the truest sense of the continuity of corporate existence and of the corresponding responsibilities, and who is the most familiar with the economical conditions, as exhibited on a clear and wide platform, on which all civilised society and therefore all government ultimately rests, starts with a political education to which the isolated dweller or worker amidst purely rural scenes can make no pretension, and for which no book study or desultory social intercourse can make compensation.

It is for this reason that the great reforms and beneficial revolutions in such feudalised countries as England, France and Germany may be traced back to the indestructible political instinct which has often had its sole refuge in the casually protected corporations of the great towns; and that, even at this date, the characteristic political sentiment of the dwellers in the great towns of these countries is one favourable to indefinite political improvement rather than, as in country places, to the mere maintenance of existing institutions and the preservation of order.

It has been seen, however, that this clear opposition of sentiments, which may be regarded as salutary where it does not result in stagnation, cannot be treated as a permanent phenomenon. Even where the political characteristics of town and country life are on the whole maintained, the gradations of sentiment brought about by incessant motion to and fro, by migrations, and by the indefinite extension of the area of town life into the country, are becoming so numerous and fine that the distinction itself is becoming antiquated for purposes of Parliamentary representation, and will shortly be worthless in the more advanced countries.

If once the distinction of town and country becomes no longer recognisable as one of the bases of the distribution of seats, it cannot be long before an end is put to all the less startling inequalities in the electoral franchise. The extent of electoral areas has been determined not only by population but by merely accidental, local, or traditional claims to special representation. It may thus be expected that within a period not too remote for political prevision, in every country in which representative institutions are the foundation of the Government, no other principle of distributing votes and seats will be tolerated than that which makes every person—not disqualified by age, disease, or crime,—a voter, and every person's vote of exactly equal weight as affecting the composition of the Legislature.

A difficulty, however, is here encountered the elements of which must be examined with some care, because of its bearing on some political problems already adverted to and larger than itself. Though every person's vote may presumably be of equal weight, yet there are various modes of adjusting the machinery of voting by which on occasion the effective value of each vote may be disproportionately increased.

The current electoral practice in England is an illustration of this. The electoral areas in England (excepting the Universities) are a county,—or divisions of a county,—and a borough,—or (as in the case of London) divisions of a borough. One, two, or three members are apportioned to each electoral area; and— except in a very limited number of constituencies tentatively submitted to a different system,—every voter has as many votes as there are members to be elected, and he can use as many or as few of his votes as he pleases. Thus when a party issue or other clearly comprehended and sufficiently interesting question is clearly propounded to a constituency at the time of an election, the majority of the voters who are of accord on this issue or question necessarily carry all the seats, and the minority are, so far as this area is concerned, wholly unrepresented.

The misfortune is that as it usually happens that one question at a time occupies public attention and depresses all other questions, the accidental distribution of opinion on this single question at the moment of election determines the constitution of the representative Chamber so long as the Parliament lasts, while the people may be wholly unrepresented on all other questions, and the aggregate of minorities throughout the country are unrepresented on this question also. In fact, for the duration of the Parliament, on all questions but the one which predominated at the moment of the General Election, the will of the Parliamentary representatives is substituted for the will of the people, and on all questions whatever the will of the minorities is unrepresented.

The only practical correctives to this state of things are found in the inevitable competition of other questions with the prominent one; in the confidence reposed in individual candidates independently of their specific views at a given moment; and in the necessity that members desirous of re-election should defer, in their Parliamentary conduct, to the sentiments prevailing in their several constituencies. This last consideration operates most forcibly when Parliaments are elected for the shortest periods, and, naturally, with more force towards the close of a Parliament than in its early days.

Many schemes have been devised and partially resorted to in England, and in other countries, in order to bring a greater portion of the true popular will to bear upon Governments purporting to be representative, and to enable this will to operate at a greater number of points.

Shorter parliaments have been always one of the demands of an extreme democratic party when in pursuit of more complete and continuous popular representation. Long Parliaments have different disadvantages according to the modes in which they come to an end. One disadvantage is that of gradually substituting for the popular voice an adventitious, and yet highly organised, opinion generated from within by the conditions of co-operation peculiar to the Assembly itself. Another may be that of artificially prolonging the duration of an Assembly proved to contain elements too recalcitrant and irreconcilable to sustain the interests of order and progress. A third may be that of putting in the hands of the members of the Executive Authority an arbitrary right of dissolution which may be resorted to, not in the public interests, but simply in order to maintain themselves in office. But, on the other hand, too short Parliaments prevent the formation of habits of Government; favour an undue reference, at critical moments, to transitory waves of opinion and sentiment outside the House; maintain ceaseless agitation and excitement in the country; and impede the construction of a strong and lasting Executive Authority.

Some of each of these opposite disadvantages may no doubt be avoided by the American system of re-electing a third (or some other considerable fraction) of the whole House at short fixed intervals so as to ensure that within a brief, but not too brief, period,—as for instance six years,—the whole House be re-elected. But this system bears, like so much else in the American Constitution, the signs of nervous apprehension of democratic dangers, and thereby loses some of the characteristic advantages of a true popular constitution. There is the want of perpetual opportunity for a full exhibition of the public sentiment; and therefore there is always a sense that there can be no real and permanent unity in the House of Representatives, but that one portion or another will find support in the Senate or from the President, each of which departments is elected on different principles from the rest of the Legislature. The public mind is, at the most critical junctures, curbed and chained by the Constitution, and the result is that it expresses itself with most freedom on the occasion of the election of the President, who becomes, as soon as he assumes office, the most conservative and irresponsible element in the Government.

The solution of the problem of popular representation which has obtained most favour in England of late years, and has been, to some extent, put in practice, is that of the direct representation of minorities. In the actual schemes which have been propounded, the subject has usually been implicated with others, such as local representation and the machinery for expeditiously taking the votes, which are only indirectly connected with it, though of great importance in themselves. It is expedient, however, in pronouncing on the value of this solution of the problem, to reduce the mode proposed to its simplest elements.

At some point or other both inside the Legislative Assembly and outside it, it is obvious that, in case of final difference of opinion, the opinions of the more numerous must practically prevail over those of the less numerous; not by any means because the more numerous are more likely to have right on their side, but because a decision of any sort is better than no decision at all; and if the superior physical force wielded by the stronger is no longer the means of decision, the bare collected opinions of those who might otherwise wield the force form the natural and only available substitute. It is true that the very notion of force is forgotten or exploded, and the mere allusion to it savours of a deference to mob law. But, historically speaking, there can be no doubt that the practice of deferring to a majority is simply that of giving way, in time and by decent ceremonial, to those who could have their own way if they chose to take it.

The solution of merely counting the votes, and acting in the direction to which the greater number of votes incline, is rough at the best, and the only apology for persisting in its use, in a civilised condition of society, is that when action must be taken and the individual votes of the persons in whose name it is taken are presumably of equal value, the test of mere plurality is the only imaginable test to abide by. It has at least the advantage that it seems plausible, because, to the superficial observer, the greater the number of people who assent to a proposition, the more likely is that proposition to be true. In the common matters of life, which rest chiefly on wide experience easily obtained, the mere multiplication of witnesses gives credit to a statement or persuasion in which they all concur. In these matters exceptional views are, at least, as likely to be signs of mere eccentricity as of genius. But, in proportion as the question rises out of the region accessible to common experience; as it involves strict logic for its treatment; demands the casting aside of prejudices due to habit and a narrow experience; and calls for moral as well as mental equilibrium and introspection; it is the few rather than the many who are most likely to give a true reply to it.

No doubt, between the common problems of daily life on which the opinion of one average person is likely to be as good as that of another, and the questions requiring special knowledge, thoughtfulness, or moral culture, there are a class of questions which only come to the surface at moments of political emergency,—especially when some moral sentiment is involved or believed to be involved. On such occasions the conscience of the people as a corporate community may be stirred to its depths. All the ordinary ties and associations of habit are snapped asunder. The heart of the people is moved as the heart of one man, and, either with the frenzy of fanaticism or the judicial resolution of an intelligent patriotism, the large mass of the community thinks and feels together with hardly noticeable dissent.

It is seasons such as these which generate national crimes or occasion acts of heroic magnanimity which illustrate to all time the possibility of corporate virtue. It was such a *vox populi* which, by supporting the unwavering energy of the Roman Senate, steadied the nation after the defeat of Cannæ. It was the same voice which vindicated the cause of the Seven Bishops and, by anticipation, stamped the English Revolution of 1688 with popularity. It was, too, the same voice which accredited in France the military encroachments at home and abroad of the two Napoleons, and which has since again and again emphasised its acceptance of the Republic. It is the same voice which at one epoch, supported in England the Chinese aggressions of Lord Palmerston against the condemnations proceeding from both Houses of Parliament, and which, thirty years afterwards, accepted with tumultuous approbation the counter policy of Mr. Gladstone avowedly based on the principle that England must peremptorily abstain from encroachment on her weaker neighbours.

Such examples as these prove that, even when the public mind of a nation is so far shifted from its common moorings as to act with abnormal activity and concentration it is dependent, to a perilous extent, on the sort of personal influences which are brought to bear on it. The Roman Senate, the two Napoleons, M. Gambetta, Lord Palmerston, and Mr. Gladstone,—not to dwell on the more common instances of popularly exerted power which are spread over the history of Greece, of the Italian Republics, and of the United States,—severally exercised, at great national crises, an amount of widespread popular influence which for a time, or in some cases for years together, imparted a marked and uniform consistency to the policy of the country.

It is the object of a Constitution so to settle the framework of the State in harmony with the true and permanent national spirit of the country, created by its history and by the growth of all its institutions, that no casual political accident, wave of feeling, or momentary personal influence, shall have a disproportionate weight among the forces which affect the public mind. It has been seen that in ordinary times and in respect to the commoner topics of life, a majority of persons are more likely to be in the right than a minority. In similar times, as to matters requiring special thought and knowledge or specially cultivated sentiment, a minority is at least as likely to be in the right as a majority, and a properly selected minority more likely to be in the right. In times of a critical and exceptional kind the majority may be right or may be wrong, but is at all events likely to be overwhelming in numbers and irresistible in authority.

Assuming then that the constitutional machinery must harmonise with, and give effect to, the political preponderance of numerical majorities, it still remains to be settled at what point of time or of sequence in the process of election and legislation the mere weight of counted numbers, and of this alone, is to tell. Suppose, in the simplest case of all, that a single member has to be elected by the electors dwelling in a definitely circumscribed electoral area. There may be several candidates, of whom the one who obtains the greatest number of votes is chosen. All the electors who have voted for any other candidates than the one who has the majority of votes are unrepresented in Parliament altogether. Suppose the case to be the same in any number of similar areas. If these unrepresented minorities are added together throughout the country, they may largely outnumber the sum of many of the majorities which are represented.

Therefore, because the separation between the majority and the minority is made at the first moment, is irreparable, and is made for every member elected, the aggregate effect is that, on a vast variety of topics, and in respect of the competing claims of a vast number of candidates, the number of represented persons may be exceeded by that of those whose votes prove good for nothing. The latter are in fact, for many purposes, and when added together, the majority. For instance, if a particular candidate were nominated for a dozen constituencies at once, and only failed of election by a single vote, as against different successful candidates in each constituency, the aggregate majority in his favour throughout these dozen constituencies would be overwhelming, and yet he would not be elected, and the votes of his supporters in each constituency would be thrown away.

It is with the utilisation of these votes, so thrown away, that Mr. Hare, Mr. Mill, and a variety of Continental writers have occupied themselves in their schemes for what is sometimes called the Representation of Minorities, and sometimes Personal or Proportional Representation.

The most popular of these schemes provides that each voter may furnish to the returning officer a list of persons, either selected at pleasure or out of a list of candidates previously prepared, arranged in the order in which he wishes each of his votes to be turned to account. There is a fixed minimum of votes,—based on the proportion between the number of members to be elected and the number of electors in the electoral area, —needed to secure the election of any member whatever. So soon as, in counting up the votes, it appears that any member has received a sufficient number of votes to secure his election, all other votes given for him are cancelled, and the votes so given are applied in favour of other candidates, according to the order of preference in which they appear on the voters' lists. The operation of cancelling and substitution is repeated with each return of a member till the whole number of members are elected in the area, which may be as large as the area of present constituencies, or larger, or, indeed, coextensive with all the existing constituencies. The mere size of the constituencies is not of the essence of the scheme propounded, though it is an important element in estimating its value.

The writers who have advocated this scheme have laboured to show that the mechanical difficulties of counting the votes with rapidity could be got over, and that it would become as familiar and as thoroughly understood as voting by simple majorities. One obvious objection to it is that, to make it of real advantage to voters, the area must be sufficiently large to secure a large choice of candidates. The smaller the area, the smaller the number of members for that area, and the fewer the names which will appear on a voter's list with any hope of the alternative votes being turned to account. The larger the area, the greater chance that a name, though first on no list, will yet re-appear on a great number and so secure election, rather by diffused than by intense popularity. In this way the finer shades of political opinion will secure a greater chance of representation. But, according as the area is extended in this way, the notion of local connexion between a member and his constituency becomes obliterated. This not only implies a vital alteration in the Constitution of most existing States, but involves a loss of some political elements which could ill be spared.

The connexion between a member and a definite constituency has undoubtedly some disadvantages which are reaped to the full when, as in the United States, and some British Colonies, the places represented are very far apart and have very diverse interests, and when the sense of corporate national responsibility is not always strong enough to overcome the centrifugal tendency thereby created. But, on the other hand, it is scarcely possible to overrate the benefit accruing from multiplying sub-centres of Governmental responsibility. To bring a definite portion of the population, already welded together by geographical situation, hereditary antecedents, and current mutual dependence, into a close and constant connexion with the central Government must be a primary object of the Statesman's solicitude. This definite connexion with the central Legislature is at once the necessary supplement and the best corrective of local Government. The fact that, in some countries, it degenerates into a system rife with opportunities for corrupt self-seeking is one of those morbid phenomena which, while they call for the political physician, are no imputation on the general worth of the life they impair. Mere universal popularity over a large area, as was shown by the *plébiscites* which returned again and again Napoleon III., is often but a superficial indication of true personal merit; and though, under such a system of alternative voting as that described above, the mere force of notoriety would be largely corrected by the return of the nominees of accumulated small minorities, yet here again the want of connexion among the voters would rather favour the representation of worthless crotchets than of deep-rooted and wide scattered, though unobtrusive, political convictions. The personal relationship between a member and his constituency has been often made, and is capable of being made still more, the occasion of the finest species of political training for the people. In his speeches and addresses to the electors of Bristol Edmund Burke well explained the limits within which he held a mere local subserviency to be confined.

The English practice of autumnal speeches addressed by members of Parliament to their constituencies, followed by questions and varied forms of social intercourse, ought not to be omitted in taking account of the less direct machinery by which the claims of different parts of the country are reconciled with its claims as an integral unity.

Other less complete schemes of minority representation have been suggested, and to some extent put in practice, but none of them occasion the loss of so few votes as that just explained. The method of election of English School-Boards, according to which each elector in an electoral area has as many votes as there are members to be elected for that area, and can distribute them among the nominated candidates, or withhold them altogether, or accumulate them in favour of one or more, certainly secures the representation of candidates distinctly representing well marked minorities. Thus in some parts of the country it often happens that a Roman Catholic, Nonconformist, or woman candidate, is at the head of the poll, not because more persons vote for them, but because those who do vote for them give them all their votes and vote for no one else.

Another mode, in use in what are called in England the 'three-cornered constituencies,' is to allow voters to have votes numbering one fewer than the number of members to be elected, so that if there are three members to be elected the probability is that the majority of the constituency succeed in returning two out of the three and the minority the third. In these constituencies it is always the object of the majority, by economising their votes, to secure the return of all their candidates. But this is difficult; and they are usually defeated where the sides are clearly marked and the majority is not overwhelming.

The representation of a clearly marked minority of this kind in a single constituency is logically unsatisfactory because it proceeds on an assumed numerical distribution of opinions throughout the country which probably at no moment represents a real distribution of opinion. If such constituencies existed all over the country, the result might be an Assembly of which exactly two-thirds were attached to one political party,—the dominant one in the country at the day,—and the remaining third was attached partly to the direct opponents of the former and partly to an indefinite number of strongly organised but politically insignificant coteries.

Though a House of this composition presents the appearance of arithmetical fairness, yet the very sharpness of the line separating the different classes of members is unfavourable to unity and to legislative homogeneity. It is one thing for a deliberative Chamber to come together, as formed of personal elements having a history which recalls on a smaller scale the actual lines of demarcation which broadly separate political parties and opinions in the country at large. It is another thing to attempt to reproduce, in exact numerical proportions, the quantity of opinion on one side or another arbitrarily presumed to exist outside. In the one case, the sense of political responsibility, the mere fact and habit of companionship, and the necessities of co-operation, all tend to develope a unity of purpose and action which is quite consistent with the broad and sharp opposition, at proper moments, of party policy. In the other case the Members for the same constituency bring with them into the House the deep-rooted oppositions of sentiment which prevailed on the spot at which the election took place, and which were exacerbated and intensified by all the incidents of a sharply contested election.

If it be true, as has been already admitted, that the mere economical distribution of society will, of itself, always maintain the existence of great political parties inclining in opposite directions, it is, furthermore, a true condition of healthy political existence that every means be exerted to render this fixed opposition as compatible as possible with the unity of State life.

This unity can be best secured not only by softening, in all forms of social intercourse and in Parliamentary manners, the asperities of party spirit, but by preventing hard party lines being drawn in the ordinary working of the Constitution. Party divisions, even where they connote true and deep differences of interests and sentiment, should be made as casual and evanescent as possible in their formal expression. They should instantly disappear before the solvent of a national call which appeals to that which is deeper and more permanent than themselves, and the utmost opportunity should be afforded for the frequent subordination of them to personal or other claims of a different kind.

On all these grounds, it seems undesirable,—that is, in other words, incompatible with the highest principles of popular government as already enunciated,—that minorities should be so represented as to reproduce with microscopic precision the unstable divisions of political feeling stereotyped at the moment of a general election. The claims for the representation of minorities are not properly based on the notion that the less popular opinions outside the House should be entitled, through their concentration in a narrow field, to tell with reduplicated force in the actual performance of the task of Legislation and Government.

These claims really rest on the fact that, according to the recognised methods of counting only the majority-vote in each electoral area, the country is not polled at all in respect to a vast number of questions. Such questions are those which, either owing to the special circumstances of the country at the moment of the election or to the necessity of choosing candidates likely to command general confidence, are inevitably treated, at that moment only, as secondary questions. Thus the complaint is that the majority-vote only accidentally represents, even in form, a majority. It may happen that the number of aggregate minorities throughout the country would, on some other question than that temporarily uppermost, coalesce with a sufficient number of those now opposed to them to form a majority still greater than that now dominant.

Thus a really adequate representation of even a majority of the electors would mean the representation of all the majorities which would be obtained by taking the votes successively on a large variety of urgent political questions, capable of being propounded in a clear shape to persons not specially instructed.

It is customary in 'election addresses' for candidates to announce their views on a series of questions which they consider urgent or interesting to the constituency at the moment, and to arrange them in the order of the importance they attach to them. It depends on the quality of the party divisions at the time whether a number of such questions hang together and can be treated in the lump as a portion of the party programme, or whether significance attaches to only one or only a few of them. Thus each elector, in comparing the claims of candidates to his vote, may have to determine whether he shall make the party question prevail in his mind over all the others, or whether,— —through indifference to party claims, through personal predilection for a particular candidate, or through superior concern in other questions in which a candidate would represent him more closely than he does on the party question,—he will refuse to be bound merely by his party ties.

As it may be assumed, by the very hypothesis, that the dominant question of the moment will most interest most electors, there are strong inducements for an elector to subordinate his concern in all other questions, and even in the personality of the candidate, in order to make his vote tell at all. In this way a certain violence is done to freedom; and this is especially true when a Minister dissolves the House suddenly on a question on which the country has concentrated its whole attention for the moment,—as, for instance, that of his own retention of office or that of a foreign war. In these cases, all those electors who do not rate the dominant question at the same value as the average electors do are not only out-voted, but are never asked to vote at all on any subject but one. These disappointed electors are often more numerous than is supposed, because, as they find it worth while to vote on one side or the other rather than be temporarily disfranchised, their indisposition to sacrifice all their strong opinions to one opinion, which to them is almost colourless, never appears.

It is obvious that such a scheme as that of naming alternative candidates,—worked with electoral areas large enough to secure a plentiful supply of varied candidates and yet not so large as to lose the advantage of a local connexion between a member and his constituency,—would go some way to secure a representation of a far larger number of the population on a far larger number of questions. This would be done without representing minorities, and so, perhaps, indurating and intensifying within the House the antipathies already more than sufficiently well marked outside it.

Having ascertained the principles which determine how the people are to be represented, it remains to consider how far the efficiency of the representative Chamber itself and the conduct of Government are affected by the various modes of representation to which attention has just been drawn.

Some part of this subject has been anticipated in the remarks which have been made on the aggravation of party-spirit within the House likely to be promoted by positively representing minorities as such. There is a cardinal objection to all modes of minority-representation, even to those which have for their supreme object the most complete attainable representation of the majority of the electoral body on the largest number of separable topics. It is that the less uniform and narrowly confined are the political sentiments of members of the House, the more difficult does it become to secure promptness and decision in legislative action, and the more incalculable are the obstacles which, at unforeseen points, are likely to obstruct the path of the Executive Authority. Thus it is feared that, in a House representing a breadth and diversity of opinion at all corresponding to the multiform interests and tastes pervading the community, debates would be indefinitely prolonged, party discipline would be slackened, and important measures would be carried by such insignificant majorities that small and compact sections of the House would be able to make the whole policy of the country sway from side to side at their pleasure.

This evil indeed is no imaginary one; and it represents, undoubtedly, the characteristic danger to which an assembly with a thoroughly popular constitution is always prone. It was, in spite of Mr. Grote's apologies (which are, in many respects, unanswerable), the main constitutional drawback to those popular bodies in Athens and in early Rome which not so much represented as were constituted out of the citizen body.

Mr. Grote has sufficiently shown that the Athenian people, assembled in their Ecclesia, were neither fickle nor unjust; but on the contrary had attained the habit of listening patiently to arguments from all sides, and practised the self-restraint needed to re-consider again and again their determinations. But this very process of re-opening decided questions and of sustaining a condition of protracted doubt is not favourable to the rapid despatch of business or to the maintenance of an uniform policy. The widening area of Roman Government,—which opened out an experience to which Athens had not time to attain,—rendered the concentration of the powers of Government in the hands of a homogeneous aristocratic Senate an essential condition of further political existence, though (as Professor Mommsen has fully proved) it was the corruption and internal discord of this Senate which brought the Republic to the brink of ruin, from which it could only be saved by the institution of Imperial rule.

In modern States the best hope for uniformity,

strength, and stability in the executive Government need not be placed in the narrowness of the range of interests or questions to which representation is extended. It may be expected that, according as the constitution is so modified as to admit of a more complete representation of every voter,—not in respect of one subject only but of many,—political activity will be developed in the country at large. Already, in countries in which tolerably free institutions are found, the cheap daily and weekly Press has an extraordinary influence both in diffusing political information through the length and breadth of a land and in concentrating attention on questions which from moment to moment specially invite popular interference.

This influence of the Press is emphasized by the large use of public meetings, the proceedings of which,—often aided by the presence of members of Parliament or even of the Executive Government,—are again reported in the daily papers and are thus shared by innumerable persons in distant parts of the country. The result is that the subjects on which large classes of electors are simultaneously and sympathetically interested become not only more numerous but of a more exalted kind. Large associations are formed for the purpose of pressing on certain classes of measures in Parliament, and committees are formed for the preparation of draft bills and of taking counsel with Members in charge of them with a view to their being brought before the House in the most advantageous way.

In this way, a great deal of work, which, in an earlier condition of society, would be performed within the walls of the House,—where perhaps would then be found the only persons in the community competent for legislative duties,—is done outside the Houses by interested, philanthropic, or patriotic persons availing themselves of all the modern advantages of a free press, and a free right of public meeting and of association. The advantage of legislative work prepared in this way is that it is done under conditions of unrestrained liberty, even to a greater extent than is possible in the House itself by Members acting under the eye of constituents who may some day call them to account.

Thus when a claim is made for a more complete representation by enabling wasted minority-votes to be in some measure utilised, the result of conceding the claim would not be, it may be fairly presumed, to fill the House with Members concerned only to advocate narrow and ill-digested crotchets, but to favour the discussion in the House of a far larger number of questions than at present, while presenting them in a form in which all the initial steps of fitting them for precise debate and prompt decision have been already taken.

It cannot be a gain that a Legislative Chamber should be forced by its own constitution to ignore whole classes of important questions which are found to interest the people at large; and it may well be expected that, in proportion as, under a more complete representative system, a larger range of subjects are brought under the effectual notice of the Legislature, the House will not exhibit more instability and vacillation of purpose in dealing with them by a consistent policy than in dealing with the present narrower range. The previous work of elaboration performed outside the House, the aroused public interest, the publicity of all modern legislation, and the ever-widening public of educated political critics, all guarantee a representative House that will not allow itself to be brought into disrepute by the caprices of small sections of its members, and that will exhibit a higher rather than a lower capacity of adhering to a steady and uniform policy.

The subject of the superior advisability of having one or more Chambers is part of the general question how to secure all the benefits of the most complete popular representation without sacrificing any of the advantages supposed to belong peculiarly to Constitutions resting on less broad foundations.

The subject must be distinguished at the outset from that of the discussion of the political value of the English House of Lords, though the two subjects are often confounded.

The English House of Lords, in its modern shape, is an institution wholly *sui generis*, of a character quite unprecedented, and one which never can be reproduced. It is by attempts to copy it or to imitate some of its characteristics, erroneously supposed to be the most essential ones, that modern States,—and more especially the Australian Colonies,—have plunged themselves into inextricable perplexities. The truth is that the House of Lords owes its distinguished constitutional position, and even efficacy in the face of every adverse popular criticism, to those very facts which cannot be transferred to another country and other circumstances. The House of Lords, being a scarcely less ancient part of the Constitution than the Monarchy itself, is so implicated in the rest of the Constitution that no competent political reformer can think of simply expunging it or of radically altering it, without being prepared with an entire reconstruction of the most essential parts of the whole Legislative framework. The House of Lords, as an hereditary Chamber, is, in fact, and still more in popular apprehension, a protest in favour of that law of hereditary descent on which both the Monarchical succession and the institution of a titled Peerage is based. Furthermore, by occupying a situation intermediate, both in rank and in actual power, between the Crown and the representatives of the people, it maintains a hierarchical gradation of Governmental influence which obscures the otherwise too patent facts of the omnipotency of the people and the impotency of the Crown. But the maintenance of such a post of resistance is only rendered possible by the fact of possession,—guaranteed, at least temporarily, by a sentimental indisposition to disturb a state of things having its roots in the far past.

Lastly, the House of Lords is largely composed of powerful landholders, who, by family connexion, as well as by identity of interest, are in close relationship and sympathy with a large, if not a dominant, section of the House of Commons. Thus, in the case of any conflict between the Houses, there are always found in each House a sufficient number of members who care still more for the maintenance of the existing character and of the mutual relations of the two Houses than they do for the point in dispute; and these persons, by throwing (perhaps under the politest and most self-respectful of forms) all their weight into the scale of peace, prevent the strain from proving excessive.

It will be noted that relationships such as these are

the product of innumerable causes of a wholly special kind, which are bound up with the very core of English life and history in their most characteristic aspects. These merits (if such they are) have little to do with the benefits attributable to a second Chamber or to the individual merits of the hereditary legislators. They are an indigenous growth of the country, and cannot be transported elsewhere. It may, then, be laid down at once that the questions of the value and of the reform of the House of Lords only belong to the Science of Politics so far as that Assembly is a specimen of a second Chamber; but to estimate it properly from this point of view it must first be abstracted from all that is most characteristic of it.

In discussing a second Chamber, two topics have to be kept distinct, though they intermingle at some points. One is the general value of such a Chamber, and the other its best constitution. The topics are so far related that it may be advantageous only to have a second Chamber if it be well constituted.

The usual arguments in favour of a second Chamber are (1) that it affords a check upon the characteristic tendency of a democratic assembly to hasty and precipitate legislation; (2) that, unless the constitution of the second Chamber exactly repeats the constitution of the first, its existence affords the opportunity of approaching a legislative problem from a new point of view and throwing, perhaps, fresh lights upon it; (3) that by prolonging and complicating the process of legislation it affords multiplied opportunities for correcting the oversights, supplying the defects, and improving the structure, of legislative measures; (4) that, in the case of the second Chamber being representative like the first, but representative of other classes of the community, it affords a security that the interests of these classes are not overlooked.

The answers made to these arguments in favour of a second Chamber of some sort are (1) that the enormously increased legislative business of modern times (the discharge of which may be facilitated by the division of labour which the existence of two co-ordinate Chambers renders possible) is, on the whole, delayed, hampered, and interrupted to an extent wholly disproportionate to any benefits derived by a second discussion conducted in a different assembly. (2) As a barrier against the tempestuous current of democracy, the second Chamber is worse than useless, because if the more popular Chamber is practically omnipotent, resistance will only be persisted in in matters on which the mind of the people is not fully made up, and therefore on which no legislation ought to take place at all;—which is only saying that the popular Chamber is badly composed, not efficiently representing the people, and being prone to reckless legislation: or if, on the other hand, the popular Chamber is not omnipotent, and the two Chambers are of co-equal efficiency, legislation will either be the result of a series of compromises, or be barred altogether by a succession of dead-locks, as it has been in the British Colony of Victoria. (3) So far as, like the Senate of the United States and of France and the Legislative Councils of the Australian Colonies, it represents a different class of interests or sentiments, it is pure legislative loss,—without any compensating gain,—to have one class of interests or views represented at one discussion of a measure and another class at another discussion, instead of having both represented simultaneously to the great gain of the debate and the saving of time, expense, and labour.

4 With respect to the class of arguments adduced in favour of two Chambers, those numbered (1) and (3) (which relate to the beneficial impediments a second Chamber is calculated to oppose to the progress of democratic caprice, and which recommend it for preventing errors and accidental blemishes in legislation), they can be disposed of at once. Such arguments mark a transitional state of mind, in which really popular institutions are not yet accepted without distrust, and in which what is called democracy is regarded as a fatal political miasma which must envelop all States some day, but may by cautious preventive measures be staved off for a time.

5 The true and sufficient remedy for bad or rash legislation is the improvement of the constitution of the Assembly which really represents the people, and the amendment of its legislative machinery. Such amendments would be concerned with the length of notice which must be given of a proposed law, with the number of times it has to be discussed, with the information to be procured by Committees and Special Commissioners on its bearings, with the rules of debate, and with the opportunities afforded to persons outside the House to make their views on the proposal known.

The phases which an ordinary Bill has to pass through in the British House of Commons are tolerably familiar to all. As a means of showing the possible or endless variety of such phases which are available to persons who wish to oppose obstacles to the precipitate flood of popular energy in a Legislative Assembly the following extract is given from the French *Figaro* relating to the stages which a sanatory Bill for Paris, decided on in the Ministerial Council, would have to pass through:—

'(1) The bill will be drawn up by the Minister of Public Works; (2) submitted to the *Conseil d'Etat*; (3) which will appoint a committee; (4) which will appoint a reporter; (5) who will make a report; (6) which will be submitted to the committee; (7) which will approve it; (8) the report will be discussed, approved and sent back to the minister; (9) who will lay it on the table of the Chamber; (10) which will appoint another committee; (11) which will appoint a reporter; (12) who will make a report; (13) which will be discussed by the committee; (14) laid again on the table of the Chamber; (15) printed; (16) distributed to the deputies; (17) put on the order of the day; (18) put off; (19) adjourned; (20) discussed; (21) there will be speeches; (22) amendments; (23) additional paragraphs; (24) perhaps a change of ministry; (25) then it will be voted; (26) the bill will be sent up to the Senate; (27) which will refer it to the bureaux; (28) new committee; (29) new reporter; (30) new report; (31) report read to the committee; (32) laid on the table of the Senate.'

It surely is not needed to have a second Chamber for the sole purpose of interrupting and checking the too easy flow of popular legislation when such difficulties as these may have to be surmounted even in the case of a Bill which cannot excite much political opposition and has already been approved by the Executive Government.

But, further, this terror of what are called democratic institutions to which, in some measure, the late M. de Tocqueville gave colour by some of his criticisms is wholly unworthy of a statesman who takes a true view of the elements with which he has to deal. It is confessed that all Governments in the future will have to be conducted with full popular consent, if not by direct popular intervention. An Assembly or body of persons which is truly representative of the whole people — or which, even if not professedly representative, commands the confidence of the whole people — is not likely to be more fanatical, more selfish, more incompetent than some of the Assembly or body of persons existing side by side with it, and may well be assumed to be less so.

It is the first object of a statesman not to be domineered over by a mob; but it is equally an object with him to become the organ of the people, truly announcing their deliberate judgment, and the organ of the people only. Thus the temporary subterfuges by which it is sought to counterfeit deafness to the popular voice under the name of arresting impetuous legislation must certainly be swept away, as M. de Tocqueville foresaw, yet with gain in all ways rather than loss,—which he did not foresee.

Even in the case in which a second Chamber reverses a vote in the popular Chamber on the ground that the course of the discussion disclosed such differences of opinion that time ought to be afforded for the constituencies to be heard, the advantage that is gained by a seeming deference to the true intention of the people is lost by the extremely capricious and accidental way in which this check is sure to act. It will only act at moments when, for other reasons, some political antipathy is aroused or grudge entertained. It would never be allowed for one Assembly less popularly constituted habitually to reverse the decisions of another Assembly more popularly constituted, simply on the ground that a vote was not that of a sufficiently large majority, or from a casual and wholly arbitrary conjecture that the other House did not in this matter represent the body of Electors. Thus, here again, the true remedy for legislation out of harmony with the wishes of the people is to be sought in some improved constitutional machinery, — such as that examined above,—for representing the whole people on as many distinct questions as possible.

There remain the two arguments in favour of a second Chamber, based on the supposed necessity of representing certain special elements in the country not adequately represented in a purely popular assembly, or on the advantage of having each piece of legislation exposed to the criticism of a body quite differently constituted from that which has first approved it or must join in approving it. All the second Chambers at present existing are constructed on the basis either of their representing entirely different elements of the population from those represented in the first Chamber, or of their being themselves composed of elements selected on a principle which disposes the second Chamber to apply to the judgment of measures a scale very different from that in use in the first Chamber.

On one or other of these bases are constituted the Senate of the United States, which rather represents the component States of the Union than the population of each State; the French Senate, which represents a number of corporate rather than individual electors; the Legislative Council of New South Wales, which is nominated by the Crown; the Legislative Council of

Victoria, which especially represents the rich pastoral occupiers of large tracts of land, and the larger capitalists; and, lastly, the British House of Lords, which pre-eminently represents the interests of the larger landed proprietors and of the Established Church.

So far as the opposition of rival interests goes, it is not,—as has been proved by very extended experience,—a convenient solution of the real difficulties of the case to have one class of interests represented exclusively in one Chamber and the opposite class of interests in the other. By such a seclusion and agglomeration of persons all feeling in the same way and in a way which, from the nature of the case, is not always, if ever, in harmony with the general interests of the country, every opportunity is afforded for obstinate confederacy and none for placable concession.

The separation for legislative purposes of the two Houses of the British Parliament was an accidental though inevitable consequence of their distribution for the purpose of taxing, according to their several dispositions, themselves or their constituents. In some countries, as in France, special provision is made in the Constitution for the two Chambers, in certain emergencies, sitting and voting together. The same expedient has been advocated by some eminent Victorian politicians as a mode of bringing the two Houses of the Victorian legislature more constantly into accord. Even in the British Parliament provision is made for what is called a Conference between the Houses in case of an otherwise insoluble difference of opinion. But the procedure is antique and almost obsolete, and does not involve the whole body of the two Houses being brought together face to face.

According to the older English Constitution, the Clergy were represented in Parliament as an essential part of the Body Politic, and it was here again a mere financial accident that they broke away in order to tax themselves in their own Houses of Convocation and thus lost all direct voice in Government, except so far as they continued to be represented by the Abbots, and Spiritual Peers in the House of Lords.

It has already been laid down that where there are conflicting interests to be represented in the Legislature, two objects have to be attained,—one, that of their real and effectual representation; the other, that of each being only represented in proportion to its importance relative to all other interests; so that every opportunity is provided for proper concessions and compromises, for personal sacrifices, and for a fine correlation of ends and means. Now, on behalf of all these objects, —that is, of effective representation, harmonious co-operation, timely concession, apt adjustment, and habitual preference of the more pressing to the less pressing claim,—a common discussion in one broadly representative Chamber must surpass in value any series of discussions conducted first by persons having exclusively one order of interests and afterwards by those having exclusively another order. When the two alternative courses are contrasted in this way, it seems almost absurd that there should be any doubt as to the side on which the advantage lies.

And what is here said of the superior value of having all classes of interests represented simultaneously instead of successively, applies with no less force to the value of having various modes of thought, prepossessions, and habitual standards of opinion, all brought to bear in all the discussions of a measure, instead of having some exclusively recognised and enforced at one period of the discussion and the opposite or different ones exclusively recognised on a quite different occasion when the measure has reached a different stage. Nothing but the actual—and, so to speak, accidental— historical evolution of the British Houses of Parliament could have made that appear so natural and familiar which is, in fact, wholly alien to all principles of discussion as recognised in other fields of enquiry, and which can never be part of a permanent political system.

There is no subject which has more exercised the ingenuity of modern founders of Constitutions, beginning with the writers in the 'Federalist,' than the relations of the Executive (including the Administrative) and the Legislative Authority. Some light may be thrown on the question by reflecting on the circumstances of the evolution of the existing relations of the Executive and the Legislative Authority in the older countries of modern Europe which have had the most continuous Constitutional history. In these countries the King or Queen is the Supreme Executive Authority; but this function is not one which has been gradually attained to or arbitrarily cast upon the monarch for constitutional convenience. It is the last relic of far more ample powers, which included Legislative authority as well, and which, in early feudal days, were limited only by the close rivalry of powerful vassals and by occasional obligations to a superior but, usually, far removed feudal lord.

The tale of Constitutional History is that of incessant hemming in, at all points, both of the Legislative and Executive omnipotence of the Crown, though in earlier times Legislation was of comparatively small importance and the Executive authority of the Crown was disputed not so much between the Crown and the people as between the Crown and its greater vassals. In France the final subordination of all the greater vassals was the reverse of a gain to popular rights, while in England it was the greater vassals who allied themselves with the people, and even with the towns, to extort concessions from the Crown.

The result has been that, after some hundred years' struggle, the so-called 'limited' monarch of modern days has carried off from the fight a real and not inconsiderable portion of Legislative power, and the whole of the Executive power. This is subject, however, to two serious limitations,—one, that every act done by the monarch personally, either in his Legislative or Executive activity, is presumed to have been done by a particular minister or ministers approved by, and responsible to, a popular Legislature; and the other, that the Legislative authority, even as so circumscribed, cannot be exerted at all so as to contravene the judgment of the Legislative Assemblies; while the exertion of every part of his Executive authority is exposed to the constant criticism and vigilance of the same Assemblies.

Of course this summary and broad description of the state of things is not designed to describe exactly any existing constitutional condition,—not even that of England,—and it would require many limitations and qualifications before it would conform to any. But every one will recognise that this is the framework which presents all that is most characteristic of the relation between the modern European Monarch and the people, as more or less perfectly represented in Legislative Assemblies. So far as the most recently organised Constitutions go, whether on a professedly Republican basis, —such as those of the United States and of France; or on a Monarchical basis,—such as those of Belgium, Holland, Italy, Greece, and Spain; or on what may be called a quasi-monarchical basis,—such as those of the British Colonies having Parliamentary institutions; the same type reappears everywhere, the most interesting variations being those of the present French Constitution and the Constitution of the United States.

The position of the President in these two Constitutions, with his remarkable personal prerogatives, his fixed term of office, and almost complete exemption from constitutional or legal control during that term, is a wholly new and peculiar political experiment, which is still on its trial. The executive functions of the Senate of the United States through which, in a limited number of cases, it becomes a sharer in the President's executive power, is also a novel factor in politics, and the value of it can hardly be estimated till more materials are supplied by future history for a comparative inquiry.

The question which at the time of the foundation of the United States Constitution especially perplexed the great statesmen and writers of the period, as to the true position of the Judicature, may be held to be now settled in theory, if not in practice. It is now widely recognised, in accordance with the constitutional development of English History, that public liberty demands an independent Judicature more than almost any other guarantee; that this Judicature must not be dependent on the mere will of the head of the Executive for its nomination, for its casual amount of remuneration or reward, or for its retention in office; and that,—a provision upon which the United States have not always acted,—the Judicature must be rendered no less independent of the people than of the Executive.

These several propositions, which are truisms in England and the English dependencies, are scarcely admitted to the full in any other country. But they are propositions which hardly need the support of an unbroken line of historical testimony. When once announced, they commend themselves as by a sort of overbearing logical necessity.

The questions which are open to much controversy, and on which modern experience is too recent and too narrow to pronounce with decision, are questions as to the relations which ought to exist, first, between the Executive and the Legislative Authority, and, secondly, between the Executive Authority and the people.

In the working of the modern Parliamentary system the Executive Authority has a most important part to play. The more truly popular and broadly representative a Parliament becomes the more does it need for the conduct of its legislative functions a body of persons who command its confidence and who direct its activity into the necessary channels. There is no sacrifice of independence in requiring that the best opportunities of doing independent acts without economic loss of time or energy should be opened out. To do this constitutes what may be called the Legislative functions of the Executive Authority. The play of party spirit or of other less distinctly manifested forces designates the persons whom the majority of a Parliament are disposed to follow and trust, and in following them the Parliament makes no small sacrifice of the claims of its individual members.

But, out of this relationship necessarily springs a reciprocal one which is not without its important constitutional consequences. The Executive Authority which subserves the pleasure and prepares the work of Parliament tends to become its master. It is in a competition for mastery between the Legislative and the Executive Power, and in an incessant struggle between them, that a large and most important part of modern constitutional life exists. The typical way in which the struggle is conducted is something of the following kind.

According to one form, the Legislative Assembly in the course of its own debates and divisions, which may or may not be characterised as of a true 'party' kind, brings to the surface a certain number of its own members in whom the Assembly, represented by the permanent majority of its members, is disposed to repose implicit confidence for the discharge of such administrative work as the Assembly cannot directly interpose in, but can superintend and control. Or, according to the form which prevails in the United States, a prominent portion of the Executive Authority is selected by methods wholly independent of the action of the popular Assembly, and this Assembly only maintains its hold on the Executive through its command of the national finances, its capacity of legislation, and its power of adverse criticism. According to the written theory even of the English Constitution the

Monarch is under no obligation to select his Ministers from the ranks of the members of either House of Parliament, and it has occasionally happened within the last few years that a Member of Parliament has, in accordance with a well-known Statute of Queen Anne's reign, vacated his seat on being appointed to an Executive office and has not succeeded in obtaining another seat for months together, while continuing in office all the time.

According to the letter of the English Constitution, the Privy Council is the true Executive authority in which alone are reposed all the Executive functions of the Crown, and the Monarch is under no kind of obligation to call to his council only members of the Legislature, and, in fact, a considerable number of members of the Privy Council, including many of the Judges, have never sat in Parliament.

In most Continental countries, which in the general constitution of the Legislature have followed British precedents, the choice of the Executive is far more dependent on the arbitrary will of the Monarch or President than it is in England on any authority but that of the House of Commons. In England, at the present time it is notorious that the choice of a Prime Minister, and, incidentally, of all his Cabinet, is determined only by the majority of the House of Commons as evolved by a series of divisions sufficient to manifest its reality and solidity, and proceeding on the lines marked out by strict party organisation. It is only in the very exceptional cases in which there are more than two parties strongly marked and considerable in point of numbers that the direct personal influence of the Monarch may be invoked to determine who, as

Prime Minister, shall undertake the formation of a Government.

Thus, in ordinary cases, in England the initiative of forming the Executive Government proceeds from the popular Assembly; in some Continental countries having representative institutions, either from the Monarch,—as in Germany,—or from the two Assemblies sitting together and the popular Assembly alone,—as in France; or from the people directly supplemented by the popular Assembly,—as in the United States.

There is no country in which the continual presence of every important member of the Executive Government, and especially of the Chief of the Cabinet, in one or other of the two Chambers is held to be so indispensable as it is in England. In America the distance of the President from Congress, with which he only communicates in occasionally written utterances of a strictly formal kind, is said to present one of the most serious impediments to facility of political action especially at critical times. His irremovability and his provisional Legislative veto tend of themselves to make him a power in the State wholly exempt from either Parliamentary or popular control. The position was, no doubt, specially created as a counterpoise to what at the time of the foundation of the Constitution, was believed to be a hazardous experiment in democracy.

In the present day, when popular legislatures based on a widely extended suffrage have become little less than universal, the irresponsible and autocratic powers of the President, coupled with his firm tenure of office, can only produce anomalies in Government which nothing but the exceptional wisdom and self-restraint of particular Presidents can prevent from becoming disastrous.

The United States have been able to defer the consideration of a remedy for this confessed flaw in their constitution because of the remarkable sequence of able men who have occupied the Presidential office, and also because of the absorbing problems of reconstruction and financial recovery which have called for and found an exceptional amount of patriotic co-operation and self-renunciation in all quarters.

But it can hardly be expected, that in ordinary times the population of the States will continue to be content to put into commission for so long a period together so large a proportion of their indisputable right of control over Legislation and more particularly over Administration, especially when the Monarchical States of Europe have become one and all governed at every point by purely popular institutions, and when the character of the nation is deeply involved in the prevention and exemplary punishment of Executive abuses.

Thus the control of the Executive Authority by the English House of Commons, and the exemption of the President of the United States from any such control, present the two poles of possible relationship between the Authority which makes the law and the Authority which sees to its execution and conducts the administrative task of Government.

It is, however, scarcely possible to devise any theoretical constitution which should, at all times and in all circumstances, maintain a due balance between the Legislative and the Executive Authority. There are some departments in which, from the very nature of the case, they are always tending to encroach on each other, and the occasional mischiefs or even calamities resulting from this tendency, if unchecked, can only be kept at a distance or remedied by a thorough recognition of the perils at hand.

There are, for instance, some departments of administration for the supervision of which a popular Assembly cannot be suited, if it is broadly constituted enough to do its own appropriate work well. Such departments are the management of the Army, Navy, and Police, the conduct of Foreign Relations, and the Government of Dependencies, especially when,—as in the case of India,—the Dependency can supply very little material for its own Government and calls for a special amount of knowledge and skill of the highest kind in those who rule it.

In some countries, and especially in France, the management of the Police has been, for years, so entirely withdrawn from the intervention of the Legislative that the department of Government which deals with it has acquired a degree of irresponsible authority which is a dangerous menace to public liberty. The peril is all the more serious in countries in which there is no Habeas Corpus process, and in which the methods of criminal procedure concede to the police engaged in investigating a crime an amount of licence in secretly examining any number of persons on the barest suspicion, which would be scouted in countries which have followed the English type of criminal proceedings.

The evil is intensified in countries where a highly centralised system of administration prevails; and here the local and municipal control of the police (though this has been much infringed upon of late in England by the Metropolitan Police Acts) may present effectual barriers to the development of an uncontrolled central police Agency. It is obvious that a police system, to be really effective, must have extensive ramifications, must be inspired by a common spirit and subjected to an unity of management, and must have a large portion of its most important work habitually concealed from view.

In all this, however, there are abundant opportunities for the growth of a government within, and yet only too much outside, the general Government of the State. The more silent, prompt, and elastic are its movements, the more effective it is likely to be for its own peculiar ends, and yet all these requirements wholly unfit it to satisfy the scrutinising requirements of a popular Assembly which does all its work in the broad light of day. The result of a compromise between public justice and public liberty is that the scrutiny is less close than is needed for the one end and the prosecution of offences is less vigorous than is needed for the other.

Nevertheless there is no reason for an Assembly of popular representatives to ignore their functions, as the sole and last refuge of the obscure and dependent classes of society, on the ground that the police must be irresponsible if crime is to be checked at all. As in all other political matters, a balance must be struck between different and incompatible ends. The first duty will be to provide by Legislation, and by the creation of fit institutions, that the Police force be not centralised more than is absolutely needed for the public safety,—and that every opportunity is afforded by the intervention of a local and independent magistracy for proper publicity and for the vindication of innocence. The next duty is that of securing that all abuses are brought to light, and that the responsible members of the Executive Government are vigilantly checked and criticised by the popular Assembly.

It is well-known that, in Paris, the sole institution which has survived from the days of the old monarchy, throughout all the storms of revolution and repeated changes in the form of Government, is that of the organisation controlled by the Prefect of Police. The secret methods of French criminal procedure enabled the police to become masters for successive generations of the private affairs of a large number of persons, some of them in influential positions, and most of them interested in purchasing silence by connivance at police usurpations. There is reason to believe that it was against this network of subtle and irresponsible despotism that much of the popular indignation which, at the close of the Franco-German war, took the form of 'the Commune' was directed; and some of the leading Communists have alleged that the incendiarism which destroyed public buildings had for its original object the annihilation of the records of domiciliary espionage treasured up in the archives of the Police. Certainly, it is notorious that one aspect, and that the least exceptionable one, of the Communist movement was that of substituting local for central Government in a large class of matters of which the Police was the most prominent.

It may be laid down then as a fixed political principle that under all forms of Government the management of the Police force will be a lasting and justifiable object of popular jealousy and watchfulness. In proportion to the numbers of the police, as demanded by the growth of population and by the multiplication of transactions and relationships, will be their individual incompetency and their corporate strength when highly organised. Nothing but just laws, publicly and strictly executed by a high class of educated magistrates exposed at every moment to public surveillance, and abundant opportunities for bringing to light every abuse committed against the most insignificant member of the population, can ever afford sufficient guarantees against public liberty being eaten away in secret all the while that constitutional principles and democratic forms make the loudest protestations in its favour.

The management of the Army and Navy has long been recognised as affording a chief opening for Executive aggression. In England up to Charles I.'s time, a standing army in time of peace was regarded as the symbol of despotic as opposed to constitutional rule. The earlier English Constitution had done its utmost to render the forces of the country subject to local control in the counties, and to ensure all special levies for foreign wars being subject, financially, to strict Parliamentary control. The tradition of this control has been handed down to the present day, when the grant for the two services is renewed year by year, and the Mutiny Act empowering the Crown to levy soldiers up to an accurately computated number, and to make Articles of War for their discipline, has to be passed year by year.

It is usually the object in more military countries, such as Germany, to obtain a Parliamentary grant reaching over some years, so as to be, in the interval, exempt from popular criticism, in respect of the use to which the army is put, and the details of the mode in which the levy is made. Indeed, in Continental countries, where the conscription universally exists, and where the practice of passing the whole male population through the Army is becoming more and more habitual, the command of the Army during the years for which Parliament has surrendered its right even of financial control, puts an inordinate power in the hands of the Executive.

It is not merely that the soldiery form a physical support to the Executive against resistance, but that the hand of the Executive is made to be felt, through countless subordinates and delegated agents, in every spot and hamlet of the country. Even in times of profound peace, the whole population has more to do with the central military than with the local civil authority. If there are complaints of abuse or of trespass on constitutional rights, the matter becomes one of military order and discipline, and is taken out of the range of the common civil courts. The arbitrary will of a capricious petty officer becomes substituted for fixed and well-understood laws. Remedies have to be begged by servile petition, by ignominious compromise, by corrupt purchase, not demanded, as of right, in a public Court of Justice. The sense of self-respect and self-reliance is weakened to the lowest point, and popular Government becomes merely the shadow of a tyrannical dominion which has its centre in a very different quarter.

What is described here as the peculiar characteristic of those countries in which the levy is universal, and where Parliament abandons its control for a definite term of years, is only true to a very small degree in such countries as England and the United States, in which military service is free and the popular Assembly retains a sufficiently firm hold on the War department of the Executive Government to prevent the arbitrary rule which is an inevitable adherent of all military institutions from crystallising into permanent principles. But in these countries, the danger, though comparatively slight and remote, is still real. The use of the Army in times of alleged sedition, and even of riot, is a matter in respect of which the Executive needs to be watched with the utmost vigilance.

Even apart from the physical strengthening of the Executive by the Army, the political influence which the Executive exerts through this medium is not inconsiderable. The officers of all grades, and the more intelligent soldiers, are likely to be much at one on large classes of questions either political or closely allied to politics, and to agree in being indifferent to other large classes of questions. Thus at moments when it is apprehended that some national affront has been received from another State, or when the popular conscience demands that some concession of territory be made, or that a long pending controversy be closed by a conciliating adjustment of rights, or that arbitration be preferred to war, it usually happens that the military profession are all on the side of belligerency rather than of peace. This may be of small consequence, unless the people are only just so far roused that strongly expressed divisions of sentiment manifest themselves. In such circumstances, if the Executive Government chances to favour a warlike rather than a peaceful policy, it is of no small account that it has with it so large, so generally intelligent, and so compact a body of opinion as that represented by the military profession and all closely connected with it by ties of blood or of interest.

In speaking of the watchfulness with which the Executive Government has to be regarded on the ground of the support it may derive, at certain emergencies, from the military classes, it must not be forgotten, furthermore, that in the management of the Army and Navy the Government is the greatest employer of labour in the country, and in the employment of this labour has the command of the greatest amount of capital. Every one knows the influence, social and political, which is wielded by employers, and of which no electoral or other restrictive laws can rob them. The larger the army and navy, the more numerous are the functionaries, of every degree of hierarchical subordination, through whom the Government has to act.

Even where gross abuses are avoided and the Government is, on the whole, disposed to do its best and to act honestly, it is almost impossible to check all the officials who have to choose whom to employ, whom to contract with, whose pay to increase and whose to diminish, whom to retain and whom to discharge, whom to reward and whom to punish. Here, too, again, an innumerable quantity of interlacing interests are deeply concerned in labour being plentiful and uninterrupted. A new fortification or dockyard or arsenal; the breaking out of war; the despatch of troops in large masses to a dependency in disorder; any of these means the well-being and regular means of livelihood for thousands and thousands of families, as the opposite of them means their loss and suffering.

It is impossible then to expect political impartiality from the classes of society which have so vast a stake in the game of life and death. No doubt miracles of patriotism and of self-abnegation have been found, again and again, at memorable crises, as in America and the North of England during the War of Secession; but the statesman cannot act as if human nature would in all similar emergencies attain the same elevated range of sentiment. In ordinary times, the physical claims of a man's wife and children are at least as near to him as any other interests, and usually far nearer than all other interests put together.

If, then, this is true when the Executive Government acts honestly and abstains from using unfair pressure on the myriads of persons it employs, it is obvious how easy it is for it to operate on public sentiment in all those cases in which its views are really at one with the interests of those who work for it. It is against this fallacious exhibition of public opinion, turned to account by an unscrupulous Executive, that a popular Assembly must be upon its guard. The remedy is to test the allegation that public opinion is on the side of the Government, by examining in what quarters that opinion is manifested; by referring to the printed organs favoured by the labouring classes; by attending to the sort of arguments which have weight at public meetings; by studying election addresses to such classes as dockyard labourers and constituencies in garrison and sea-port towns; and by watching the course of deputations to responsible Ministers.

In a country in which the expression of opinion is really free, it will be easy, in a short time after the public mind is fairly roused, to distinguish a real from a factitious popularity of a Governmental act; and if, on applying such tests, the act is discredited, the

Government can then only justify it by reference to the intrinsic merits of the case.

It should be needless to supplement these remarks on the perils, incident to the position of the Executive Government as an employer of Labour, by noticing the importance, on the one hand, of providing innumerable checks,—of the nature of strict accounts, audits, inspections, publication of quarterly statements of the most minute accuracy in detail,—upon extravagance and corruption ; and, on the other hand, of following up by a special legal machinery every alleged irregularity, and of remorselessly punishing every underhand transaction, and, still more, every species of fraud, whether committed by the highest or the lowest official.

It would seem from some miserable passages in the recent history of the United States that the complication of modern Government has surpassed the powers of the republican institutions, introduced a century ago, to grapple with the widespread corruption to which an opening is given. Here again the independence of the head of the Executive Government and its remoteness from Congress render the exercise of the popular judgment far too ineffective.

There is another mode in which, in modern times, and to an extent which is ever increasing with economical progress, the Executive Authority exerts a political influence which needs not only counteracting institutions but also unresting vigilance of control on the part of the Legislature. The Executive Authority is not only the greatest capitalist in the country so far as the employment of labour and the making of contracts are concerned, but is also the greatest capitalist so far as the power of operating on the money-market is

THE EXECUTIVE AS A CAPITALIST. 263

concerned. This latter power is almost more important than the former one, because it reaches into foreign countries; it reposes on a very subtle connexion of political and economical duties equally incumbent on the Executive Authority; and it involves so much secrecy of action that it almost defies the scrutiny of the most vigilant members of the Legislature as well as of the intelligent public outside.

In the communities of the ancient world almost the only mode in which the Executive Government could operate on the value of money and on prices was by debasement or alteration in value of the current coin; and the repeated recourse had by Rome to measures of this sort, from the period of the troubles introduced by the Punic wars, are well remembered as forming some of the causes of national disorganisation which culminated in the Empire. In modern times the mode of operating on the coinage is of the more seductive kind rendered possible by the general use of paper money. The difficulties of restraining Executive abuses in the creation of paper money have tested to the utmost modern political invention.

These difficulties have their root in the inseparable connexion between the political activity which the Executive Authority is bound to exhibit, and the money needed to carry it on. Thus in time of war or at an apparent critical emergency at which the national honour, order, or safety seems ever so indirectly involved, the Executive is always held bound to do its utmost, and even, if necessary, to pledge the national credit to an extent to which no legislative limit could ever be put by anticipation. The mode in which this is most easily done is by issuing paper money or promises to pay at or after a certain date. These promises may or may not be punctually redeemed or else renewed when the crisis is over; but the fact that it is the Executive which, at the outset, was responsible for them, and that it is the Executive which may be presumed to have the best means of information as to the advisability of redeeming, renewing, or supplementing these pecuniary engagements, and as to the times and ways and means for doing so, puts the Executive in a position which it requires all the energy and vigilance of the Legislature to cope with.

Apart, indeed, from the supreme crises here alluded to, even in the ordinary administration of the country, the Executive must be allowed a very large discretion as to the contracting of debts and as to the modes and times of their payment, as well as the securities to be demanded from debtors to the State, and as to larger commercial transactions (such as the purchase of the bulk of the Suez Canal shares by the British Government) which have to be decided on without a day's delay. The practice in England of allowing the Executive to issue Treasury Bonds at a high rate of interest, redeemable within the year, for the purpose of meeting merely temporary deficiencies due to financial accidents, or to the necessity of making payments before the receipt of the taxes designed to meet them, is a recognition of this discretionary power.

It is most of all in its relation to national taxation that the Executive Authority occupies a position of the highest financial responsibility, and this position is made all the more important in modern times through the practice of contracting unredeemable Public Debts. The amount of those debts in some of the countries of the

Old World is such that a large proportion of the taxation of the country (in England about a third of the imperial taxes) is wholly absorbed in paying the interest of debt. It is thus a subject of yearly recurrent concern whether any and what portion of this debt can be conveniently paid off at particular periods, and by what devices this can be most economically done. The purely political question is always involved as to whether future generations should be relieved at the cost of the present generation, and this depends, partly, on the view taken of the comparative wealth of the tax-payers now and hereafter (so far as this can be prognosticated), and, partly, on the facilities presented, at a given moment, by the state of the money-market for providing the funds needed to pay off debts.

Now the initiative of paying off portions of debt must necessarily be left in the hands of the Executive Government, because any public movement of the sort on a grand scale debated and voted by Parliament would, of itself, operate on the money market in such a way as to change all the conditions of the problem and, perhaps, render immediate liquidation no longer expedient. Thus it will rest with the Executive Government to make engagements with the creditors of the State at its own pleasure and in the exercise of its own discretion. It will have to choose the opportune moment, the agents, the terms of arrangement; and in respect of each of these matters there are opportunities for infinite abuses, not so much on the part of the Executive Authority, as a corporate body, as on that of corrupt individual members of it who are always liable to creep into its ranks.

There have been too many charges of abuse of their

financial position made in recent times against Executive Governments or their agents for dangers of this class to be treated as nothing better than theoretical hallucinations. The accusations against Financial Ministers in the United States for abuse of their authority as collectors of customs; the deplorable revelations of the State frauds on which so much of the Executive action and personal Government of Napoleon III. in France seems to have been based; the imputations, right or wrong, that the disorder in Tunis in 1881 was craftily designed, as a money-making plot, to pave the way first to anarchy, when certain funds would go down, and afterwards to French annexation, when they would go up higher than ever; the implication in certain quarters of the purchase by British Executive Authority of the Suez Canal shares with a vague scheme of Oriental policy to which the British Parliament had never been asked to assent; all these tokens,—which might be multiplied indefinitely,—sufficiently prove that the modern relations of an Executive Authority to Finance present political perils which will be likely to increase with time rather than to diminish.

Dangers of this class are further aggravated through the practice which so largely prevails in modern States of maintaining a National Bank in peculiar relations with the Executive Government. This subject, on one side of it, belongs to the topic of the province of Government, under which head it will be discussed at length. But, on another side of it, and as a political fact which actually exists and is likely to exist far into future time, some observations must be made upon it here.

The general nature of these National Banks will be

understood from a reference to the constitutional situations of the Bank of England and of the Bank of France. The Bank of England was at its origin a mere company of merchants who obtained from the Crown certain exclusive privileges in return for the services they agreed to render as the intermediate agents of the Government for paying the national creditors and for receiving the taxes out of which the payments had, at fixed intervals, to be made. These privileges and corresponding obligations have been repeatedly confirmed, defined, and enlarged by successive Charters, usually granted in conformity with special Acts of Parliament, the most important of which is the Bank Charter Act of 1844. The effect of this Act was entirely to separate the business of the issue of notes from all the other banking business,—a certain limit being affixed to the amount of the issue determined by the amount of bullion actually in the coffers of the bank at the time of issue. The notes of the Bank of England are convertible on demand, and are legal tender. They thus operate as current coin within the country.

The Bank of France was constituted mainly for the purpose of facilitating commerce by affording to merchants a sure means of obtaining advances on good security. It has the power of issuing notes payable to the bearer at sight, up to the amount of three times its cash in hand; but these bills are only legal tender by special and occasional legislation, which the Court of Cassation has declared to be a matter only of police and public safety which special contracts can avoid. (*Cass.* 11, *Feb.* 1873.)

With respect both to these banks and to other banks of this sort, it is obvious that the point at which

Government pressure is most felt is that which limits the right of issue and either enforces the convertibility of the notes or,—what amounts to nearly the same thing,—makes an inconvertible note legal tender. In England the history of repeated commercial crises has proved that, while the crisis has been aggravated and precipitated by the legal impossibility of the Bank increasing its issue to meet the emergency, the sudden interference of the Executive Government to suspend the Bank Charter Act and to enlarge the powers of the Bank, which that Act alone restricted, has been instantly attended by a relaxation of the strain,—even when the Bank has not actually had occasion to avail itself of its extended rights.

This fact may or may not be used as an argument against the policy of the Act itself; and many of the ablest authorities on the subject have employed the argument both ways, but especially against the desirability of the Government implicating itself at all in the control of the commercial community with a view to protect those who ought to be able to protect themselves.

But, whatever may be said from the purely economical point of view, there can be no doubt that the recognised right of the Executive Authority to interpose or not to interpose, or to choose the moment and the degree of its interposition, deserves the most jealous watchfulness at the hands of the Legislature. The two occasions on which the notes of the Bank of France were made legal tender (March 16, 1848, and August 7, 1870) were times of revolutionary change, when the Executive of the hour must, unavoidably, be in supreme command of the situation.

The suspension of the Bank Charter Act by the

English Executive is, constitutionally speaking, an encroachment on the rights of the Legislature which would be tolerated in no other department of affairs; and it has only been endured hitherto because its good results are manifest to all, while its indirect bad results, in making the vicissitudes of commerce dependent, in the last crisis,—and therefore, through the expectation aroused, even from the first,—on the will of the Executive Authority are less obvious. It must not be forgotten that the Executive Authority must, by the nature of the case, consist of a number of persons in confidential relations to each other, and likely, many of them, to have strong personal, social, or family interests involved at the occurrence of every monetary catastrophe. At such epochs a few hours' advance in obtaining information,—and, still more, the slightest capacity to direct the springs of action,—may mean even for respectable commercial men all the difference between disastrous failure and conspicuous enrichment. The temptation to abuse such opportunities, though in some healthy conditions of society it will be generally resisted, will yet too often prevail, and the possibility of its prevailing in any case should be absolutely provided against.

The only mode of providing against such moral hazards is to withdraw from the Executive, to the greatest extent possible, all power of directly influencing the money market, even at the moment of the most severe strain of public credit. If it be determined to persist, on principles to be discussed hereafter, in recognising an interference with Commerce and the maintenance of National Banks as belonging to the province of Government, it will be found necessary to provide some standing Committee of the Legislature,—such as that of the House of Commons for Public Accounts,—which shall take advice with the Executive even in the interval of the Parliamentary vacation, and share the responsibility of all its acts. This Committee would keep a minute of all its transactions from day to day and from hour to hour, and through its close relations with Parliament would have facilities for discussing openly the grounds of any exceptional action without involving the Executive Government in the fate of its measures.

It is most difficult to maintain a proper check on the pecuniary discretion of the Executive in relation to Foreign Policy. The subject of Foreign Policy as a department of scientific Politics will be discussed, independently, later on. But one aspect of it belongs to this place. In cases in which the main conduct of Foreign affairs belongs, at least so far as the initiative is concerned, to the Executive Authority, it is almost impossible to prevent that Authority involving the country in pecuniary liabilities which the Legislature, if fully consulted, might well have shrunk from encountering.

The purchase by England of the bulk of the Suez Canal shares, already alluded to in other connexions, is an apposite illustration of this danger. If the purchase had to be made at all, it must have been made, as in fact it was, precipitately and secretly, by the Executive Authority. There was no time for delay or for prolonged negotiations, and publicity would have been fatal to the transaction. But, owing to the haste of the proceeding and the absence of full Parliamentary discussion, the country found itself irretrievably committed to a commercial enterprise wholly unprecedented and involving almost indefinite pecuniary risk. There was absolutely no precedent for the Government of one country becoming the main proprietor of an industrial and commercial undertaking conducted in the territory of another Government and wholly subject to its control.

The Suez Canal Company was a French Company having its domicile in France, though, no doubt, it had also a domicile of Jurisdiction in Egypt. One result was that a Government, the greatest shareholder of all, might have to depend upon Foreign Judges sitting in a Foreign country (not even that of the enterprise itself) for the ascertaining and vindication of its rights. The alternative was that of dependence on the Egyptian Courts, which by the accident of the International Tribunals established there, were in themselves an unobjectionable tribunal.

Questions appertaining to the rights of the shareholders, to the debts on the undertaking, to the latent and ulterior rights of the Khedive, and even, in some emergencies, of the Sultan, (who was one of the parties to the original concession,) were numerous and complicated, and the solution of them one way or other might not only be productive of international embarrassments but involve serious pecuniary consequences.

Yet to none of these matters was the attention of the British Legislature ever called; nor was there opportunity for it to be called. The Executive Authority availed themselves of their actual power and committed the country to engagements the nature and extent of which it could not itself possibly divine at the moment.

It is needless to recur to the case of Foreign wars brought about by Executive diplomacy, or of commercial Treaties which, though often discussed in Parliament, are just as often negotiated by the Executive on its own responsibility. In superintending and checking the Executive Authority in such matters the Legislature will have to bear in mind more and more that, quite apart from the more obvious dangers to Parliamentary freedom involved in trusting too implicitly to the Executive of the day, there is hidden the danger that the Executive in a popular Government may carry with it the show of popular assent and confidence, through its command of the numerical majority of votes. But the majority themselves will do well to be ware of the Frankenstein-monster that they themselves have called into being. What they allow to-day may become a precedent to-morrow and be used against them when the Parliamentary tables are turned a few days hence.

The Executive Authority, by the necessities of its composition and of the continued co-operation of its members, has a tendency to acquire rapidly a compactness which itself is full of danger to free Parliamentary life. Where this tendency is aggravated by the prominent influence of an autocratically-disposed chief, or by the weak servility of a Parliamentary majority, or by the undue dominance in the country of bureaucratic institutions (as in France and Germany), the perils to public liberty are almost inevitable. The Executive possesses itself of the Legislative power, ensures the acceptance of a series of measures favourable to its own pretensions, and does its utmost even to sap the foundations of an independent judiciary and of the last bulwarks of public liberty residing in such institutions as Trial by Jury, the writ of Habeas Corpus, and regular Magisterial procedure.

The story is an old one, tracing back to the times of Greek Tyrants and Roman Cæsars. It has yet to be seen whether the story is to be perpetual as well as old; or whether the popular constitutions of modern States will suffice to maintain a permanent barrier against the aggression of an Executive dressed in the little brief authority imparted by a fluctuating majority vote.

Besides the parts of a Constitution which admit of being expressed in the formal structure of the Government and in provisions for securing its proper operation, there are other parts which are of even greater importance but do not admit of being so expressed. They rather exist as fluid principles, only occasionally congealed into fixed institutions, such as, in England, the processes which regulate trial for libel and treason. Parts of the Constitution like these have usually been handed down from early times, and are attributable to specified documents or grants or memorable historical events. They are cherished with fond popular affection, and, in healthy periods, on no other subjects is it so easy to stir the national jealousy.

In early England soon after the Conquest, 'the laws of Edward the Confessor,' as supposed to have been guaranteed by the Norman invaders, seem to have been regarded as a fixed basis of the Constitution which the people were entitled to claim, even from a new dynasty,

T

as their national birthright. It was not long till Magna Charta and the other Charters which preceded or succeeded it acquired an almost sacred efficacy, and even to this day it is believed by countless persons who have never read a word of the original documents, nor could translate them if they once succeeded in reading them, that they announced, and that for the first time, all the most characteristic doctrines of the English Constitution.

At a still later date the Bill of Rights, the Act of Settlement, the Act of Union with Scotland, and even the terms of the Coronation Oath, have been regarded as possessing a certain constitutional cogency over and above their mere force as Acts of Parliament or solemn personal engagements of the Sovereign. In the same way each other country, in which a traditional constitution exists at all, reverts to special documents and written manifestoes which, at the least, are treated as supplying the best evidence of the antiquity of a political claim.

In France and Italy 'Concordats' between the civil Authority and the Authorities of the Catholic Church; in Germany and neighbouring States the settlement brought about by Treaties at the Peace of Westphalia; in the United States the Declaration of Independence, and in the British Colonies the first constitutive Act of the British Parliament; are documents the validity of which it is scarcely possible by any later legislative measure to supersede or call in question.

Such documents draw their force, in truth, not from their scant and often irrelevant verbiage, but from their stamping, in visible and lasting forms for ever, resolutions, concessions, compromises, and arrangements, which were at the time,—and were thereby made to continue for all time,—essential parts of the political consciousness of the whole people expressing themselves by their proper representatives. It is by a long series of such material proofs that the constitutional sentiment of a people is framed, and it is far more the strength of this sentiment itself than the mere words of the documents, interpreted like any other written law, that constitutes their political efficacy.

The mode in which the growing and increasingly settled constitutional instincts of a people manifest themselves in the detail of common life is through the decisions of Courts of Justice. This has been especially the case in England, where the Judges have not been restrained by the precedents of a legal system already fully developed, as was Roman law, and where, consequently, they have been free to seek for the principles of their judgments in the moral traditions of the people themselves. It was such moral traditions, brought, as far as possible, into harmony with actual usages, and with such written law as there was, which enabled the English Judges to pronounce against the right of the Crown to impose arbitrary taxes, against monopolies, against the use of torture for the purpose of eliciting evidence, against irregular trespasses on person and property by the police, against the right of the Crown to call Juries to account for their verdicts, against the one-sided interpretation of treason statutes, and in favour of free speech, free right of public meeting, and free association.

The doctrines of public liberty, so evolved and laid down by Courts of Justice in England, have been generally translated into written law in the various

States of the American Union and into the constitutional Charters of new States which have taken the English Constitution as their type. It may be expected, hereafter, that most of these doctrines, which have been wrought out by slow degrees and painful effort by England, will prove to be henceforth part of the world's heritage. They will be universally incorporated in all written constitutions; and, side by side with the provisions for popular representation, and for defining the mutual relationships of the Executive and the Legislative Authority, there will be found a series of declarations as to what neither the Legislature nor the Executive Authority is, by the Constitution, entitled to do. It will be recognised in formal terms that there are certain inalienable human rights which no majority vote, at any crisis in the fortunes of the people, has a right to infringe upon ever so slightly. It may require a longer political experience before the full reach of these rights can be even approximately ascertained; and they will never be so absolutely determined as to be beyond the reach of further constitutional evolution. But the world cannot go back, and those countries alone will continue to advance with it which secure for themselves in the firmest manner each step which has been already gained by any one of them.

CHAPTER VII.

LOCAL GOVERNMENT.

THERE is nothing in the political structure of the States of the ancient world which corresponds with what is now meant by 'Local Government.'

It is true that, so often as a State comprehended within its dominions territories far removed from each other or from the seat of Government, various devices were resorted to for making the hand of the Government felt at the extremities, and for securing not merely order but in some measure harmonious contribution to common ends. The favourite Oriental mode of bringing this about was by the formation of quasi-independent satrapies, in the government of which the delegate of the sovereign was supreme within the limits of the province entrusted to him, and only responsible to his superior for the provision of a military contingent, for handing over revenue received, and for maintaining order. He was usually liable to be arbitrarily deposed and superseded.

This mode of Government seems to have obtained in the middle period of Ancient Egypt, at the time of the Semitic invasions and lengthened usurpation; in Persia under the immediate successors of Cyrus the Great; and is well known to be the occasion of the political embarrassments of the modern Ottoman Empire and of the Empire of China.

The Roman Republic and Empire resorted to the same method of administration, though in a qualified form, in the government of the provinces successively annexed. The period of the appointment was usually for only a year, though it was occasionally prolonged. Its continued prolongation for an unprecedented period in the case of Julius Cæsar was, in fact, the most serious omen of the coming reconstruction of the very basis of government.

Furthermore, in the Roman dominions, the numerous colonial settlements scattered about, and the various corporate and personal rights of Roman citizenship conceded to the residents in the different classes of towns, all tended to restrict the autocratic power of the Proconsul or Procurator, and to bring the subject people into direct relation with the central Government.

At successive intervals under Augustus, under Diocletian, and under Justinian, the whole system of Provincial administration,—especially in respect of the administration of justice,—was recast, but always with the object of avoiding the local irresponsibility which was becoming so disastrous in the later days of the Republic, and which has become a byword in characterising the despotisms of the East.

Nevertheless, at all periods of the Roman Empire the conditions were lacking for combining local free-agency with central unity of control; and this was one of the chief causes why the efforts of the Roman Empire to govern such vast dominions were premature and destined to failure. What these conditions are will shortly appear.

Another class of tentative efforts, in the old as well as in the newer world, to reconcile the claims of local independence with central unity is that known under the name of 'Federation.' The idea and the practice of Federation are at least as old as the supremacy of Athens over her Ionian allies, and as the Achæan league; and the numerous political and commercial leagues of the Middle Ages all expressed the same necessity of combining the advantages of corporate strength and individual freedom.

The numerous attempts at Federation among the American colonies, previous to the final one ushered in at Philadelphia, sprang from the same necessities which the United States Government find it at this day no light task duly to recognise and provide for. It was the war of Independence which, with extraordinary rapidity, brought to a head both the advantages and the embarrassments of a system of Federal government; and a Federal constitution was hardly created before it was modified in the direction adverse to true Federal principles and favourable to the supremacy of the Central Authority. As time went on the adequacy of a Federal system for the government of so large a part of North America, in the face of the compactly organised Governments of Europe, was tested again and again by all varieties of constitutional crises at home and of diplomatic hazards abroad. The Secession War brought the question to a head, and it was decided against the Federal system and in favour of a system of Local Government, the forms only of an extinct Federalism being retained.

It has, then, to be determined, as a matter of scientific investigation, what are the conditions,—

social, economical, and national,—which recommend a system of Local Government in preference either to a rule by provincial deputies or to a true federal organisation. It is assumed that the essence of a system of Local Government consists in a distribution being effected between the governmental, legislative, and executive powers, in such proportions as that the claims of unity of control and of supervision are reconciled, or presumed to be reconciled, with the claims of independent management and self-taxation on the part of all the groups of persons locally associated who, taken together, constitute the population of the country.

It is, indeed, not so much a distribution of all the powers of government which really takes place, as a delegation of certain powers of government; and in describing what Local Government is in its essence, it must be remembered that the actual forms of it which are manifested on every side seldom fulfil the logical conception. Thus where the interference and supervision of the Central Government becomes incessant and no important act can be done by a Local Authority without the acquiescence of the central department, or where the assessment of a tax has to be approved by that department, or where the chief officials in the different local seats of administration are appointed by a central authority and for short periods and under stringent control by that authority, Local Government may exist only in name. It is only by understanding what are the broad characteristic features of Local Government as contrasted with a purely centralised system of government, on the one hand, and, on the other, with such peculiar phases of decentralised government as Federation or Provincial delegacy, that its existence in any particular case can be detected and its merits and demerits assigned.

The history of Local Government in England may, without any imputation of illogical patriotic conceit, be fairly resorted to for the purpose of throwing light upon the essential conditions of Local Government generally. Besides England itself, the countries in which Local Government has already naturally developed itself with the greatest exuberance and promise are the United States, the British Australian Colonies, and the German Empire.

In the United States the local institutions more distinctly than any other part of the system of Government spring from an English stock. In the Australian Colonies the English people established all their native institutions, so far as they were at all applicable, in their most mature form. In Germany, in spite of the Imperial traditions and the autocratic military organisation which, for the present, tends to stifle all popular freedom, the Local Government of England is that part of the English Constitution which has most profoundly impressed theoretical writers of authority, and is being used as a type in the constitutional transformation which every part of the Empire is rapidly undergoing. Professor Gneist published a treatise on 'Self-Government in England,' the result of long and patient enquiry on the spot, which serves even for Englishmen as the best and most exhaustive authority on the minutest problem or surviving antiquarian curiosity on which it may be consulted.

The reasons of this pre-eminence of England as an authoritative precedent on the theory and practice of

Local Government are two. One reason is that the primitive circumstances of the political settlement of England,—first by those who (in spite of current criticism) are most conveniently denominated by the name of Saxons and then by the Normans,—concurred to bring the Local Government of parishes and counties into a special relation with the Central Government of the King and the King's Council which has had no exact parallel elsewhere.

The other reason is that this special relation has been maintained intact, in spite of all sorts of modifications and developments in point of detail for 800 years without interruption from civil strife or external foe. There is no other country, not even Japan, of which two similar propositions could be laid down.

The history of the English parish is traceable so far back that its origin is lost in that period when the Romans had scarcely yet withdrawn, and when the institutions of the British Church were still the most influential elements in the civilisation of the island. At this period, which intervened between the publication of the Codex Theodosius II. in the West in 438 A.D. and that of the Code of Justinian in the East in 529 A.D., it is well known that the Roman Empire was throughout its length and breadth almost as elaborately organised for purposes of ecclesiastical as for those of civil Government. Indeed the Bishops and Clergy had civic functions of the utmost importance cast upon them by the Secular Government, and Christian assemblies and Churches were freely turned to account for witnessing the performance of civil acts.

Recent writers on Ecclesiastical antiquities have pointed out that the ecclesiastical dioceses and divisions survived the civil, as is conspicuous in the names of many French Bishoprics in the present day. In England indeed the inroads or rather the violent colonising raids of the pagan Teutons from the European Continent not only drove the native Britons into the Western fastnesses of Wales and Cornwall but broke up the already tottering fabric of Roman civilisation in the cities, and with it the crumbling relics of ecclesiastical organisation. It is still a moot point how far the Teutonic invaders, as they became settled, revived the expiring life of Roman and Ecclesiastical order, or how far they simply introduced their own institutions as existing in their Continental homes. They certainly adhered to the general sites of the Roman towns though not to the identical spot previously occupied. It may be at least supposed, that, when the Christian Church was organised afresh by Augustine and his successors, the more enduring of the landmarks of the primitive British Church were rather re-invigorated than superseded.

The history of the County and the 'Hundred,' and of the Courts and Assembly which belong to them, has been carefully investigated of late years by Professor Stubbs and Mr. Freeman, and the result of their enquiries seems to establish that these divisions have their origin not in any artificial organisation devised by any particular King or Government, but in the original separation from each other of the different sections of settlers, and in the habitual organisation (of the kind described by Tacitus) which prevailed among the German tribes.

If this be true, it is evident that, just as parochial organisation traces back to the Church and to the joint civil and ecclesiastical organisation of the Roman period, so County and other local divisions trace back to the peculiar circumstances of the Teutonic settlement and to the home traditions of the settlers. It appears then that in England all the main units of Local Government now in force,—that is, the County, the Parish, and the Hundred,—were anterior to the consolidation of the English Monarchy and have a continuous history which is older, and so longer, than that of the English Parliament.

The effect of the Norman Conquest,—as is now well known through the amount of erudition which has been expended on this special topic,—was not to destroy or weaken the local organisation which it found in existence, but to use it to the utmost, while bringing it into closer relation with the Central Government and into harmony with the stricter feudalisation of the country.

The general effect of the Conquest, from a judicial and from an administrative, and soon from a financial, point of view, was that of increased centralisation. But when once the supremacy of the King in all causes, ecclesiastical as well as civil, was duly protected against local (if not against priestly) insubordination the County and parochial organisation could work together in excellent concert with the characteristic feudal institutions for the keeping of the peace and for the military defence of the country which were introduced by the Norman Kings in an improved, if not a totally new, form.

This historical review serves to explain the peculiar conditions under which Local Government has thriven to the extent it has in England. The first of these conditions is that its arrangements oe as naturally congenial to the habits and tastes of the people as are the common incidents of domestic life. The smallness of the circle within which Local Government, as contrasted with central government, is conducted, while it brings its responsibilities and charges more closely home to each person found within the circle, also claims from him an amount of individual practical activity from which ordinary persons, in the larger circle of central government, usually find themselves exempt. The Parish Vestry, the Hundred Mote, the Court Baron, the Local Board, the Court of Quarter Sessions, are each of them small Parliaments or judicial benches in one or other of which the most insignificant householder, as well as the wealthiest territorial proprietor, may find his place. There is needed a certain amount of training, moral self-restraint, public spirit, capacity for co-operation, which cannot be called forth in a day at the will of a legislator, but which may require generations for their diffusion throughout every portion, even the remotest, of a country.

It need not be said that these local institutions themselves, if they require, as their primary conditions, a certain natural disposition and capacity in the people themselves for their due operation, also react powerfully back on those who take part in their operation. There could be no better school for the acquisition of genuine political habits, though it must be remembered it is, at best, only a school, and he who brings to bear on the Government of a great country nothing but the limited ideas and resources to which he has been accustomed to in a narrower area is properly stigmatised as exhibiting only the talent of a 'vestryman.'

Again, for the effectual working of Local Government in harmony with the exigencies of the central government, it is necessary that a certain community of sentiment, national spirit, moral conscientiousness, and economical information be found in all parts of the country. The greater the community in all these respects the better, and it is the tendency of a broad and effective system of national education to produce this community to an ever greater extent. It cannot be expected that identity in these respects will ever be reached, any more than that the time will ever come when people will always think and feel alike even in exactly similar conditions. But it may be expected, that, taking one part of the country with another, the main divergencies of thought and sentiment will be due only to real and important local peculiarities of the kind for which independent Local Government is specially needed as a supplement to central government. So long as the people are unequally civilised or as education is only partially diffused, the real differences due to important local diversities are obscured, and the Central Administration remains uninformed as to the requirements of particular districts.

It is one beneficial consequence of a centralised administration that it tends to prevent the different portions of the population advancing at such an unequal rate that Local Government might become rather an aggravation of a social disease than a manifestation and means of health. Everything that tends to weld the population together in thought, sentiment, habits of life, and moral instincts renders them fit rather than unfit for Local Government. In England such influences as the Church and Clergy, the diffusion of the Bible after the Reformation period, the popular literature at all times broadly circulated, the very community of sentiment brought about by the French wars, and the feudal burdens, all tended to produce an extraordinary amount of national uniformity, in spite of much provincial ignorance, rudeness of manners and tastes, and even dialectical peculiarities.

In recent times, indeed, England has shared, in an unusual degree, in all the extraordinary advantages in the way of means of locomotion and of mutual communication which modern inventions have introduced in all civilised countries. The railway, the telegraph, the newspaper press, are all means for equalising the knowledge as well as the tastes and opinions of the people, in all parts of the country. This does not imply, what is so much feared in some quarters, the production of a dull uniformity of type or the obliteration of all originality and specific genius. The gain is obtained not by levelling down but by levelling up. No political advantage accrues from retaining ignorance or brutishness under the name of independent thought.

The more men think alike in respect of all the problems which admit of demonstrative proof, the more likely are they to be sagacious and discriminating, and therefore to have fine differences among themselves, in respect of matters which, at present, are only matters of probable conjecture. The more they agree in comprehending the needs and situation of all parts of the country, the more acute is likely to be their sensibility to the special wants of the part which is nearest to them. Thus one of the most important conditions for the existence of Local Government in a beneficial form is an equality of mental and moral attainments in the population resident in all parts of the country, even those the most removed from each other.

A last condition of Local Government is that of a sufficiency of topographical area to prevent it being a needless excrescence on the central government. It is obvious that much of the advantages of Local Government must depend on the amount of work to be done by the central government and on the convenience of delegating some of it to local bodies. But the case might present itself,—and in fact does in some very diminutive States such as Belgium, Holland, and the Hawaiian Islands,—of the whole territory of the State being no greater than can be conveniently administered, for all purposes, by the central government. In these cases, it is quite possible that Local Government may exist, as it does in those countries especially in the Towns; but its characteristic advantages are scarcely perceived, and all the possible disadvantages of inequality of conditions, uncertainty of rules, and perplexity as to jurisdiction, are felt in an enhanced degree.

It has been already seen that the area may be so large that on this account alone Local Government is inapplicable, and some such device must be resorted to as the Federal system lately introduced into the British Colonies in North America, and the division into several distinctly organised Presidencies of the British territories in India. It is, of course, impossible to lay down any distinct limits to the area for which, and for which alone, the utmost advantages of Local Government would be obtained. It depends not merely on the area as measured but on the area regarded in its relation to the actual habits and condition of the people who populate it. Thus it might come about, in England, say, that communication between all the parts of the country was so incessant, and the practice of living in towns having an identity of conditions and wants had become so persistent as largely to depopulate the country places, and that the economic saving effected by a central organisation had become so widely appreciated that the local areas should be constantly enlarged till they were nearly co-extensive with that of the central government. The experience already obtained in the case of the extension of Highway districts, of Poor Law Unions, Local Government Districts, and of School Board Districts, and the call for County Boards of a representative kind, seem to point to the antique area of the parish being gradually superseded, and Local Government itself undergoing an entire transformation which, in fact, though not in appearance, tends towards increased centralisation. In every change that is made, the newly created authority is brought into the closest possible relation with the central administrative department.

Having ascertained the conditions in which Local Government, properly so called, is possible, the next class of questions which present themselves relate to the principles which determine the actual mode in which, at any time and in any country, the distribution of the task of Government between the Central and the Local Authorities ought to be effected.

It is necessary, at the outset, to remove a certain ambiguity which attaches to the term *Centralisation*, an ambiguity which the late Mr. John Austin did his best to explain and get rid of in an article specially devoted to the subject in the number of the *Edinburgh Review* for January 1847.

The term *Centralisation* may be used merely to describe certain constitutional arrangements by which the central government is brought into direct connexion with all local authorities throughout the country, and is able to make its power felt to the utmost extremities of the land with the smallest loss of time or energy occasioned by the interposition of intermediate agencies. The word in this sense means nothing either good or bad. The system of government implied by the word may be compatible either with a very large amount of local independence or with a very small amount of it. It only means that inasmuch as all local authority is, in theory, subordinate to the central authority, the dependence of the one on the other is not weakened by the accidental or artificial intervention of official obstacles of a purely mechanical sort. The structure of the whole government, if it be likened to a machine, is so perfectly constructed that wherever the hand of the central agency is entitled to exert itself, there it can exert itself at once and effectually without loss of power from interruptions or needless friction.

In the other sense of the term *Centralisation*, it means that which the person who uses it wishes thereby to condemn as politically vicious. He implies, in using the term, that the government of which he speaks has drawn into its own hands so large a part of the direct forces of control and administration that local authorities have no free play. They are hampered and arrested at every point. Local officials, like the French Mayors under the Second Empire, are the nominees of the sovereign power; all the details of executive work in the smallest village, town, or district, are supervised and checked by a system of incessant inspection; one uniform body of rules for education, for sanitary control, and even for the regulation of the use of libraries, parks, and public institutions of all sorts, is imposed from above, and not the smallest deviation is allowed even when dictated by varieties of climate or of ancestral practice. The whole population is governed like the army, and precision, uniformity, and submission are purchased at the expense of the free national life. This is the system which is most favourable to an autocratic government, such as that of Napoleon III., of Augustus, and of Diocletian, and of the British Government in India. It enables the central authority to feel the pulse of the people from moment to moment, to check disaffection even before it has manifested itself, to secure the return to the popular Assembly of a disproportionate number of its own creatures, to give to its more demonstrative acts and manifestoes an outward show of popularity, and, in the case of actual insurrection, to repress it with concentrated energy.

Nevertheless, history is full of instances, from the days of the Cæsars to those of the Napoleons, of the real instability of centralised government of this sort. The very unity of mind and spirit which expresses itself in every act and institution and the real simplicity of the political organisation lead to the instant imputation of every national check and disaster to the Government, while it makes the entire removal of a dynasty, or the change in the succession, or the substitution of a fresh body of ministers, alarmingly easy. The bureaucratic efficiency of the government mechanism is shown to be independent of all merely personal considerations. Any amount of change can be risked without fear of prolonged disorder or anarchy.

After the defeat of Sédan, the republic of M. Thiers instantly stepped into the place of the Empire of the defeated captive, and the smallest possible shock to the constitution was experienced from the change. There is an advantage in this species of stability; but it is not the sort of advantage which autocratic rulers seek for themselves; and it is purchased for the country by the loss of the sense of independence, and by the imposition of a tyrannical uniformity which forces all local arrangements into an unyielding Procrustean type.

In determining on the principles applicable to the construction of a system of local Government, a decision has to be arrived at on the following points:—

(1) The Distribution of Work to be done by the Central and by the Local Government.

(2) The Distribution of Workers.

(3) The Modes of connexion between the Central and the Local Work and Workers.

(1) The principles on which work has to be distributed between the central and the local authorities will be best evolved by setting over against each other the characteristic advantages of local free government and those of the enforced uniformity which comes from the superposition of a higher authority. Of course it is not necessary for the argument that the regulations imposed by a central authority should be uniform for all parts of the country, but they must not fail to be uniform in policy and in spirit; and generally speaking, for the mere sake of economising time and labour,

all directions appertaining to the same class of matters, and which come from a central authority, will be monotonously identical for all parts of the country.

The characteristic advantages of local independence in the matter of government are that the persons who legislate have an ever present, and often life-long, knowledge of the persons, things, and facts, of the most exact and detailed sort, to an extent which no persons living at a distance can ever rival. Furthermore, local legislators and administrators are able to watch with minute and incessant vigilance over the operation of their own regulations, and are able to change, supersede, or supplement them, or derogate from them from one short period to another with a facility and propriety which cannot be attained by even the most omniscient and sagacious of central governments.

Again, in respect of taxation, for many local purposes, there is the greatest advantage in visibly connecting in the popular mind the necessity for the tax with the fact of its exaction. Thus it is well for people clearly to understand that if they grudge a poor-tax they must bestir themselves to remove poverty from their midst. If they want good roads, or the luxury of a free library, or parks, or public gardens, it is they, and not some indefinite class of persons somewhere else, who must make sacrifices to obtain them.

Lastly, there are many matters,—especially those touching on the private, religious and moral life of the people,—in respect of which a natural and proper sensibility indisposes them to conform to any dispositions in the public interest the true policy of which they do not thoroughly understand. A local debate in a vestry or common-council hall, a discussion in the local papers, and free conversation at all places of public resort, gradually tend to bring out the true merits and issues of a really complex measure. When once it is understood, more than half the obstacles to carrying it through are out of the way, and the probability of its being thoroughly and loyally complied with is vastly increased.

These arguments in favour of committing to local Authority a very large share of independent legislation of a particular kind, when stated together, are so forcible, that it would almost seem that local government might one day absorb the large mass of all legislation. It will be seen, however, that these advantages of local legislation are not without serious drawbacks which, if they do not wholly impair its value, at least largely restrict the topics to which it is properly applicable.

One chief objection to all local legislation is that it is not likely to be undertaken in what may be called a true political spirit. This means that the area, at the largest,—being yet, by the hypothesis, less than that of the State itself,—is insufficient to call into existence that conscientious sentiment towards posterity, in respect of similar surrounding areas, and in respect of the corporate requirements of the State as a whole, which is the essential characteristic of the true statesman. For the creation and nurturing of such sentiments, not only is the local area wanting in size, in self-dependent distinctiveness, and in continuity of traditions, but the only available legislators are too few and are likely to be drawn, for the most part, from too little cultivated a class, to generate such sentiments among themselves.

These remarks apply least of all to the case of capital towns in which,—as in the case of London, Manchester, Liverpool, Birmingham, Glasgow, Paris, and New York,—the local government, even when at its worst, may sin in a statesmanlike way, and, at its best, has done acts of true and memorable statesmanship.

Again, there is the further vice attaching to all local government which is due to some of the very advantages which have just been enumerated. If it be true that the legislators and those legislated for are at one in being wide awake to the necessity for, and to the effect of, a tax or of a severe regulation, it is also true that the direct and immediate interests of all concerned tend to cover the whole legislative vista. Every one becomes accustomed to calculate with precision his own exact loss and gain by each measure, and the result is that a utilitarianism of the narrowest kind swallows up all higher and broader political methods.

The local management of poor-law unions in London has been, within recent years, a scandal of selfish administration; and if the recently instituted School Boards throughout the country have exhibited a higher standard of public sentiment, it is because the domestic instincts of the members have, in this respect, specially educated them to a higher moral sensitiveness than that which responds to nothing better than a sharply apprehended balance of profit and loss.

Lastly, in respect of certain matters there is an advantage in uniformity which is a counterpoise to many of the undoubted benefits which belong to local independence. Every traveller appreciates the advantage of the consolidation of the German Empire by which the necessity of showing passports, the use of different currencies, the examination of baggage at the frontiers, and the interrupted postal and railway service have been put an end to.

On a smaller scale, local independence means an amount of local heterogeneity which is an obstacle to social convenience and to the free and simple progress of trade. It means, besides, the want on the part of the central government of that facility for obtaining instant information, and for making prompt administrative changes, on which at certain crises public order and security may depend for their maintenance.

Furthermore, through the variety of rules and practices which local freedom introduces there are all the losses which come from excessive friction at moments when co-operation is needed for strictly national ends, and all the increased expense and possible extravagance which are due to a number of tentative efforts on a small scale in the place of one highly organised effort on the largest scale. It is true that it is difficult to check the expenditure of any Government; but it is not much more hard to expose financial excesses committed on a large scale than those committed on a small one, and when once it is done, the whole country is relieved at once, instead of the operation having, by possibility, to be repeated for every centre of local administration.

The condition of the poor-law administration in England, before the introduction of what was known as the 'New Poor Law' in 1834, illustrates some of the social and political disadvantages of an exaggerated attachment to local government. Owing to the smallness of the administrative area, a struggle was always going on between adjoining parishes to avoid being burdened by each other's poor; and it was inevitable that a law, itself economically condemned, should be executed in a spirit wholly unaffected by broad considerations of national policy. The remedy introduced was to enlarge the area, to secure uniformity in the administration of a law, itself largely amended, and especially to bring the reconstituted local authority into direct and constant connexion with the central government.

In pronouncing a judgment, then, on the class of matters which can alone with advantage be left to a local authority, it is evident that a statesman will refuse to hand over to such subordinate legislatures all the affairs in which the characteristic defects of local rule are likely to be exhibited in the most prominent form. He will, at the same time, reserve to the central authority all those departments of government in which the requirements of uniformity, despatch, economic organisation, and efficiency of provision, and vindication of national character, are more important than a deference to local taste and peculiarities.

In applying these principles in detail, it appears at once that a certain class of matters scarcely involve political considerations of a broad kind at all, nor do they in any significant degree touch the national character. Nor is it of much importance, either financially or as a matter of social organisation, that the regulations appertaining to them should be uniform. At the same time it may be of importance that the regulations should be popular, well-understood by those concerned, and easily modified from time to time without involving too wide-reaching changes.

Such matters are (1) sanitary arrangements,—including under this head all that relates to the healthful enjoyment of life and not merely to the prevention or cure of disease; (2) all that relates to the artistic embellishment of a town or of a village,—including the construction of public buildings, the improvement of streets, and the restraint of eccentricity in the fashioning of private houses; (3) all that relates to the education and mental training and occupation of the people, reserving it, however, to the central government to insist on a certain *minimum* of education being enforced universally in every part of the country; (4) all that relates to the necessary conditions of industrial and commercial life, such as the provision or superintendence of market-places, cattle-markets, bridges, roads, water-supply, lighting, and, in some districts, canals. This is not intended, by any means, as an exhaustive list either of a positive or of a negative kind. It is only illustrative of the principles laid down.

On the corresponding principles, the central government will reserve to itself such matters as the general superintendence of the main means of locomotion and communication throughout the country, the enforcement of its own methods of general taxation, the manipulation of the currency, and, of course, the administration of Justice in all but the humblest departments of it.

The most difficult and pressing problem as to the relations of the central and local government concerns the Police. In this case all the arguments in favour both of central and of local control are at their strongest; and the only solution is by distributing the control between the central and local authorities.

Public liberty is endangered by nothing more than by a highly centralised police system wholly out of correspondence and relationship to the local magistracy. It is at the same time necessary, for tracking out crime and carrying out comprehensive legislation in an uniform way, to attain the highest possible unity in police management and mutual understanding.

In England, indeed, a large portion of the liberties of the people are due to the fact that the maintenance of order has—up to quite recent times and to the era of the modern Metropolitan Police Acts,—been always entrusted to a local constabulary having its centres in the parish, the borough, or the county. The result was that the local magistracy who appointed, managed, and dismissed the constables, had them entirely under their control, and could prevent any excesses of official zeal. The magistrates themselves, of course, were always directly subjected, in such matters, to the censure of that public opinion which was nearest and, therefore, most stringent.

Considering the importance of the police being a popular force and of the people willingly co-operating with them in case of need, it is a misfortune where, merely in pursuit of a higher amount of organisation, the people are habitually pitted against the police. This is more likely to be the case when the police are introduced from without than when they are nominated from within; when they are only believed to be subject to an unknown and indefinite authority at a distance, instead of being obviously responsible to magistrates or a town-council close at hand; when they are seen and known to share the common sympathies and even prejudices of the neighbourhood in which they have been brought up, instead of being, or seeming to be, alien in all their sentiments and antecedents.

Another topic, in relation to the distribution of work between the central and local authorities, which has, of late years, excited much interest in England and America, is that of the liquor traffic. It is claimed, in some quarters, that the right of restricting or of absolutely preventing the sale of spirituous liquors should be put into the hands of local authorities, even though, for the purpose of such subordinate legislation, the authority were constituted in such a way as to require the concurrence of some number of householders exceeding the bare majority. In behalf of this demand it is alleged that the amount of the local poor-law, sanitary, and penal charges due directly to drunkenness invest those who directly suffer from these charges with the moral right and the political claim to be free to agree to remove the causes of drunkenness out of the way by absolutely forbidding, within the district, the sale of intoxicating liquors.

The only replies to this forcibly worded argument are that the right to sell spirituous liquors is one which may be regulated but cannot be wholly abrogated without an undue assault on public liberty; that the wrong-doing of some is no excuse for abridging the independence of all, even with the consent of a large proportion of them; and that this is one of the matters in which extreme inconvenience and some disorder would be encountered by having a different practice in two adjoining districts.

It is difficult to deny that, where drunkenness does really exist to an extent which obviously aggravates the local taxation and imposes other disagreeable burdens, the sober part of the population ought to have a remedy; and that the remedy proposed is an obvious and easy one. If the restricting law were carefully worded, it would have the advantage of being so far elastic that it could only be applied when the evil was so great that the great bulk of the inhabitants did not hesitate to apply it, and the mere threat of applying it might of itself bring sufficient pressure to bear on the authority which grants the licences to sell. It is said that in countries where such laws exist they either become a dead letter or are immorally evaded by all persons concerned. The possibility of such a consequence has to be avoided, and, it would appear, could easily be avoided by affording frequent opportunities for the will of the people to be ascertained.

Another expedient for the purpose of reducing the sale of intoxicating drinks which has recently been advocated is that of the Local Authority, such as a Town Council, purchasing all the public-houses, and vested rights of sale attaching to them, and constituting itself the sole dealer in intoxicating liquors within the district. The political objection to this measure is that, inasmuch as the Local Authority cannot afford to lose by the speculation, though it might be content not to make much or any profit, it always would have a certain interest in the maintenance of habits of drinking intoxicating liquors. The interest may be ever so small, but it is there. In times of financial difficulty there will always be found a party who will demand, in place of aggravated taxation, improved receipts from the liquor-houses. Sometimes this policy will be acquiesced in, and the scandal will be manifested of the Government itself fostering habits of intoxication with one hand and punishing the offences of drunkards with the other.

It has already been seen that an exception to the general propositions here laid down has occasionally to be made in the case of towns, especially those which are large and densely populated. The only genuine experiments in true Local Government made by the Romans were those exhibited in the free towns or *Municipia*, in which the resident inhabitants enjoyed at once all the advantages of self-government and corporate independence, without losing any of their rights as Roman citizens.

But in the ancient world the methods of locomotion and of communication were too little advanced to admit of the full problems of Local Government being propounded;. nor in the free towns of the Middle Ages in Italy and Germany could these special problems emerge, owing to the want of an effective Central Government. The problem of Local Government as applied to towns is, in fact, a new one, inasmuch as never till now have towns attained such size, such commercial importance, and such density of population, without seriously encroaching on the force of the central government.

It is only in the exceptional and, probably, transitory circumstances of the United States that towns like San Francisco, Salt Lake City, and Chicago,—owing to their distance from the seat of the Central Government and the intermittent communication (rapid as that already is),—secure to themselves an amount of autonomy which is not always compatible with the interests, or even with the character, of the American nation as a whole. In fact the difficulty of bringing these active but distant centres of political, as well as of commercial, activity into constant harmony with the will of the Union, as represented in Congress, is one of the most pressing problems with which the United States have to deal. It may be solved, of itself, by the rapid increase of population and the multiplication of towns of all sizes and degrees of importance, which will operate as uninterrupted links in the chain of communication and of political interest and sympathy. Or it may have to be solved by some re-constitution of the Union which will create large provincial areas of Government, sufficient in extent to satisfy the demands created by peculiarities of climate and condition but not large enough to foster ambitious proclivities or to promote rivalries with the Central Government. Such areas would, in fact, correspond to the provinces of the Canadian Confederation.

Looking to the future in Europe, the problem of the growth of towns is a sufficiently difficult and anxious one. It is probable that the progress of education and of commerce will enhance the attractions of town life, and diffuse the appreciation of them, while, in many countries, the multiplication and enlargements of factories will continue to maintain and produce a congestion of population in towns new or old. The only compensation for these tendencies will be found in the leisure that comes of accumulated capital, and the indulgence in country occupations and tastes which will result from it. The greater division of labour, and the practice of free-trade principles, also operate in the direction of the abolition of agriculture as a general means of livelihood in countries having no special advantages for its profitable pursuit, and of the restriction of the population of villages and of the smaller towns.

It may thus be expected that in many countries of Europe, and, not least, in England, the problem of the Local Government of towns will become the most absorbing, if not the most embarrassing, of all political problems. It will, however, be found in one respect easier than the problem of Local Government in less intelligent and less well populated regions of the country. It may always be expected that in a town of a certain magnitude there will be found a considerable number of persons gifted with a genuine political spirit and conforming themselves to a high standard of moral responsibility. In many towns the available knowledge and skill will be found superior to much which is at the service of the Central Government in the capital.

In the older towns and villages (as those of the United States which soon attain to what is for this purpose a venerable antiquity) lofty traditions and sentimental associations of a stirring kind acquire an ever increasing hold on the imagination of each successive generation, which is of the highest service to the statesman who has to deal with it. He has the finest elements of human nature in its proper social development to deal with. He can always appeal with confidence to an overwhelming majority of the townsmen, whenever the supreme interests of public safety, order, or honour, entitle him to expect a more than usual amount of individual sacrifice or more than common co-operation. The very conditions of social and commercial life, the publicity of such life, the value set on personal credit, the sincerity which comes from all real interests being habitually evaluated in exact money's worth, the very impatience with the conditions which turns so much of existence into a calculation, and the desire to escape from them at every fit opportunity,— are all the finest material for the judicious statesman to handle.

Whatever lethargy, selfish indolence, or slow creeping corruption, may do in the less densely inhabited parts of the country to drag it down, the true statesman will ever be able to find in the dense manufacturing or trading towns of the country a response to his patriotic appeal, and to elicit the means of national recovery.

(2.) The question of the distribution of the workers, as distinguished from that of the work, between the Central and the Local Government can only be answered by referring to the actual circumstances of the country concerned. The obvious answer to give is that the task of central government will be performed by the members of the popular or other Assemblies which constitute the Legislature from among whom the members of the Executive will (under most constitutions) be largely chosen. In addition to them other persons, habitually resident at the seat of government, may be specially designated for Executive tasks in connexion with the central government. Of course some of the residents at the seat of government will be occupied with the Local Government of the capital town which usually forms that seat.

Similarly, those who engage in the task of Local Government will be residents dwelling on the spot. As society progresses, and the different areas of Local Government are brought nearer together, and the habits of locomotion increase, it will be found more and more difficult, even where desirable, to insist on any tests of actual residence and even of habitual residence. Both in towns and country places the local franchise will be determined, as it was in the earlier days of the towns of Europe, by the fact of being held liable to contribute to the local burdens; and this liability will be practically ascertained by the fact of profiting from the produce of them. There are always a certain number of persons who habitually benefit from a closed market, an Exchange, well paved and lighted streets, a fund and organisation for the relief of urgent cases of distress, and from that indefinite use of social conveniences which is roughly indicated merely by being a householder. These persons then properly form the body of local taxpayers, and thereby constitute the local electoral constituency. The constituency may either be the same for all offices, as when a Town Council is elected by the ratepayers of the town and the Town Council delegates its several functions to special boards, or those who are taxed for a special object may form a distinct constituency for electing the Board to carry out that object. It is needless here to dwell further on the various principles of election which may be adopted.

(3.) The modes of connexion between the central and local work and workers suggest some questions of considerable importance, because, while some connexion must be maintained in order to prevent pure autonomy, which may mean anarchy, the nature and extent of the connexion may determine whether there is real local Government or whether it exists only in name.

The most recent invention, on this subject, in England, is that of a special department of the central executive authority, denominated the 'Local Government Board,' the functions of which are to maintain constant correspondence with Local Boards all over the country; to provide for their due election in cases which seem to call for it and yet in which the people are lethargic or divided in opinion; and to supervise the action of such Governments so far as the claims of the Central Government, or of financial security and of justice, seem to call for it.

It is not the object of this invention to supersede the functions of the Local Board in respect of initiating improvements, or to override the views of the people on the spot in matters within their competence. This Central Board is, in fact, a mere extension of what was formerly the Poor Law Board, and it has also assumed to itself the functions of a Board of Health. It may thus be taken as a characteristic specimen of one mode of connexion between the Central and the Local Governments. The range, however, of this Board is limited; and it occupies itself mainly with 'sanitary' matters, in a large sense of the term, and with the administration of the Poor Laws.

The large department of Municipal Government is only indirectly affected by the institution of a Local Government Board. In many countries the Central Government does its best to retain in its own hands the election of the Mayor, and some of the most scandalous abuses of electoral corruption and fraud exhibited during the reign of Napoleon III. in France came from this cause. In England the right of the citizens of London to elect their own Mayor was one of the earliest and most cherished liberties wrung from the Norman Kings through their financial dependence on the rich municipality. In modern times, English towns having corporate institutions have retained something more than the right to elect all their civic functionaries. They have succeeded, many of them, in almost escaping all central control.

The Municipal Corporation Act, passed in 1835, defined the modes of election of all the officers of the corporations which adopted it; but many have not yet adopted it, and the City of London was not contemplated in its provisions. By this Act the Town Council was forbidden, except by approval of the Lords of the Treasury, to sell or mortgage the land or public stock of the Borough or to demise them for more than a certain time. The accounts of the Town Council were to be at all times open to inspection, and to be regularly audited and printed for the use of the ratepayers. They were, furthermore, to be submitted to the Secretary of State and laid by him before both Houses of Parliament. The terms of the local franchise were laid down with the greatest precision.

It may be observed that in such a case as this the central government reserves to itself the right to interfere negatively and for preventive purposes. So far as rights of making minor internal regulations go, of taxing themselves, and of expending the product of the taxes, the Town Council is wholly unfettered from without. It is difficult to conceive a more independent form of Local Government, a due connexion with the Central Government being none the less retained.

One mode of enforcing the claims of the central government which has been resorted to is that employed in England in the government of Poor Law Unions, in which certain special officers, such as 'inspectors,' 'collectors,' and 'assistant overseers,' are either nominated by the central authority or have in cases of special emergency or necessity, of which the Local Government Board has become cognisant, to be elected according to rules prescribed by law, and in conformity with the arrangements made by the Board.

Another specimen of modes of maintaining the connexion between a Central Authority and Local Authority is supplied by the constitution of the French Senate, which awards a certain number of seats to the representatives of communes and municipalities. The communes and municipalities each elect, by a majority of their members, one of a body or college of electors; and these in their turn choose the senators. 225 of the whole 300 Senators are elected in this way, and 75, that is a third of them, retire every three years.

This mode of representation was no doubt suggested by the practice of electing the Senate of the United States, which is, pre-eminently, a representative Assembly of the Governments of the component States of the Union, the Legislature of each State of the Union electing two members for six years. The rapid changes which the United States are undergoing must render it uncertain for a long time to come how far an electoral practice, originally dictated solely by ideas of confederation, will be found consistent with the notion, which is succeeding to it, of centralisation modified by great independence in Local Government. If this form of the constitution is permanent, it will be a remarkable instance of the most complete harmony being maintained between central and local institutions, without loss either to local independence or to the claims of uniformity.

Both in England and in the United States the circuit judiciary system has always done much to overcome the centrifugal influences of local institutions; and it is one of the current signs of the close approximation to each other of all parts of the country in England, —which means the restriction of the sphere of Local Government,—that the County Court, the Quarter or Borough Sessions, and the Metropolitan superior Civil and Criminal Courts, are year by year making fresh inroads into the ancient province of the County Assizes.

CHAPTER VIII.

THE GOVERNMENT OF DEPENDENCIES.

It has already been pointed out that the subject of the Government of Dependencies has to be distinguished, on more grounds than one, from that of Local Government, though it is not always easy, as a matter of practical application, to determine which subject is concerned, and though there are many principles of Government which are equally applicable to both subjects. In ancient times the physical conditions of the civilised world scarcely admitted of the existence of true local government, though the administration of the Roman free towns very nearly amounts to it. In modern times the rapid means of communication tend to convert all provincial, federal, and colonial administration into special problems of local government. Nevertheless, there will always be certain conditions in which the relations between a State and some remote but connected parts of it are such that, in some respects, it is necessary to concede a greater amount of independence, and in others a less amount, than comports with the true notion of local government.

In modern times the occasions for investigation of the principles applicable to the Government of Dependencies are of two descriptions, and of two descriptions only. The question is one of colonisation either conducted in an uninhabited country or in a country only inhabited by uncivilised and unsettled races; or it is a question of the acquisition of territory already populated by civilised races, though of a race, religion, language, and form of culture more or less different from those of the acquiring State.

The first is the case of the British Australian Colonies and of the original Colonial settlements in the part of North America now occupied by the United States. The second is the case of the Canadian Confederation, the British Colonies in South Africa, British India, and the French Colony of Algiers.

It thus appears that the topic of the Government of Dependencies has the highest possible interest for England; and, though France and even Germany are said to be desirous of acquiring extended colonial possessions for the sake of disposing of their surplus population, yet there is no prospect of any State ever again acquiring such an extent of colonial and subject territory as is included in Australia, British India, and Canada. England may lose part, but it is singularly improbable that any other single State will ever gain as much.

There have been two notable attempts made in the history of the world to govern dependencies, and they both signally failed, either through the political backwardness of the age in which the attempt was made, or through the reckless neglect of principles which were theoretically acknowledged. These two attempts were that of the Roman Empire to govern its provinces, and that of England to govern the thirteen American colonies.

It was the accident and misfortune of Rome, rather

than the promptings of ambition, which led to the successive annexations of provinces beyond the limits within which the political resources of the period admitted of their being governed by a single Power. The story of Rome is that of a commercial State, led on by the necessities of securing quiet, first to occupy Italy, and then to secure Italy by expelling the Carthaginians from Sicily; then to win a province in Africa and in Spain, as a mere consequence of the necessity to crush the maritime rivalry of Carthage; then to add successively Greece, Asia Minor, and Syria, and fresh African provinces, merely for the purpose of securing already acquired territories against the invasions of such enterprising patriots as Pyrrhus, Mithridates, Antiochus, and Jugurtha, and to reinstate order and quiet. The same was the tale in Germany, Gaul, and Britain, till the Empire was founded, and the same work of forced and incessant annexation went on,—sometimes at the price of such desperate reverses as those at the hands of the Parthians and the Persians. Augustus is said to have left to his descendants a warning not to extend the bounds of the Empire further, and his successors fully appreciated the danger. But it was more difficult to govern without further conquest than it had been to conquer in order to govern.

There is no more interesting or instructive subject of political study than the government of the Roman provinces; and the numerous inscriptions that have lately been brought to light have done much to illustrate a subject which, from the comparative barbarism of many of the countries concerned, has but few historical monuments.

Undoubtedly the general intentions disclosed in the

Roman Provincial policy were good and wise. The Romans appreciated to the full the advantages of not interfering with the native institutions and habits of the people more than the necessities of public order required. They took immense pains not only to secure the regular, prompt, and impartial administration of justice, but to promote appeals to the Central Government against the decrees of the Provincial judges. They displayed much political adroitness in preventing combinations among large groups of subject people by attaching the different provinces and towns to the Central Government by a great variety of different ties and privileges. Hence, as there was no identity of sentiment having its roots in a monotonous centralisation, universal simultaneous insurrection was impossible.

But there were two obstacles to the success of Roman Provincial Government which proved insuperable, in spite of genuine efforts to withstand them. One of these obstacles was due to the time and circumstances of the world at and amidst which a premature experiment in governing widely scattered races of men was made. The other obstacle was due to the misfortunes and shortcomings of the Roman State itself.

The obstacle which belonged to the time and circumstances was that created by the primitive savagery of most of the races which constituted the several provinces, coupled with the absence of sufficient means of ready communication with the Central Government. These races, indeed, occasionally produced noble and courageous leaders, and sometimes, as in the case of Sertorius of Spain, patriots gifted with a true political sagacity. But, for the most part, the virtues even of the best men and races, from the Pillars of Hercules to the Euphrates, were of the harsh kind which belongs to a warlike and not to a political condition of society. The Gauls were the most advanced, and it was with them that the Roman Provincial Government was most successful.

The other obstacle was the impoverishment of the Roman State, which not only prevented the Government from adequately remunerating their Provincial Governors and so putting them beyond temptation, but made the acquisition of revenue from the Provinces a far too prominent object in all their policy.

The result of these two hindrances acting in concert was, that the case most frequently (though, happily, not quite universally) presented was that of a grasping Proconsul administering his province for no other purpose than, first, the enrichment of himself, and secondly, the securing of such a revenue as might satisfy the expectations of his employers. The general brutality of the people and their remoteness from the Roman centre of civilisation permanently excluded them from such influence on the part of their conquerors as might have gradually brought about amalgamation between the races.

In some parts of the Empire, where the races were in an advanced stage, or were of the best type, as in Egypt, Gaul, Germany, Britain, Spain, and Greece, some little progress was made in Romanising the provinces, or at least in making the Roman rule congenial and acceptable. But in other parts, as in the provinces near the Danube, in Asia Minor, in the lands bordering on the Euphrates, in Africa (excepting Egypt), and even in Syria, the Provincial history of Rome is little else than a long narrative of conspiracies, insurrections, military enterprises, and, as often as not, disastrous Imperial calamities.

The experience of England in the government of her American colonies was of an entirely different character, though equally illustrative of the nature of the problem concerned. The thirteen American colonies were constituted of persons of the same race as those inhabiting the parent country; and so far were the colonists from being below the average standard of moral and intellectual cultivation in their old home, that they were above it. The original immigrating stock consisted of those who,—considering their exceptional commercial and industrial energy, peculiar fortitude in grappling with physical obstacles, or rare conscientiousness in preferring banishment to the want of religious freedom,—may be presumed to have surpassed, in the most valuable qualities, the great mass of their English contemporaries. But their great distance from the seat of central government,—a distance far greater, for all political purposes, at that day than the distance of the Australasian colonies from England now,—rendered all true government from England an impossibility.

Owing, however, to specially favourable circumstances, it took some two hundred years to disclose the futility of the political connexion between the mother country and the colonies. These circumstances were the orderly and constitutionally trained habits of the colonists; the excellent provisions which were generally contained in the charters of the colonies and which communicated, in a compact and definite form, all the most cherished and liberal institutions which had been developed in England; and the spontaneous arrangements made by the colonies themselves from time to time in the direction of partial confederation and self-government on an ever larger and larger scale.

So long as Navigation Laws prevailed which not only confined commerce with England to British ships, but otherwise largely restricted the trade of the colonies with any other country than England, and so long as the commercial policy of all countries was that of a jealous protection of native and colonial produce, the possession of Colonies must have been, on the whole, economically profitable to the mother country. From such gains, the expenses of maintaining a large, efficient, and ubiquitous navy, and of occasionally conducting a land war for Colonial defence, ought to be deducted.

But, in spite of the economic advantages of colonial possessions, especially when magnified by slave labour, it cannot be said that the governing policy of England in respect of her colonies was that of obtaining from them the utmost pecuniary profit. The ties which bound England to her Colonies in America were those of genuine sentiment and of blood relationship, and it is a mistaken view of the War of Independence to suppose that the prominent thought on one side was that of acquiring revenue and on the other that of escaping fiscal burdens. The whole history of that conflict, both on its social and on its constitutional side, demonstrates that there were, deep down in the breasts of the colonists and in those of the dominant political party in England, sentiments of pique, of personal irritation, and even of vindictiveness, which had their roots far more in a consciousness of outraged and yet indestructible relationship than in the mere crossing of economical interests.

Some intelligent Americans of the present day have given it as their opinion that the true offence of England which brought about the war was not the mere claim to tax the colonies for Imperial purposes, but the mode in which it was attempted to impose the tax, by violating the colonial constitution which,— owing, in a great measure, to the apathy of England,— had gradually evolved itself during the past two hundred years. This constitution was based partly on local government, partly on a system of confederation. In imposing a stamp tax by a mere fiat of the British Parliament, without deferring to colonial rights of self-assessment, the British Government was violating a relationship which had acquired all the fixity and dignity of constitutional prescription.

The real grounds for the breach with the American colonies have such a close connexion with new colonial problems, and the precedent is always so readily cited in the case of any serious controversy between England and one of her colonies, that it is important that there should be no misapprehension on the subject. The teaching involved in the precedent is not that colonies ought never to be required to contribute to the general expenses of the central Home Government, and still less that, if they are so required, it is their right and duty instantly to revolt from their connexion with the mother country. The true lesson rather is that while, on the one hand, a merely selfish use of great dependencies for purposes of revenue was shown by the Roman precedent to be incompatible with any stability in political organisation, the English precedent in America shows that mere indifference to, and, still more, an ignorant or contemptuous encroachment on, time-honoured political institutions must entail either the anarchy of dissolution or the pangs of forced separation.

The Government of the great dependency of India for a hundred years by the East India Company, acting under a succession of Charters from the English Government and acting therefore as its agent, illustrates, though in a more agreeable way, some other important doctrines relative to the government of Dependencies. The English settlement in India presents the peculiar case of a colonisation (if so it can be called) begun for one purpose, and continued for a wholly different, if not opposed, class of purposes.

At first the sole purpose was that of forming an *entrepôt* of trade at an Indian port, where Oriental products could be collected from the interior and re-packed with a view to their being distributed among European countries. But a flourishing and expanding trade of this sort, first of all needed political securities for the unhampered conduct of its own operations and against spasmodic breaches of civil order in the vicinity of the commercial settlement; and, secondly, it brought rivals from other European countries into the field, and so raised up special political complications. The history of the political and military efforts to protect their commerce against the consequences of internal disorder, and against foreign rivalry, is the history of the English in India from Clive to Lord Canning.

The government of India by the East India Company presents, in many respects, a favourable contrast to that of the government of the Roman provinces, and of the American colonies. The problem was certainly as great as that which lay before Rome. The countries were won either by the sword or by pacific engagements with autocratic governments without any simulation of popular consent. The general condition of the people, so far as political attainments went, was backward in the extreme; and their language, religion, and race differed widely from that of their conquerors. Furthermore, the actual and direct agent of government, the East India Company, was essentially a trading association representing numerous shareholders whose prime concern must have been, in average cases, the safety and improvement of their investments. Thus the inducements to sacrifice political to economical considerations might seem to have been scarcely less than those of the pauperised Government of Imperial Rome.

In the face, however, of all these difficulties, and in spite of temptations to a sordid abuse of financial responsibilities, the result of the hundred years' possession of British India by the English has been the gradual substitution of a wide-reaching and stable political relationship for a casual commercial link; the establishment of perpetual internal peace and order; the severe maintenance of religious toleration; the enormous industrial development of the country; and (except in some fanatical and irrepressibly wild sections of the population) general political content. This is not intended as an optimistic view of the position of the English in India. Every one knows there has been, and is still, abundant ground there for seasonable criticisms; and the political responsibility of the English Government does not end with simply keeping at a distance Powers which might compete with itself for supremacy, nor even with reducing the periodic famines and securing the material well-being of the people. Higher and ulterior objects must be increasingly recognised; and when once they are recognised, there is good ground for hoping that they will be pursued as unintermittently and attained as successfully as the lower objects already reached.

It will serve as a guide to the true principles applicable to the Government of Dependencies to reflect on the objects which it may be supposed a State has in view in retaining or in acquiring dependencies and colonies, and on the real advantages and disadvantages which attach to such possessions.

It is not necessary to say much on the mere national prestige which at one time formed one of the main attractions of an extended dominion, and which, even at this day, retains some of its glamour. By this time, however, historical and, still more, economical knowledge has sown a wide distrust of mere breadth or empire, apart from special considerations which give it value. If there is always a fever of annexation prevailing in some sections of a national community, there are other sections quite as strongly in favour of surrendering what has been already won or even long held. Extent of topographical area is being more and more valued for what it is really worth—that is, for the opportunity it gives to national expansion and to the increased means of support it supplies to a growing population, who are thereby saved from the necessity of seeking in foreign countries, and perhaps among institutions less congenial than their own, a refuge and a home.

The mere glory of extended empire belongs especially to the Middle Age monarchical *régime*. The utter and felt inadequacy of ancient constitutions to grapple with the class of problems now being considered prevented a sense of spurious magnificence deluding the Ancient in the same way in which it deludes much of the Modern world. It is probably the feudal system which has associated so deeply, in the minds both of monarchs and of people, the notion that breadth of territory means power and wealth. It is becoming better recognised that, often enough, it means only weakness and impoverishment.

Up to a certain point indeed, as in the case of modern Greece, a certain amount of good cultivable area of land is needed to supply the primary elements of political self-support and independence; and, again, up to a certain but different point, the larger the area of cultivable land, especially when found under different climatic condition, the richer and more independent, and consequently the more powerful, the State. But beyond this point, extent of area may mean the disintegration and scattering of the population, bad and superficial agriculture, want of sufficient concentration in towns and connected political centres, intricate problems of local or colonial government, expense for defence and for the maintenance of civil order, and disproportionately small returns in the way of revenue.

Such is often the condition of a new country, though,—as in the case of Australia and Canada,— a compensation is obtained in the superior energy of a population suddenly plunged into new conditions of life, and in the immense returns from some unexhausted but not inexhaustible sources of wealth. But even now the large pastoral ranges in Australia, while they

VALUE OF EXTENT OF TERRITORY. 323

afford enormous fortunes to individual settlers, are far from being a pure economical or political advantage to the colonies themselves. If agriculture is thwarted, if towns are retarded in their growth, and if the accumulated fortunes are removed out of the country, it does not appear how, at present, the vast territories of the Australian colonies are other than an obstruction to their development.

The case of Russia, though it is not a new country in the same sense, is a parallel one. It is difficult, however, as yet to draw any profitable conclusions from it, inasmuch as the recent emancipation of the serfs, followed, perhaps, hereafter by the growth of a true middle class, may prove that its territories, in Europe at least, are not incommensurate with the national resources for turning them to the fullest account. But, so far as its Asiatic territories go, it may be expected that, but for some fortuitous combination of circumstances which cannot as yet be predicted, its width of Empire will prove its weakness rather than its strength.

A more legitimate object, already adverted to, in acquiring extended territorial possessions, is that of providing a field for Emigration. This is a topic which, in view of the limitation of the area of the older European States and the growth of population, has of late been acquiring an importance of the first magnitude; and it is from the point of view of prospective emigration on an ever increasing scale, that the subject of the methods of governing dependencies is becoming proportionately interesting.

The modern reasons for treating Emigration as a

subject of political concern are different from those which prevailed either in the ancient world or at any period in the history of the modern world earlier than the present century. Before the present century, Emigration and that which included it,—Colonisation,—were rather the indulgence of a taste, or, at the most, the consequence of some momentary social pressure or congestion. Or, perhaps, it may have been a recognised avenue to wealth for which, as in the case of the Spanish American settlements, exceptional opportunities suddenly presented themselves.

It is only quite recently that emigration and attendant colonisation have been treated as one of the natural, and almost indispensable, outlets for an overflowing population. It might always have been anticipated that the strict geographical limits of most European States must become too narrow for the support of their population, so soon as the habit of engaging in internecine conflicts ceased to be perpetual, and in proportion as improved methods of existence at once increased the number of births and reduced the death-rate. The growth of factory labour on a stupendous scale, and superior skill and energy in cultivating the soil, have done much to counteract this pressure of the population against the bars of their territorial prison.

But where,—as in Ireland,—factories have not absorbed the surplus labour and, from one cause and another, physical, political, or moral, the culture of the soil has come to a standstill, the necessity for providing means of existence for a redundantly prolific population has been felt in all its force. The occurrence of famines, which are rather symptoms than exceptional accidents, brought the problem to a head, and the result was such a stream of emigration from Ireland as, within some ten years, reduced the population from eight to five millions.

It is well known that though some of these emigrants went to the Australian colonies, and some to Canada, yet a very large proportion betook themselves to the United States, and have since become an element of no small political importance both to their new Government and to the Government of Great Britain. In fact, the perplexities which this wholesale emigration of a dissatisfied population to a foreign country have caused in the political world are an instructive illustration of some doctrines which apply to emigration generally as a topic of political concern.

It is the misfortune of England that, in spite of the enormous and unprecedented colonial territory which her people have settled and are populating, there are scarcely more than two colonies—that is, New Zealand and South Australia—which from the first have been settled with reference to broad and enduring principles of economy and public policy. Ordinarily speaking, the colonial policy of the country has been left entirely to the hap-hazard accident and claims of the moment, or else to the idiosyncrasies of some individual Minister of State.

When it was a question of getting rid of surplus population, facilities were contrived for shipping emigrants away to distant shores, with little care where they went to, or what became of them. When it was a question of occupying new territory, convicts and the progeny of convicts, and the associates of convicts, had every facility provided them for laying the foundations of the future State, and considerations of personal character, internal organisation, and political capacity were thrown to the winds. It is these initial disasters which it is so hard to repair; though it may still be hoped that the constant renewal of the population by fresh immigration, and the potency of constitutional government, coupled with better understood principles of economical and social organisation, will combine to constitute new points of favourable departure.

The same necessity of promoting emigration for the mere purpose of providing an outlet for a population which is overpassing the territorial capacities of the State is already pressing, as never before, on Continental States such as France, Germany, and Italy, and, in many affairs, affects their political action. This is being especially felt in the eager competition which has been going on for the last few years for the territories of the North African sea-board which are so congenial to European settlers. But it is also manifested in the novel phenomena of the occupation, or attempted occupation, by Continental States of islands in the southern seas.

One difficulty in all emigration schemes is that, except at such conspicuous national crises as that presented in the Irish famines, when all the usual bonds of society are momentarily relaxed, the classes who are most disposed to emigrate and who form the best colonists are just those classes whom, from the point of view of internal policy, it is most desirable to keep at home. Nor will even the progress and diffusion of education and public grants for purposes of emigration improve this state of things, so long as so little pains is taken to organise emigration at home, and to devise measures for more adequately meeting the moral, as well as the material, exigencies of the colonists in their new home.

The prevalent notion of colonisation is that it is a means of individual security against poverty, and possibly of self-enrichment and aggrandisement. But an appeal based on such a notion can only reach the more enterprising and independent members of society, — those who from physical health, acquired capital, or special skill, know that they can stand alone without the support of a complex social edifice all around them. Those who are not more enterprising and independent than the average of mankind are, as things are, right to shrink from removing to a colony.

Even in the best administered modern colonies the utmost that is,—or, according to existing arrangements, can be,—done for a new-comer or a family of new-comers is to supply them with food and shelter while they are waiting for work, to help them towards the obtaining of that work, and possibly, if the work fails, to help them over a period of struggle and anxiety and find for them fresh work. Beyond this, they have to fit themselves into an active, forward-pressing, yet imperfectly organised, society as best they may. They may find friends ready made, a place for their own form of worship, religious guides, and familiar institutions, or they may not. In the remoter parts of the country, of course, they cannot find these things, and they are scarcely less alone and thrown on their own resources than the original settlers.

Those who are content with a system of colonisation of this sort both underrate the moral and political conditions by which men live, and ignore the responsibility of the State in respect of the population which, in pursuance of the general welfare, it, practically, deports from its shores. The poorer and the less well educated members of society who, by the nature of the case, would emigrate with most advantage to the home country can, less than any other class, dispense with the ubiquitous presence of all those moral and political conditions which fold them round from their birth, and which serve to elevate in the scale of humanity the most insignificant and destitute of men. These conditions have been the product of ages of struggle and evolution, while they are connected in the subtlest of ways with places and personal memories and visible associations which can never be transplanted elsewhere. The absence of these brings on that "home-sickness" which, from the days of Ovid to those of the last transported convict, is no sentimental appetite but a deep and genuine hunger for the first necessaries of human existence. This craving for home passes away indeed, but it is disguised and blunted without being appeased or transmuted into anything better.

The State which finds it politically convenient to disembarrass itself year by year of thousands of the population it has called into being has no right to hide from itself the terrible temptations and difficulties to which life away from home will expose its outcasts, nor to flinch, indolently, from its duties in respect of them. In ancient days, there was scarcely a more solemn tie than that which bound a colony to its parent State; and if it be true that a colony then was not the same as a colony now, the difference is one which casts a heavier burden now than of old on the parent State. Then it was a voluntary departure of an enthusiastic and highly organised few, rather recalling the Pilgrim Fathers than the modern emigrant ship. Now it is the enforced disruption of countless family and social ties, and the exclusion of those who fail in the race at home, simply in order to secure ease and plenty to those who are allowed to stay behind. The least that the State, in such an emergency, can do is to extend its protecting and organising hand even to the most distant parts of the earth, if it may be, in order to ensure the reception of its outcasts in a worthy and true home.

This view of the duties of a State towards its emigrant populations throws some light on a class of problems as to the relations of a parent State with its Colonies which in recent times have attracted much attention. It demonstrates, for instance, that a State has no right to treat it as a matter of indifference whether its people emigrate to its own colonies or elsewhere. It is not a question of national vanity in respect of the amount of enumerated population, nor a question of economical interest in respect of the continued maintenance of profitable relations between the State and its prosperous colonies. It is a question how far the State has fulfilled its duties to its people when it indolently allows or encourages them to commit themselves and their fortunes to the care of alien people and institutions over which their own father-State has no control.

The prevalent laxity of relationship, and still more the prevalent ideas as to the essential laxity of relationship, between a State and its colonies, are, indeed, making such considerations as these seem irrelevant anachronisms. But it may be that they are anachronisms only because their time has not yet come, rather than because their time is gone by. It may happen, indeed, as it has long happened with Germany and, in some measure, with France, that there is emigration without proportionate opportunities for colonisation, and that, consequently, the emigrants must necessarily pass under a new dominion. But, even in this case, it is possible for the parent State to acknowledge its continuing duties to its emigrants, and,—both in securing for them a proper reception, and in obtaining guarantees for their civil rights and independence,—to avail itself to the uttermost of its diplomatic resources.

Another consequence of this view of the responsibilities of a State is that it should not be treated as a matter of indifference and of mere accidental taste or caprice on the part of a colony whether it is to continue to form part of the parent State or not. Of late years, and, in some measure, as a consequence of the abolition of restrictions on colonial trade, a reaction has set in against that spirit of attaching the colonies, at any hazard, to the parent State which precipitated the American War of Independence.

It is being argued, in some quarters, that a modern State receives little economical benefit from its colonies, and such as it does receive it would procure from them equally if they were politically independent, or even if they were subjected to a foreign State. It is alleged that the expense of protecting distant colonial possessions is a serious drain on the resources of the people at home, while the constant risk of losing them hampers political international relations in far more important respects. It is also urged, on grounds the general truth of which has been already admitted, that mere extent of territory is no proof of real power or dignity, and that, by scattering the population, and by opening out endless facilities for escaping from liabilities to the central Government, it may be a cause and a sign of national decay.

To all these arguments it is sufficient to reply that, although a time may come at which the necessities for absolute colonial independence exceed those for a continuance of the political connexion between the State and its colonies, till that time has come, the parent State is bound to treat the connexion as one of the utmost importance and value. No one could now deny that the time has gone by for attempting to fasten a colony to its parent State by any other hooks than those of moral obligation, reciprocal interest, and mutual affection. But this is very different from admitting either that the connexion is one of a wholly indifferent sort, or that its continuance or severance ought to be determined by nothing else than the casual freak of a particular generation of colonists. The mere admission of the frailty of the relationship tends to propagate freaks in the same way that free doctrines of divorce, which, while establishing marriage as a matter of sentiment and interest, impair the practice as resting on reciprocal moral duties.

Inasmuch, then, as the colonies of a State form that part of the national territory to which, implicitly or explicitly, it invites its surplus population to betake themselves, or has in past times invited them, it behoves the State to do its utmost, within the limits of political prudence, to retain its colonial territories generally within its own control, and to exercise control by providing such institutions as may best tend to obviate the disadvantages of isolation and banishment. Of course such a policy is not only compatible with, but demands, the speedy generation of self-governing institutions of a kind to effectually supersede interference from the central Government at home.

In proportion to the largeness of the colonial area, the distance from home, and the importance of the issues requiring prompt and irresponsible determination, the delegated powers must far exceed in magnitude those which belong to Local Government at home. At the present day even customs-duties are regarded as belonging to the region of colonial freedom, and it is only as to questions of colonial defence that the Central Government has absolutely reserved to itself the initiative in any one department of administration. It is to be regretted that, with respect to the great Australasian and Canadian groups of colonies, which are so important from an emigration point of view, England has only reserved to herself a negative control exercised through the Governor appointed by the executive authority at home and responsible only to it.

The distance of the Australasian colonies and the propinquity and attractive force of the United States in the case of the Canadian Dominion would, in any case, render constant intervention from England peculiarly difficult. But if the practice of intervention had never, in deference to false analogies between local and colonial independence and under the haunting memory of the breach with the thirteen American Colonies, been abandoned, it would not have been found insupportable. Indeed, it would, when exercised in behalf of emigrants and the children and grandchildren of emigrants to whom the parent State owed a lasting debt, have been seen to be founded in reason and justice.

It has, however, been admitted that a time may come when the question of separation from the parent State seriously presents itself. It has yet to be seen how far a substitute for actual separation will be found in the erection of great and nearly independent Confederations such as that which has already been formed in North America and legislatively provided for in South Africa. Nothing but further experience, for which the world must wait, can decide whether such a colonial system as that of England will continue much as it is now; or will resolve itself into a multitude of independent States of the type of the present States of Europe; or will be transformed into new political units in which England will simply preside over an aggregate of co-equal communities, in somewhat the way in which Prussia has a certain precedence in the constitution of the German Empire.

Nevertheless the case is more clear in respect of countries like British India, in which, through a series of fortuitous circumstances, England has been called to govern a population of alien race, language, and customs, out of all numerical proportion to the English residing in the country. In such a case, the duties of Government can neither be ignored nor resigned nor transferred. They are a trust for a coming generation and for a new age. Every opportunity must be taken, as it is being taken in practice more and more, to habituate the native population to the duties of self-government and to prepare them for a time when the imposed and alien rule can prudently be first relaxed, then shared, and finally withdrawn.

Between the obvious case of prospective independence because the inhabitants can never amalgamate with their rulers, and the equally obvious case of the possible independence of the Australasian and North American colonies because of the identity of race and attainments between the inhabitants of the Colonies and those of the Mother Country, there are the mixed cases of the Cape Colonies, of the West India Colonies, and of foreign settlements such as Hong-Kong, Malta, Gibraltar, and Aden, retained only for purely commercial or military objects. The questions appertaining to these several cases will probably be found more soluble than they were when selfish economical doctrines, now obsolete, and vainglorious military sentiments, favoured the retention of colonial possessions at any expense to the legitimate national pride of other countries, and even when they cost more than the maintenance of them was worth.

There are two questions relative to the general subject, not altogether of a speculative nature, which have attracted some interest of late, and which may hereafter assume a practical importance. One question is, whether the principle and machinery of direct representation are available in the government of an extended Colonial Empire. The other question is, whether in any novel form of extended confederation which may be adopted, it will be possible to draw, in advance, a permanent line of separation between the legislative or administrative topics of mainly local concern, and those which either ought to be treated in an uniform manner for all the parts of the system, or which, at the least, ought not to be treated in one part independently of reference to the interests of all the other parts.

The two classes of obstacles in the way of the extension to a vast colonial empire of the principles of representative government, are, first, those due to the inevitable delay occasioned by distance, and, secondly, those due to the presumed incompetency of a representative of a remote colony to take part in legislation for other colonies and for the Empire as a whole.

The essence of representative government, as now applied in all constitutionally governed countries, is, that each deputy, though specially conversant (it may be) with the wants of a particular area of territory and section of the population, is none the less held to represent the nation as a whole, and is bound to legislate for the good of the whole, while seeing that the interests of his own constituents are neither misunderstood nor overlooked.

Even in Assemblies which have most of the Federal character and, historically at least, have been based on Federal institutions in the past,—such as the Legislatures of the Swiss Confederation and of the German Empire and the United States Senate,—this is the fixed constitutional doctrine. The members are reputed to be not merely delegates bound each to contend for the claims of his own constituents at any cost. They are rather statesmen, enjoying, indeed, the special confidence of a definite portion of the population of the State, peculiarly cognisant of its situation and needs, and bound to advocate its proper interests. But they are none the less responsible to the country at large, as well as to their own constituents, for the general government of the country in the interests of all, by the subordination of what is small to what is great, of the few to the many, and, it may be, of what is lasting in the future to what is only an ephemeral, though conspicuous, advantage in the present.

This theory of representative government has existed in England from the early days when the House of

Commons, as a condition of its assent, on behalf of the constituencies, to grants of subsidies, insisted on concerning itself with the conduct of the general government and on obtaining remedies for general grievances. Indeed this spirit of subordinating the personal to the general interest, and of connecting the demands of special classes with the common policy, may be traced back at least as far as the action of the Barons at Runnymede. The latest and most profound exhibition of the same doctrines is found in the resistance made by Edmund Burke against attempts in his own constituency of Bristol to convert him from a representative into a delegate.

The same conception of representative government has travelled into all continental legislatures, and may now be treated as of the essence of what is understood by that form of government. It constitutes, in fact, its main ground of distinction from true federal government, as was found in the various attempts at confederacy made by the thirteen American Colonies before the establishment of the existing constitution of the United States.

But for representative government of this sort, it is indispensable that each deputy should have sufficient opportunities to inform himself of the circumstances of other parts of the national dominions besides that which he specially personates; that he should have leisure, skill, and disposition to avail himself of these opportunities; and that there be sufficient correspondence in the needs and circumstances of all parts of the dominions represented in the same Assembly for time not to be unduly wasted nor energy dissipated in bringing all the diverse peculiarities of opposite regions adequately under the notice of the general legislature. The case of the French, German, and Italian Cantons of Switzerland (the last across the Alps) probably marks the limit of possibility with respect to satisfying these conditions; though the representation of States so remote from each other as California, Virginia, and New York in the United States Congress, and, still more, the representation of Algiers and other Colonial possessions of France in the French Chambers, would seem to go beyond this limit.

Nevertheless, neither the Italian Cantons of Switzerland, nor California, nor Algiers, present such differences of needs and position, coupled with such remoteness from the more geographically integral parts of the national dominions to which they respectively belong, as do the Australasian, and even the South African and the Canadian, colonies of Great Britain. It is not so much that a colonial-born deputy from one of these colonies could not easily master all the political questions which immediately concern Englishmen at home, and might not give as just and impartial a judgment upon them as an Englishman, as that he would not seem to be doing this in the eyes of the English people at home; nor could he do this efficiently without proportionately sacrificing the claims of his own colony on his time and attention; while, at the same time, the representatives of English constituencies could only master the political circumstances of all the Colonies represented by similarly sacrificing the claims of their own constituents.

The only alternative would be that of having a special Assembly formed exclusively of colonial representatives, which would, at least, have the advantage of securing attention to colonial needs and would afford an intermediate agency for sifting them and for grouping them and bringing them into relation with each other before the debate in the central Legislature.

What is here said is, of course, no disparagement to the suggestion that the colonies should be represented, simply for the purpose of imparting information to the central Legislature, something in the way in which organised territories, not yet erected into 'States,' are represented in the United States House of Representatives by 'delegates,' who have a limited right to debate without a right to vote. It may be noted, incidentally, that in two territories, Wyoming and Utah, the franchise for the election of these delegates extends to women.

If the colonial dominions of Great Britain assumed the form of a confederacy (and even to the extent to which they tend towards the assumption of such a form —as they certainly do now—), it becomes a prominent question how far Colonial can be separated from what are sometimes called Imperial concerns. Attempts have already been made in such embryonic confederacies as those of North America and of South Africa to settle a list of topics for which the central colonial Legislature is alone competent, and another list of topics left to the determination of the provincial Legislatures.

But, outside lists of this sort there must be a third list of topics in respect of which only the central Legislature of all is competent,—be that body the Parliament of Great Britain, or be it some new federal body of representatives, or of delegates, which time may call into being.

GOVERNMENT OF DEPENDENCIES. 339

It seems to be admitted that if a common foreign policy is indispensable to maintaining unity in the organisation, the cost and administration of the Army and Navy beyond the point needed to maintain internal order and, perhaps, protection against marauding native tribes, is a matter of common and not of private concern. On the other hand, customs-laws and commercial regulations are recognised as of private and not of common concern. It may be presumed that the utmost pains would be taken to promote the formation of a common criminal code, admitting, possibly, a few local peculiarities adjusted to national habits, a common procedure, and the utmost facilities in bringing criminals to justice.

With respect to the conduct of great public works between colony and colony, or in which two or a few colonies have some preponderant interest, the arrangements and distribution of the expense would lie outside the cognisance of the supreme Legislature, unless some universal interests were also at stake. Nevertheless that legislature would always be available for the purpose of supplying the needful organisation or, in case of dispute, facilitating settlement by voluntary arbitration. It need not be said that international, postal, telegraphic, and locomotive arrangements generally would properly fall under the control of the central Legislature.

Before leaving the subject of the Government of Dependencies, some special remarks must be made on the peculiar case of British India, which has already been referred to from an historical point of view. This subject can only belong to Scientific Politics (which deals with universal principles) so far as universal principles are implicated.

But such principles are directly concerned in answering the question whether a large dependency,—requiring for its Government the special knowledge and attainments required by those who govern, or affect to govern, a people so ancient, gifted with so rare a form of civilisation, and so remote in language, religion, and temperament from their rulers,—can be justly and wisely governed by a popular Legislature, elected for quite different purposes, in a country thousands of miles away. The question, when thus put in the abstract, can only have a negative answer; and it was some such answer as this which the late Mr. John Stuart Mill (who, equally with his father, had an exceptional knowledge of Indian administration) made to the question when it was proposed to transfer the direct government of India from the East India Company to the Crown,—that is, to ministers of the Crown chosen and supervised by the House of Commons.

Later experience has gone far to justify Mr. Mill's answer, because the House of Commons has shown an amount of indifference to the good government of the great dependency which could hardly have been expected; and, step by step, the preservatives, at first legislatively provided through the medium of the Indian Council, against undue concentration of power in the hands of the Central Executive Authority,—that is, of the Secretary of State for India and the Cabinet,—have been removed one by one. An almost irresponsible Secretary of State has been substituted for the Directors of a Company, themselves having special knowledge, and being directly responsible to an intelligent and keenly critical body of interested shareholders.

No doubt, in theory, the new state of things is better than the old, and it was an anomaly for one of the most important possessions of the Crown to be administered, in peace and in war, by a commercial company, only indirectly controlled by the supreme government. Possibly the only remedy is to be found in the mode already becoming too prevalent, that of wars, famines, and commercial losses, which bring home to the popular imagination the truth that the duties of Government cannot be neglected without early and condign punishment.

In such a case the best services that an unskilled body of popular representatives, sitting at a vast distance from the scene of action, can render, are to secure fitting governors on the spot, to insist on their accountability to itself, and to exact statements of the condition of the revenue at such periods as may afford ample time for consideration and discussion. It is almost certain that misgovernment will disclose itself at an early stage through the medium of finance, and now, as of old, it will be through its right of inspecting and checking a common-place balance-sheet that the House of Commons will most effectually exert its constitutional authority, and lift the scrutiny up to a higher and nobler platform.

CHAPTER IX.

FOREIGN RELATIONS.

It needs but a superficial glance at the altered constitutional condition, and the change in mutual relationships of the leading States of the world during the present century, and even during the last half century, to be assured that a new era in international policy has been entered on, of a kind to which history presents no parallel.

How far this era is an exceptional and transitory one, destined, in a shorter or longer time, to give way to unexpected developments, there are, of course, few materials for judging. There is, however, this promise in favour of stability for so much as seems good and desirable in the new state of things, that each modification which has taken place, if look&d at singly by itself, results rather from the removal of artificial fetters than from the adoption of artificial institutions. Each modification harmonises with the marks of human progress in individual, domestic, and social life. It purports, on the face of it, to be 'natural' in the only true sense of that word, that is, being in conformity with the trained and fully developed nature of man as a social being.

In searching, then, for those principles in politics which are lasting, ubiquitous and independent of arbitrary interference by rulers or statesmen, it may be expected that a brief review of the sort of changes which have passed over the international relations of the chief European States since the Congress of Vienna may exhibit the direction and force of tendencies still at work. These, if scientific foresight be not disappointed by some new and unlooked-for development, may be treated as supplying the laws of political motion in the future.

The settlement resulting from the Congress of Vienna, and expressed in the Treaty of Paris of 1814 and its contemporary Annexes, was based not on the interests,—from a national point of view,—of the populations concerned, nor,—still less,— from any transcendental consideration for the claims of justice and right, but solely on the necessity for making such a compromise of pressing claims as might seem likely to secure the longest duration of peace.

The main causes of war in Europe during the past fifty years were traceable to the dislocation of the German Empire as a barrier against France; the facilities which, first, the centralised French monarchy and then the imperfectly organised Republic afforded to military enterprises and the rise of military adventurers; the weakness of Austria as the recognised leader of Germany; and the want of tenacity in the constitutions of the smaller States which rendered them too easily subservient to an invader or to intriguing diplomatists.

In spite of all the cross-purposes, personal aims, and diplomatic designs of a sinister kind, of which the memoirs and despatches of the great diplomatists,— especially the representatives of Austria, France, and

England, are full,—the assemblage of Treaties which constitute what is usually known as the Treaty of Paris certainly succeeded in doing away with these causes of war; and it is no small credit to the arrangement not only that peace endured for forty years after it, but that when it was first broken by the Crimean War, the cause was the misgovernment of Turkey, followed by the aggressions of Russia,—a cause not provided for by the Treaty,—while the succeeding series of wars for the aggrandisement of Prussia and the depression of Austria were waged in direct reversal of the policy of the Treaty, in consequence of a change of circumstances since its date.

Nor is it true, as is often said, that that Treaty had been so often set at nought that it was, forty years afterwards, treated as if it were not in existence.

Considering what intractable, and at the same time soluble, material the Treaty dealt with at the moment of the greatest exhaustion of the States concerned, when peace and order were peremptory necessities, it is extraordinary how durable the arrangements of the Treaty were. It is no discredit to an arrangement made for the purpose merely of ascertaining existing legal relations and rights, and consolidating a *status quo* at one epoch, if within half a century the political pendulum has made a fresh oscillation and the preponderating forces have passed from one side to another.

New dangers were indeed beginning soon after the settlement was made; but they came, not from the infirmity of the settlement itself, nor from doubts as to the original wisdom of its provisions, but from a number of social and moral causes soon destined to reflect themselves on the political mirror with a clearness for

DOCTRINE OF NATIONALITY. 345

which statesmen had not been prepared by previous experience.

The secondary influence of the ideas and aspirations set free in France and Germany,—many of the soberest of which England had long before incorporated, for herself and the United States, in a constitutional form, —told with silent though sure rapidity in France herself under her reinstated monarchy, in Italy, and in Germany.

Another idea traceable to a different origin, but of potency equal to that of the revolutionary doctrines of France, proved a momentous ally of these latter. This was the doctrine of Nationality. It was an idea which when once broached, and especially when allied with a growing apprehension of the rights of Protestant independence, was fatal to the dominion of Austria on the other side of the Alps, and of the Bourbons in Naples, as well as to the ascendency of Catholic Austria over Protestant Prussia and Northern Germany.

The solution was obtained through the partly astute, partly knight-errant, and partly corrupt, policy of France, in the hands, for the time, of that same dynasty which it was one main aim of the Treaty of Paris to exclude for ever from the throne. There remained the final controversy between the two final aspirants for European leadership; and it was emphatically decided, for the time, in favour of Prussia, and of what was immediately erected into the 'German Empire.'

Such have been the outward movements of States since the settlement of the Treaty of Paris; and it is to be noted that, while military in form, they have been less determined by such superficial causes as dynastical ambition, religious fanaticism, or complicated statecraft, than any corresponding movements in times past.

The wars of the third quarter of the nineteenth century, beginning with the Crimean war, and ending with the Russo-Turkish war, have not been mainly if at all due to far-sighted apprehensions of a change in the balance of power; nor to antipathy of Protestant to Catholic, of Catholic to Orthodox, of Christian to Mussulman; nor to the mere personal ambition of the King of Prussia to be dubbed an Emperor, or of the Princes of Servia and Roumania to be crowned Kings; nor to the covetous desire of Savoy and Nice by France, or of Lombardy by Italy; nor even to a momentary freak or personal necessity on the part of Napoleon III., leading him to distract the attention of his people by a popular war. All such motives have been hitherto the sole ones in the case of all European wars which have not strictly fallen under the head of wars of Independence; and it is well known that one or another of these motives did enter into the consideration of those who were responsible for the wars which have just led to the reconstitution of the central European States. But what is important to notice is that in the case of all these wars, national, social or religious feelings of a rational kind,—diffused in each case throughout the whole extent of the population,—were for the first time appealed to. These were in fact the causes which alone rendered the wars possible, and in every case determined their success on the side of national independence and progress.

The least progressive State of Europe,—Austro-Hungary—has suffered most. Next to her, the greatest sufferer was France, who was in danger of bartering her dearly-won republican spirit and institutions for military glory and the glitter of an Empire. Italy, Prussia, and the European provinces of the Ottoman Empire—all of which were representatives both of a strict and broadly diffused sentiment of nationality and of the cause, not of religious fanaticism or antipathy, but of religious freedom,—have gained most.

The reconstitution of Europe on such a new and apparently sound basis has been accompanied, as might have been anticipated, by certain novelties in the principles and conduct of international relationships which connote the enlarged functions now performed by the population of States, as contrasted with the limited concern in such matters conceded to the people by the professional diplomatist of former days.

One novelty is a certain modification in the strictness of the older doctrine as to the independence of every true State and the equality of all States to each other. The doctrine of the Independence of States was, indeed, always subject to considerable qualifications from the feudal relationships which frequently existed between the sovereign monarchs of different States. But, nevertheless, the definite legal character of the feudal tie and the feudal obligations rather tended to intensify the distinction between State and State than to obliterate or weaken it.

There was brought about in the States of continental Europe a general substitution of constitutional and popular government for the system of government prevailing at the time of the Congress of Vienna, which was based solely on antique and spontaneously vanishing dynastical assumptions. This substitution favoured the demolition of a notion of independence of a narrowly legal kind, resting rather on a sentiment of isolation and mutual distrust than on the true needs of uninterrupted national existence.

In fact, the advance of popular Government, and the proportionately increased interest which the mass of the population now take in questions of foreign politics and in international relationships, have tended to increase the political dependence of State on State. No doubt such theories as that of the 'Balance of Power' and the systematic policy of grouping States together on principles traditionally handed down through generations of statesmen, tended to call into existence a vast number of treaties of alliance, of marriage, of succession, of partition, and for the settlement of disputed claims which had, as their offspring, a vast assemblage of mutual obligations of a complicated and usually embarrassing kind.

But all these obligations assumed a strictly legal form; and the common training in the Civil and Canon Law of those who usually conducted those negotiations conduced to the same result. The consequence was that, in spite of all these multiplied and formal ties, the notion of legal, and thereby of political, independence was retained in quite as unmutilated a shape as is the notion of his personal freedom by a modern citizen, in spite of all the multifarious contracts by which he has bound himself, or the obligation of which has accrued to him by succession.

The difference lately brought about is that, owing to the closer approximation in thought, speech, habits of life, and, above all, in forms of government, of the populations of different States, coupled with the increased influence of these populations on their several

Governments, the relations of States to each other are found to be much more numerous and important than was at any previous time imagined. It is disclosed that not only are the large sections of humanity, personated by the different States, morally bound to concern themselves actively in each other's welfare and progress, but that, economically, the advance of each is the advance of all, and, politically, disorder or retrogression existing anywhere tends to diffuse itself everywhere. It is being found less and less possible for a State, however signal its geographical advantages in separation from its neighbours, to venture to ask whether it is its brother's keeper?

Not only generally accepted (though as yet imperfectly applied) doctrines of trade and commerce, but incessant improvements in locomotion, in means of communication, in the use of the journalistic press, and in the facilities of travel, are bringing the populations of States, traditionally enemies, and destined always to be rivals, closer and closer to each other. This closer approach is signalised in the progressive assimilation of political institutions, and still more emphatically in the acceptance of a common standard of moral and political obligation. International Law is no longer cited as the last test of what a righteous State ought to do, but only as the standard to fix what even an unrighteously disposed State must at least do.

A new sense of moral and social relationship between the populations of different States is not restricted in its effects to the prevention of gross political wrongs which the larger meshes of International Law might in other days have allowed to pass uncensured. The same sense is beginning to act positively in bringing States together for the achievement of higher and ever higher ends. The recollections of such hypocritical and tyrannical associations as the Holy Alliance are still sufficiently lively to produce a genuine and wholesome caution in the minds of statesmen invited to take part in extended coalitions; and even in the numerous political Congresses for which this century will be memorable the States represented have usually shrunk at the last from bending themselves to any corporate action.

Nevertheless, there are many symptoms which show that politically, as well as socially, many States are being drawn together by the strong attractions of common political sentiments, common aspirations, and common interests of a permanent kind. These common grounds of cohesion are likely to grow out of all proportion to the grounds of repulsion, though the latter will always be liable to reappear and, for a time, to disappoint the hopes of mankind. The main obstacle, however, to increased union and co-operation will not be found in the more advanced States, but in the unequal rate of growth of some States and in the inevitable mixture of the sound and unsound States in one common society.

The main hindrances to a final European settlement are disclosed not so much in the antipathies of France and Germany,—which might one day be as satisfactorily adjusted by pacific settlement as by a fresh treaty of peace following on a war,—as in the composite and feebly organised constitution of Austro-Hungary, in the backwardness of Russia, and the intrusion of Turkish principles of government and

Mussulman institutions into an advanced European society. Such infirm or putrefying elements form centres round which every disorderly and selfish instinct in well-ordered States gathers ; and the interests concerned are great enough to afford a constant temptation to the aggressive spirit which is latent somewhere in all States and cannot always resist the neighbourhood of an easy and too seductive prey.

Thus the notion of the independence of a State no longer means exemption from moral responsibility to other States, any more than it has meant, since the days of Grotius, the exemption from legal responsibility. The conception of moral relationships of a distinct and positive kind, reaching far beyond the rights and duties alone recognised by International Law, has been much fortified of late years,—and will, probably, be still more so in the future,—by the inducements to commercial and industrial co-operation which increasingly prevail.

No doubt the universal acceptance of Free Trade doctrines will do away with commercial treaties and customs-unions, together with all like instruments for drawing together particular groups of States. But the existence of such instruments is a modern phenomenon, and when they are finally superseded by perfect freedom of commerce, the gain to political association, generally and on the whole, will be far greater than the loss, as estimated by the disuse of special and artificial ties.

To the class of subjects in respect of which industrial and commercial co-operation between State and State is becoming conspicuous, belong international canals, tunnels, railways, navigable rivers, and postal and telegraph communication. Many of these enterprises involve the construction of great works and the subscription of a considerable amount of capital, and, sometimes, years of labour before they are completed. All this demands a high amount of economic organisation, mutual trust and financial credit, and the contribution of capital, labour, and skill, from all the States concerned. The multiplication of such works and projects is the best testimony that a reign of perpetual peace, if not yet quite arrived, is, nevertheless, a more familiar idea and hope than the expectation of incessant war.

There still are, indeed, military authorities who regard some of these improved means of international communication as fraught with peril to their own States, and they have influence on the minds of the people and of statesmen. But the disposition to annihilate the repellant effects of all artificial and material boundaries between State and State is far too strong to be allayed by terrors which are every day more obviously fanciful. The boundaries themselves still remain as testimonies to State-independence and as supports of the individuality of national character.

There is, in all this, a transmutation of the older notion of political independence. The newer aspect of political independence, which may be assumed to be the permanent one, rests upon real and not upon fictitious, accidental, and temporary, foundations. It has deep roots in distinct geographical lines of demarcation, in language, in race, in community of religion, and of political antecedents. But it is not restricted by any limits, arbitrarily imposed by such elements, nor by any assemblages of them taken together. Nor is it possible to assign finality to any existing or future distribution of the population of the world into national groups. Suffice it that clear indications have already been presented that the independence of States will not hereafter rest on mere legal circumscriptions contained in treaties, nor on the frail support of dynastical relationships. It will rest on Nationality, as described, not by sharp legal definitions, but by the multifarious elements which combine to create and to nourish a living political community.

The practical form in which the notion of political Independence presents itself as requiring limitation or expansion is in connexion with Intervention on the part of one State in the affairs of another. The legal doctrine of intervention has been laid down again and again of late years with a considerable amount of precision; and it will be found, in the text-books of international law, that a number of distinct grounds are detailed on which intervention is held to be legally allowable. Among these grounds the restoration of order after protracted anarchy, and the abolition of institutions held to be inhuman, occupy a place of marked prominence. But, as a matter of fact, the legal prescriptions which it is affected to lay down with such minuteness are all founded on historical acts of intervention in recent times, especially in the case of slavery, the slave-trade, and Ottoman misgovernment, which, at the time, proceeded wholly from political, and not at all from legal, considerations. Indeed the attempt to apply, in a legal way, the test of humanity as a legitimate ground for intervention almost confesses its own inadequacy. The term must have different meanings for each progressive step in civilisation, and the use of it serves rather as an explanation of a permanent principle than as a precise limit of future action.

In fact, the grounds of intervention in the future will, as in the past, be the consequence and expression of the existing notions of political independence and of the mutual relationships of States. Intervention is but the converse of independence; and, as it has been shown that, in one sense, the dependence of State on State is largely increasing and promises to become indefinitely close as time advances, it becomes proportionately difficult to assign limits to the right of intervention. It may be expected, however, that such limits will practically be found in the general disuse of war, and in the disappearance of the secret and astute diplomacy which has characterised international relationship in the times now passing away.

The publicity of diplomacy in consequence of the popularisation of Government no doubt has a bad as well as a good side. When there is a real ground of misunderstanding or disagreement between States, or when some complicated arrangements involving compromises and fine adjustments of interests are proceeding, or when a sudden emergency presents itself, the disadvantage of popular institutions is at its highest. Nevertheless an adequate compensation is obtained in a broad popular interest in foreign policy; in the public political training which conversance with external relationships on the largest scale is sure to impart; and in the immediate responsibility of the Executive to a popular Assembly unsparing of criticism but not incapable in real emergencies, as history has shown (in Greece, in Rome, and in England times without number), of discretion, reserve, and self-restraint of the loftiest order.

The Constitution of the United States has made a happy provision for strengthening the executive authority in the conduct of foreign relations, in the appointment of ambassadors and in the conclusion of treaties, by requiring the President to obtain for some of these matters the consent of a majority—or, in certain cases, of two-thirds—of the Senate.

In England an attempt has been repeatedly made to prevent any Government of the day concluding a treaty without the knowledge and the assent, express or implied, of Parliament. Such limitations, however, on the power of the executive authority would tend unduly to hamper its action and so to prejudice the free movements of the State without obtaining advantages not to be otherwise procured. The true remedy for executive incompetency and wrong-doing in a constitutional government is not to be sought in weakening public action at home and abroad, but in increasing, if necessary, the responsibility of the Executive, or even by specially supplementing it for certain classes of work. The loss encountered through occasional abuse, which might have been checked by Parliament, if informed in time, is a small counterpoise to the weight of an Executive powerful in the possession of popular confidence. It would be a discredit to popular institutions if the energy of the State in which they were found could not compete with rival States governed in a more despotic way.

Having considered what are the essential differences which civilisation is bringing to light between popularly governed States in their mutual relations with States resting on dynastic or aristocratic interests, the next question which presents itself is whether any corresponding change is being disclosed in the objects of policy. The objects of the older time, only now slowly passing away, may be described as eminently self-regarding, jealous, suspicious, negative, and military, whether from an offensive or from a defensive point of view. The dominant purpose manifested by European diplomacy was to promote such alliances, to bring about such combinations, and to stimulate such sentiments of national cupidity or fear as might enable a State to dispense with the necessity of war, or to have a good chance of success if compelled to fight.

Of course such astute and connected aims as these, which only took form in the ablest statesmen of France, Italy, Austria, Spain, and England, were crossed over and over again by transient religious antipathies, extending, as in the case of the Thirty Years' War, over many countries; or by casual personal aspirations, as those of Edward III., Charles V., and Philip II.; or by a momentous sense of common danger, as in combinations against the Turks.

But, on the whole, the policy of the States of Europe between the times of Charlemagne and Napoleon was of a defensive and jealous kind.

If it be alleged that during this period the two successive dominions of Spain and of France came into existence as the products of successful diplomacy and offensive wars, and the kingdom of Prussia showed promise of expanding from a small stone into a great mountain destined to fill the whole world of diplomatic interest, these instances, when properly examined, only go to establish the proposition laid down. In the 15th and 16th centuries, when the characteristic policy of this age of the world was at its climax, no State could subsist unless hedged round by treaties, or protected by special alliances, or overshadowed by some more powerful State or union of States. In the weakness of law and the absence of morals, so far as political relationships went, the first necessity for a large State was to secure allies, and for a small State to secure the guardianship of a larger one. For this end all sorts of devices, of a legal kind mostly, were resorted to; of which royal marriages, the recognition and enforcement of feudal bonds (gradually becoming obsolete), royal wills, sales, and exchanges, are the most familiar.

It is a misreading of history and biography to attribute to mere personal ambition and covetousness the febrile eagerness of European monarchs and statesmen to direct the succession and to increase the territory of their States. No doubt such sentiments affected at times even the best and the most patriotic diplomatists and courtiers. But the expediency of multiplying trustworthy allies, and of attaching the populations of other States, was far too obvious for it to be necessary to have recourse to low passions and vulgar greed in order to explain policy often consistently pursued through a whole century or longer.

In the course of this constant accretion of State to State through the medium of alliances, dynastic relationships, and feudal ties, it was inevitable that the stronger elements should prevail over the weaker; that, in fact, the loosely coherent republics of Italy, and the feebly compacted States of the Holy Roman Empire, should succumb first to Austria, then to Spain, then to

Prussia, then to France, and then to England. Then a fresh distribution of power was effected by the settlement of the Congress of Vienna.

In the international political world it has always been the case that original, or assumed, necessities of self-defence, have generated wide-spreading empires. Nations which might be immortal cannot stand still in their growth without nurturing the seeds of death; though, as in the case of some Oriental States, these seeds may be of slow growth. So long as no real relationships of common interest and reciprocal moral obligation are yet discovered, nations endeavour to protect their frail existence by artificial ties and bonds one with another. But the effect of these ties and bonds is to produce new aggregates of accumulated force before which the smaller and weaker elements lose their independence. This process has been repeated again and again in the modern world as it was in the ancient, and it is the most hopeful symptom of the new era which this century has ushered in that natural ties are being everywhere substituted for those which are artificial, and that the strength of those natural ties is being made to rest on doctrines which promise them permanence.

These ties have already been described as those of *nationality*,—defining this term with reference to all the multiform and somewhat indefinite ingredients which it connotes. The novel doctrines which tend to impart to it permanent validity are the economic one, that the wealth of one nation is promoted not by the poverty but by the wealth and prosperity of its neighbours, or rather of all other nations; the utilitarian one, that, on the whole, a nation serves its own interest best by contributing to the utmost to promote the conjoint interest of all nations, including itself; and the moral one, that there is an abstract right and wrong in Politics (a subject hereafter to be separately treated), and that it is the moral duty of each State to do good rather than evil to other States, and to take pleasure— even, at certain moments, at its own expense—in the sense of a common progress and happiness for all, of which the particular gain of individual States is a reassuring token.

The prevalence of such an assemblage of doctrines as this is markedly opposed to all those sentiments which have in past times kept up incessant jealousies, irritations, and suspicions, between States, with the effect of producing unintermittent war, and of an alternate merging of small States into unwieldy Empires, and violent dissolution of the Empires so artificially composed.

This change of international sentiment has its roots not merely in the convictions of a narrow class of diplomatic statesmen. It lies deep in the minds and hearts of large classes of persons in each State capable of making their influence felt and of sustaining each other by all the agencies of publicity, of free correspondence, and of organised association for purposes not wholly selfish. The practical consequences of the change mirror themselves in a silent modification of the objects of political action. Not, indeed, that the old objects are not still present, especially in the less advanced States, and, unfortunately, too often in the intercourse between the more advanced States and the less advanced ones. But there are many unmistakable signs that international political action is concerned not merely with remote contingencies of a self-protecting kind, but with arrangements or contracts having in view contributory aid to common and worthy purposes.

The abolition or simplification of border customs-duties, the abolition of passports, and the prevalence of more and more wide-reaching commercial treaties; the combinations between States for the purposes of currency, extradition, postal and locomotive uniformity, and the convenient use of navigable rivers and harbours; the common abolition of inhuman institutions, such as slavery and the slave trade; the construction of engineering works in common, and common arrangements for facilitating exploration and scientific enterprises; the prevention of the spread of disease; and, not least of all, concert for the purpose of reducing the atrocities of war, and even for reducing its frequency or the apparent necessity for it in any case; these are a series of objects which are now being carried out on every side by the political association of State with State, and yet which have before the present century few precedents in the history of the international relations of the most civilised States.

It is impossible not to discern in all these things indications that, in spite of the enormous armies and navies which are such a startling feature of the times, many of the causes of war are being progressively, if slowly, moved out of the way, so far as the more civilised States of the world are concerned. The size of these armies and navies, and the corresponding military and naval organisation which proceeds unrestingly even in times of profound peace, are not a fair measure of the warlike disposition of the age.

It is not contended here that the warlike instincts of mankind, or even the real necessities of resorting to force, are yet obsolete; and it is the part rather of the pious prophet than of the scientific politician to fix a point on the visible horizon at which they will become so. It is sufficient that these instincts and necessities are, for the first time, finding vast classes of competing and ever strengthening claims for supremacy in the life and mutual action of States, and that the region of the grounds for war is becoming incessantly narrowed. So far as these grounds still remain, it might have been expected that war would borrow from peace all its hitherto unexampled capacity for economic concentration of capital and scientific organisation. In this way the most alarming symptoms of a new era of war are, in truth, but testimonies to the arts of peace.

It may be expected, indeed, that war will destroy itself by consuming all the resources on which the elaboration it calls for in time of peace can alone be fed. It is being felt, as never before, that war is a question of competing capital, and of competing scientific and engineering device, which can be paid for and has a fixed price in the market. The result will be, not only to rob war of its gloss, and to reduce it to a huckstering pursuit, or at the best to a ruinous police agency, but to introduce into diplomacy that habit of pecuniary calculation which is favourable to delay, negotiation, and compromise. Never, as now, have wars been anxiously shrunk from by States armed at all points, and averted at the last moments by successfully conducted overtures of peace.

The hope has of late years been gaining ground in

many quarters that a day is not far distant when political questions will find their solution in a higher form of association among civilised States amenable to the same legal discipline and to that uniform standard of moral obligation which now binds together the population of each single State. This speculation, which is captivating to the generous imagination and has found repeated expression in the writings of the most advanced thinkers of different countries, demands, at the least, that its basis should be carefully considered, and such truth as it has be brought out into clear relief.

It is no doubt true that the national differences between the existing States of the civilised western world have been largely brought about by historical accidents, and that the effects of these accidents are already being constantly modified, and might some day be almost obliterated. The vast differences of language and of religion might even become less significant than they are now, not through assimilation, but through the diffusion of a common education and a common literature, and by the general recognition of political and social principles in the application of which religious peculiarities would count for far less than they do now.

It has also been seen that a general reassortment of States has been rapidly proceeding during the present century, the effect of which will be to annihilate merely artificial divisions derived from the chance caprice of rulers, the events of war, the calculations of diplomatists, and the 'long result of time.' For these divisions are being substituted others based on community of national sentiment and on geographical convenience.

In the conception, however, of such a continuance

of the assimilative process as might ultimately abolish all national distinctions, except as sentimental recollections and rallying points, the true value of the distinctions themselves is ignored or underrated. Not only history (the teachings of which might be objected to as hitherto too partial to be available for the purposes of prevision), but the profoundest views of the constitution of man and of human nature, enforce the notion that national distinctions are indispensable to universal political progress. Beyond a certain limit, which is partly fixed by extent of territory, partly by population, and partly by accumulated elements not assignable in advance, government only gains in uniformity what it loses in worth and strength.

The example, indeed, of the enormous regions governed, not altogether unsuccessfully, by the United States Congress at Washington, and of the British Indian and British Colonial Empire, governed by a Parliament sitting in London, certainly show that any attempt to fix limits to the extent of a single dominion would be, at present, premature.

It has already been seen that it is the characteristic problem of Local Government, of the Government of Colonies, and of Federal Government, to render central control compatible with a large amount of local independence. But it is one thing to cling to a formal unity long maintained and having its roots deep in historical causes. It is quite another thing for States already enjoying an independence which the history of centuries has guaranteed to them amidst all fluctuations to sacrifice the characteristic advantages of that independence, in pursuit of the questionable good of a dominant unity.

As the area of nationality becomes extended, through causes of the nature of forced amalgamation rather than of ethical adhesiveness, the sentiment of patriotic identity handed down from generation to generation becomes weakened through diffusion and through having less and less relation to the real facts.

Even in modern Greece, with all the advantages of common records of resistance to the Turk, the common use of an ancient language consecrated by the best literature of the world, and the occupation of a soil the traditions of which the world will not willingly let die,—the struggle to maintain the sense of national continuity (with something of what it means in this special case) has proved to be of the hardest, especially as new territory is annexed. There is, probably, no sentiment more powerful for good of all sorts than the national sentiment, and the loss or general weakening of it would be irreparable.

Of course it must be expected that all the movements of the new age will tend to reduce this sentiment in many of its aspects and modes of expression. Nations will no longer value themselves on their exclusive military prowess, or on their monopoly of virtue, of intelligence, or of good manners. But each nation, so long as its limits admit of the national sentiment being duly fostered, will be conscious of its own history and of the moral and intellectual contributions which its antecedents and qualifications specially call upon it to make for the general good. It will know in what respects, through hereditary defects in the character of the population, or through physical disadvantages, or through historical misfortunes, it is at a disadvantage as compared to others. But it will also calmly and gravely, like Pericles in his Funeral Oration, ascertain and know in what its characteristic strength and excellence lie. It will use this strength and excellence, but not abuse them. It will remember that no nation is bound to be the slave, but that all are bound to be the free servants, of humanity. And humanity will gain infinitely more by this free and independent contribution from a multitude of centres, each sustaining its own national altar and worshipping its own gods and heroes, than by the best organised company of nationalities who have purchased the show of uniformity and political tolerance at the price of universal infidelity.

This prospect, however, of associated national life is limited at best to Europe and America and the European Colonies. There are still the large outlying nations of the East, which cannot be left out of the political survey; and there are the rude populations of Africa and of the Oceanic islands, and the aboriginal tribes still inhabiting territory otherwise appropriated, with whom civilised nations are brought into necessary contact.

The narrative of the political relations of nations calling themselves civilised with nations they have deemed uncivilised is a discreditable part of human history. It would seem as if the irresponsible savagery of primitive barbarism, after being expelled by the advent of law and government from the relationships of man with man, had taken refuge in the relationships of nation with nation.

The tales of the treatment of the native inhabitants of the American Continent by the Spaniards and Portuguese may perhaps be treated as exceptional barbarities due to a transient conspiracy of money-greed and intolerant superstition. But even in very recent times the persistently overbearing treatment of China by England, the dealings of France with the civilised Arab races of North Africa, and the cruel tyranny exercised over all the inhabited communities, civilised or uncivilised, capable of supplying what are known as coolie labourers specially fitted to labour in tropical countries, by some of the British Colonies, by France, and by Portugal, combine to show that mere progress in civilisation is no guarantee against the abuse of its responsibilities.

Many of the questions raised by international relations between countries at different stages of civilisation are ethical rather than political in the narrower sense, though the results of particular modes of solving them are political in all senses of the term. The sort of questions which are presented relate to the recognition of institutions in one State which are, not only alien but repugnant, to the sentiment of the inhabitants of another with which it is brought into contact. Such institutions are polygamy, slavery, torture, idolatry, and commercial exclusiveness.

In Europe, indeed, the several States grew up at very different rates of progress, and there were parts of North Germany and of Western Britain which retained pagan and inhuman customs long after Roman law and Christianity had saturated the States of Central and Southern Europe. But the centralising influences of Feudalism and of the Roman Church triumphed over the dislocating effects of diverse institutions, and the international law of the West became the expression of both the fact of, and the aspiration after, moral unity.

There has been no parallel set of influences at work to amalgamate Western and Eastern civilisation; and it has unfortunately happened, from the nature of the case, that contact between the two has been mainly conducted under the rough and ready conditions found in cosmopolitan sea-ports. Commercial relationships have often sprung up long before the character, laws, and practices of one party to national obligations are known to the other.

For a time, it may be, and so long as negotiations are strictly confined to the merchant class, all works well. But so soon as the area of transactions becomes extended, and a number of fresh persons, not originally contemplated, become involved, either through succession or through transfer of engagements, serious disputes are sure to arise. For want of a tribunal and of a definite system of laws recognised by all, legal points instantly become matters of personal recrimination. The reign of misapprehension, of confusion, and of ignorance on all sides, extends itself more and more widely; till the executive authorities on the spot are forced to interfere in order to protect life and property; and war, usually made by the stronger against the weaker, is precipitated in a day. The result of the war is, of course, endless and ignominious concessions made by the weak to the strong.

It may be, of course, that instead of the hypothesis of commercial relationships being the origin of the contact, it begins in proselytising effort, in ill-advised enterprises of travellers, in disputes as to the rights of fugitive slaves, or as to the requirements of courteous ceremonial in conducting international correspondence. Whatever be the immediate occasion of the controversy, it is inevitable that some such controversy must sooner or later arise between States the institutions of which widely differ, and yet the inhabitants of each of which happen to come into frequent contact.

The remedy will probably be found in the firm and practical retention of two political truths ; one, that a State cannot be forcibly driven ahead in such a way as to enable it to evade the necessity of passing through all the intermediate stages of progress from the first to the last; the other, that a more advanced State can, in a variety of ways, help a less advanced one to pass through these stages with a rapidity and ease it could not attain in default of such aid.

Now it will be generally admitted that the assimilation,—though not the identification,—of moral habits and institutions, and of political and legal ideas, between all the States of the World is, *primâ facie*, desirable as favourable to union and to communion. It will be quite as generally admitted by the more advanced States that the continued retention by less advanced ones of unsocial and inhuman institutions is undesirable from a purely self-interested point of view. On both these grounds it may be maintained that the most enlightened policy in the future will compel the more advanced States to do their utmost to promote and not to retard the development of the less advanced ones.

The gains of a few Portuguese merchants three centuries ago were a poor compensation for excluding China from all contact with the rest of the world from that time till a quarter of a century ago. Even the gains of English merchants, acquired in China first by smuggling connived at by the British Government, then secured by wars engaged in for their benefit, and by a Treaty imposed on China by force of arms, have poorly compensated for the political discredit attached to the British character, for the stinted commercial transactions between China and England, and for the jealousy, suspicion, and distaste, directed against Englishmen, which rob commerce with China of all its natural and healthy stimulus.

If, then, it be a well-recognised political object to hasten the time for the disappearance of barbarous institutions, the best mode of bringing this about is to facilitate to the utmost intercourse between the inhabitants of the less and of the more advanced States. This can only be done, however, by abstaining from giving rude shocks to the sensibilities of those who continue attached to their traditional institutions, however bad and even immoral these may be from a higher standpoint; by the practice of a courteous and respectful demeanour in travellers, missionaries, and merchants towards all national observances and ceremonies; by recognising, if not by actively contributing to maintain practices which may be objectionable in themselves, but which it would be premature at present, even for the Government of the State in which they are found, to endeavour to extirpate; and lastly, by going the utmost lengths in recognising the national independence even of the weakest State, so as to encourage confidence and to supersede the necessity of precautions which act as trammels on perfect freedom of association. Some such policy as this was generally pursued and recommended by the East India Company in their relations with native States, as they came into contact with them one by one; and if some of the institutions of British India and of the Native Indian States have shown an extraordinary tenacity, it is probably because the European element has been numerically small and confined to the official and commercial classes. There is also reason to fear that the British Government in India has erred on the side of positively encouraging, and thereby prolonging the vitality of, institutions which ought to have been, ere this, dying a natural death.

CHAPTER X.

THE PROVINCE OF GOVERNMENT.

A CONSIDERATION of what a Government ought to do and what it ought to abstain from doing is a topic which has attracted the attention of modern writers more than any other in the region of serious political speculation. In ancient times,—that is, in the best days of Greece and of Rome, or even in the days of the best political Greek and Roman writers, such as Aristotle and Cicero, —no doubt seems to have perplexed the thoughts of men as to the place Government ought to take in human affairs. As soon as political speculation again awoke, at the time of the growth of the Italian Republics and the collapse of the feudal system, though the source of all government, the duties of rulers, and the rights of the people shared with the topic of the best form of government the attention of such writers as Machiavelli, Bacon, Montesquieu, Harrington, Hobbes, and Locke,—yet it seems to have been assumed in theory, as it was in practice, that, provided the government was good and had an accredited authority, there was no limit to its free right of action.

Now that the other questions as to the source and even as to the form of government are approaching a solution, it may be asked why there still remains wholly unanswered the question as to the restrictions by which governmental action ought to be,—and therefore will be,—hemmed in.

Wilhelm von Humboldt's concise and remarkable work, in which he advocates the extremest governmental apathy and inaction, is perhaps the most important contribution to the statement and discussion of the question, though the consideration of the same subject by Mr. John Stuart Mill in some of the later pages of his 'Political Economy,' and by Mr. Herbert Spencer in his 'Social Statics' and his 'Essay on Over-Government,' should be studied as essential portions of the Literature of this topic.

Nevertheless these treatises and casual discussions have not exhausted the subject. Indeed they have done little more than indicate its inherent difficulties. Mr. Mill chiefly confines himself to pointing out the inconveniences which follow from too great an extension of the area of governmental interference in some directions, and from too restricted an extension of it in others. But he scarcely lingers to propound all the principles of judgment which must guide the statesman as to when to act and when to refrain from acting. Mr. Herbert Spencer again, with his masterly command of illustration, mainly confines himself to dwelling on all the disadvantages and disabling weakness which follow from reliance on government aid without considering historically how this reliance sprang up, and how, consequently, it can, as things are, be dispensed with.

Among the causes which have led to the question of the proper limits of Governmental action being opened out in England,—and thereby in all the countries which are sharing, either through inheritance or imitation, its political institutions,—are to be counted, first, the independent individuality of which the development of the English constitution is at once the cause, the effect, and the best expression; and, secondly, the economic doctrines which have attained ever increasing predominance since the days of Adam Smith.

No doubt the principles of religious independence which attained their climax in the days of the Commonwealth, which coloured the circumstances of the Revolution of 1688, and which were recalled to a second life by Wesley and Whitefield, made a favourable atmosphere for the criticism of all secular government, as an alien and purely human institution which must be submitted to just the same tests of suitability and usefulness as any other instrument contrived for definite ends.

In a similar way, in America, the shock of political thought brought about in the interior of each of the thirteen colonies, by the delegation of important prerogatives to a new-fashioned central government, rendered the criticism of that Government, of its functions, and of its rights and duties, as natural as, in other times and circumstances, was the unquestioned submission to the claims of any Government believed to be duly authorised.

The origin of a disposition to reject the pretensions of Government to occupy any field of action it chooses, without accountability to any other standard than the apparent demands of the moment, must be sought chiefly in the first of these causes. Modern political society in the West, unlike that of Greece and Rome and that of the oriental world, has been built up out of the magnificent ruins of feudalism. This system has passed through much the same stages in each of the leading countries of Western Europe, but at very different rates.

It took longer in France than in England for the feudal monarch to obtain undisputed supremacy over the Dukes, Counts, and Barons. But when that supremacy was attained the French King was nearly a despot who had annihilated his opponents, while the English King was a constitutional ruler who competed with his nobles for the loyal support of an enfranchised people. Thus in England, at an early date, the notion of individual rights against both the Crown and the Aristocracy prevailed; and the early and rapid development of the House of Commons gave practical effect to a conception which became every year more distinct and more popular.

In the times of the Edwards and the early Tudors the House of Commons, except on questions of granting supplies, was little more than an organ for enforcing on the people the capricious policy of a monarch or of his favourite adviser. By the time of the Stuarts the same House had become an organ for enforcing the will of the people on the King,—and the only progress made since has been that of annihilating more and more decisively all impediments between the expression of the people's will and the act of carrying it into effect. Thus, while a state of mind favourable to an outside criticism of the duties and claims of government has been in course of incessant cultivation, the people themselves have had cast upon them the charge of government to an extent which may well make them pause to ask whether power may not be abused in their hands as well as in the hands of an aristocracy or a monarch? Is there any limit beyond which, even in the name of an authorised government itself, they ought not to advance?

This aspect of Government has been brought into clearer relief during the present century from the development of the science of Political Economy in the hands of Adam Smith and his successors in this country up to Mr. John Stuart Mill. This science had, indeed, been cultivated with success both in England and in France before the publication of the 'Wealth of Nations'; and the bearing of some of its leading doctrines on practical politics had been appreciated, or, at least, divined. But, between the publication of Adam Smith's 'Wealth of Nations' and that of Mr. Mill's treatise on the same subject, events of an unprecedented character and on an enormous scale had happened, enforcing public attention to the mutual relations of economical and political science.

The question of the right of taxing colonies had been mooted in England and in America in a form in which it required all the genius of Adam Smith and of Edmund Burke to separate the claims of economic advantage, of moral right, and of political expediency. The collapse of the social, industrial, and financial system of France,—represented by the state of things to be known for all time as the first French Revolution,— threw into the crucible every familiar theory of the basis of government, and illustrated with only too brilliant a glare the dependence of all governments on economic conditions which they may control and conform to, but which they cannot, with impunity, ignore or defy.

In England, again, the recovery of the national

energy expended in the war with France was signally retarded by the agricultural distress following on a return to the lower prices belonging to a time of peace, by the desperate efforts to find redress in multiplied Protective duties, and by the aggravation of all the other perplexities brought about by the scandalous operation of a Poor Law system which was the inheritance of times of economic childhood, and which was successful only in the rapid manufacture of paupers.

It was in order to solve such urgent practical problems as these that such writers as Adam Smith, Ricardo and the two Mills addressed themselves to question afresh, from a purely logical standpoint, whether there were any laws governing the production and distribution of national wealth which were, in a true sense, laws of Nature, and which, as such, could not, without disaster, be trifled with by Governments.

The true purpose which scientific writers on what is now recognised under the title of Political Economy proposed to themselves has very generally been misconceived, and their labours have, consequently, been in many quarters regarded with a prejudice and distrust quite undeserved—at least so far as the most eminent of these writers is concerned. It has been supposed that they set before themselves the object not of showing on what conditions national wealth depends, but of enforcing on governments and on individual persons the obligation of creating wealth in preference (if it must be so) to the discharge of other and competing obligations.

Thus Mr. Malthus announced an economic law that, in certain countries and in certain conditions of society, population tends to increase more rapidly than the means of subsistence, and but for certain checks (which he enumerated) would, within a limited time, gain upon those means in such a measure as to involve widespread penury and misery. The consequence has been that the name of Malthus has been erroneously identified with a doctrine that it is the duty of all men everywhere, both individually and by corporate action, to devise all sorts of artificial means to restrict population.

In the same way the political economists who have pointed out how indiscriminate poor relief, whether accorded by the State or by private persons, promotes pauperism and saps the sense of independence and self-reliance, have been habitually charged with indifference to the culture of the charitable virtues, and with hardness or cruelty to the poor. Even those writers who have attempted to help working men to understand the necessary effects of Trade Combinations and strikes on wages and prices, with a view to ascertaining the principles on which these combinations and strikes can, and cannot, be resorted to in the true interest of the labourer, have been too frequently misrepresented and supposed to be the enemies, and not the friends, of working men.

No doubt the attitude occasionally adopted by some leading writers, and the want of strict adherence to the true limits of their subject-matter, have given some colour to these reproaches. But the subject of economics, —dealing with nothing else than the laws of the production and the distribution of wealth, as determined at any time and place by the constitution of man and the physical universe then and there,—has gradually been clearing itself from all complicating materials, and in the severely scientific treatises of such writers as the late Professors Cairnes and Jevons has at last attained the solid proportions of a compact and demonstrative science.

Now it happens that the main discoveries or conclusions of economical science during the last hundred years have been adverse to State interference. The doctrine favourable to recognising the claims of colonies to self-taxation; the doctrine which overthrew all such impediments to commerce as protective tariffs and navigation laws, and which abolished the old Poor Law with its artificial obstructions to a free circulation of labour, and with its monstrous system of supplementing wages out of the poor-rate, of encouraging improvident marriages, and of granting indiscriminate out-door relief; and the doctrines which have recognised, within just limits, the right of labourers to free combination;—these several doctrines have been alike in this, that they have marked out clear and definite limits to the beneficial activity of Government, and in every case this activity has been theoretically contracted rather than enlarged.

The result has been that there has gradually grown up, in the consciousness of the population of European countries generally, an entirely novel sentiment as to the position and functions of the State. In the older political systems, whether of the classical or the modern world, the only oppositions known were those of the State to the private citizen or perhaps of the State to the chartered corporation. In the new era independent forces are recognised of a kind which wholly differ from those centering in any individual person or wielded by any aggregate body of persons, and which are yet capable of assuming a position of lasting antagonism to the State. The question, indeed, is being asked whether, in view of these stupendous, yet highly organised, independent, forces, future civilisation will leave anything for government to do, except to punish occasional crimes, to protect property, to collect taxes, and to superintend the conduct of relations with foreign Powers.

The modern growth of what may be characterised under the generic name of Socialism is partly a product, and partly a contemporaneous symptom, of this novel attitude towards the State. The outburst of Socialism in its various forms in the different countries of Europe, and under the different titles of Nihilism, Internationalism, Communism, and Socialism (in a special sense), while it is directly due, in each particular country, to actual misgovernment or to well-founded or ill-founded discontent with the existing government, really has its roots in the same soil as that which, in England, favours a disparaging view of the usefulness of government in the abstract.

The discovery has been made, with almost staggering suddenness, in some countries, that government is not the mysterious circumambient entity which, by some eternal necessity, wraps in impenetrable folds the very consciousness of all men at every moment of life from its beginning to its close. It is found that government is an historical institution, like any other growth of time and circumstances; that governments can be either good or bad, and that most governments have hitherto been very bad, and that many still are so; that governments, however, as they may be criticised and compared one with another, can also be altered and improved; that the bulk of the population of all countries have, in common with each other, a more pressing interest that governments generally should not do harm than that time and energy should be expended (perhaps fruitlessly) in trying to make particular governments do all the possible good within their reach; that, finally, inasmuch as the bulk of mankind must be poor, in any dividing of the world's goods, property is, in the view of this large portion of the race, to be held a matter of subordinate account, and its interests are to be always subordinated to claims of more universal concern.

Such are the common postulates on which the socialistic conception of the world now actually held by no insignificant number of persons in Germany, Russia, Italy, and France, is based. The proportion of socialists is probably least in England, America, Belgium, Holland, Switzerland, and Greece; and these are just the countries in which government is,—in profession, if not always in fact,—most thoroughly popularised, and in which there is the least place for the notion of a standing antagonism between the people and the Government.

So far, however, as Socialism diffuses an indirect influence on countries little affected by it directly, that influence operates in favour of bringing into antithesis the organisation of the State and the spontaneous organisation, for all sorts of purposes, of the population regarded as outside the State. The conclusions of modern political economy, already adverted to, tend in the same direction; and it may be said, generally, that now for the first time government is put upon its trial, and required to justify its retention of a hold upon any part of human activity,—and to justify it on exactly such grounds as would supply a logical test of the justice of any other usurpation on human liberty.

⟨ The extreme view in favour of restricting the limits of State activity has been most ably argued for several years past by Mr. Herbert Spencer, the founder of a school of thought on the subject. He has discerned in the habits of modern society a disposition to have recourse to government for the supply of all its corporate wants, and to be neglectful of the disadvantages of all State interference, as well as the relaxed habits of mind which dependence on government creates and fosters.

⟨ The result is the multiplication of laws, and the endless generation of legal and administrative mechanism. The police force has to be indefinitely enlarged, and ever new and incompatible duties are cast upon it, the number of the officials required involving a deterioration in their quality and attainments. So soon as a popular working majority is obtained, the conversion of any project into law is only a matter of sufficient publication by the Press, and, thereupon, the minority becomes bound. It is bound, too, beyond the hope of deliverance; because, whatever the amount of opposition to a law before its enactment, after its enactment all the forces of conservative loyalty, as well as of the new interests springing from its mere operation, begin to work in its favour. ⟩

⟨ In this way it is contended that there is no limit to the possible trespasses on human liberty. The result is the more disastrous from the very insufficient knowledge and thought through which new projects obtain an extraordinary popularity. If they become encrusted upon the social system through the agency of law, all those fine modifications and delicate adaptations which increasing experience is sure to suggest, and, if unimpeded, to introduce, become impossible. The only substitute for them is found in some more or less comprehensive amendments, introduced at long intervals in a spirit of reaction, and often enough, through their inelastic character, working as much evil in the new direction as the unamended law worked in the old.

To these more latent disadvantages are to be added the greater expense involved in all work conducted by a cumbrous Government Board; the insuperable difficulty of securing effectual control in the true interests of the public; the opportunities opened out for corruption and crooked dealings of all sorts; the multiplication of officials; and the consolidation of a bureaucratic interest, which universal experience proves to operate adversely to the general welfare.

Writers of the class of which Mr. Herbert Spencer is the most eminent English representative take as an illustration of these evils the working of a government Poor-law, and of the laws which are passed from time to time for the purpose of checking the spread of disease. It is argued that any State measure for the relief of the poor must tend to nurture pauperism, by insuring every one against the consequences of his own imprudence or idleness or vice; while, from the mere fact of its assuming the form of an universal organisation, hardened and blunted by its legal form, it must fail generally to meet just those cases of undeserved misfortune and want which only the discerning hand of voluntary charity can relieve adequately and delicately without leaving any vicious results behind.

In a somewhat different way special legislation for

the prevention of any particular disease tends to perpetuate the views of that disease and its remedies which are prevalent, at the moment of legislation, among that section of the medical profession which has succeeded in gaining the ear of Government. If new views, or a modified method of treatment, gradually comes to the front,—owing to the subsidence of panic or to the larger knowledge derived from the longer pursuit of comparative methods of enquiry perhaps conducted in other countries,—they can hardly hold their footing against the robust institutions, the multiplied and interested officials, the fixedly conventional notions, which owe a fortuitous but unassailable strength to the old law.

To these obvious disadvantages of excessive governmental intervention are opposed the benefits which might flow from independent action. There are few fields of human energy, it is contended, in which perfect freedom does not in time vindicate the worth of its pretensions. The power of associated labour may be rendered as effective when wielded by private persons, freely and voluntarily combining together, as when exerted by the State. If there is wanting the compulsion of law, the defect is more than compensated by the superior discernment and not less potent pressure of a vigilant public opinion.

At the same time, voluntary agency provides for indefinitely wider openings to fresh discoveries, new departures, modified schemes, and continuous transmutations of plans, even to the finest degree of delicate variation. Habits of espionage and police tyranny are excluded, public corruption is impossible, expenses are kept within the smallest limits, and work is distributed in the way likely to promote the utmost amount of economical efficiency. Some political theorists, indeed, are so fascinated with their conception of the incomparable value of private action as to wish to withdraw from the State even the management of purely mechanical departments of the administrative authority such as the Post Office and the Telegraph department, leaving to the Government little else than the administration of Justice and the management of the Army and Navy.

The opposite view, in favour of extending to the utmost the functions of government, is professed,—practically, if not theoretically,—in some of the older Continental countries, such as France and Germany, which have only recently emerged out of the condition of a feudal monarchy, and in the Australian colonies of Great Britain. The grounds of this favour shown to government action are, however, very different in the European and in the Australian instances.

In France and Germany, in spite of the social and revolutionary storms which, in very different forms, have swept over both countries within the present century, a real constitutional opposition between the people and the Government, such as was described above as having discovered itself in England some three or four centuries ago, and as having gained strength and distinctness ever since, has hardly yet been manifested. Even in the most tempestuous crises of the first French Revolution the question was not one of popular resistance to Government as such, but of who were to get the Government into their own hands. The later Socialistic and Communistic movements, as already shown, have been of a different stamp; but their influence on the broad field of politics is only beginning to be felt.

At the latter end of the past century, and for the first half of the present one, the schemes of all political reformers, both in France and Germany, have been devised so as to work through Government and not independently of it and against it. In neither country has there been even yet witnessed, on a conspicuous platform, any of that firm resistance to the encroachments of government in the name of broad human or alleged constitutional or moral rights, with which the history of the English race, at home and on the continent of America, is so notably distinguished.

The result is that, while the form of the government is in both countries matter of urgent popular concern, and has in France undergone repeated changes, with every kind and degree of manifestation of popular enthusiasm, the functions of government and the limits of individual liberty have hardly attracted attention elsewhere than in the little-studied Treatises of such closet students as Wilhelm von Humboldt and Auguste Comte.

In France and Germany, there is to be found all the apparatus of representative government; and in France even the forms of purely republican institutions, Yet in both countries the power of the executive authority, in the shape of a highly organised and bureaucratically managed police system, renders individual liberty little less precarious than it could be under an absolute despotism; the only difference being due to the possibility of bringing outrageous trespasses on liberty under the notice of the Press and the representative assembly. But this relief can only apply to a scanty number of exceptional acts of violence, and affords no remedy to the crushing weight of fear and self-distrust which an ubiquitous and irresponsible police imposes on the most dependent,—that is, on the most numerous and needy,—classes of the community.

Both in France and Germany, again, the military habits and antecedents of the two countries co-operate with the traditional subservience of the people to the Government of the day to make it seem natural that all work that wants doing, and can be better done on a large than on a small scale, should be done, as of course, by the Government. Hence the extent of government interference in all the affairs of life, the recognised right and duty of Government to manage the locomotion of the country, the restrictions on the right of free testamentary disposition, and the highly centralised superintendence of education, of health, and of purely local affairs, scarcely even excites discontent or criticism. The right of absorbing such affairs into its own hands is practically assumed to be of the essence of all government, and if any field of action is to be cut off from the government domain a presumption has to be rebutted which is of considerable, and often of insuperable, strength.

The case of the Australian colonies, in which, likewise, the extension of government activity is very wide, is different and peculiar. The habit of depending on Government was formed in the oldest colony,—that of New South Wales,—during the existence of the colony as a convict settlement. In those days the whole country was a diffused prison, the free emigrants being only scattered loosely about among a population consisting of prisoners, soldiers, officers, magistrates, and gaolers.

In this state of things all public works were naturally and necessarily undertaken by Government, and were almost exclusively constructed by convict labour. The older public buildings, the harbour works, and the fine broad roads stretching for hundreds of miles across the Blue Mountains into the interior, and from one end of what was then Van Diemen's Land to the other, were thus called into being. The provision for Public Worship and for Education, such as it was, was solely governmental; and the financial economy of the country was managed almost as directly from the centre of government at home as in the case of the convict establishments at Portland and Dartmoor.

So soon as, in 1855, New South Wales and its separated sister colony, Victoria, obtained the grant of free parliamentary institutions and a popular representative government, -the Crown yielding to the Colonial Government its prerogative rights in the soil,— the population of the colony, as represented in the Colonial Legislatures, instantly stepped into the place of the British Government at home. But, as soon as this transformation was effected the new colonial Government acquired all the rights, privileges, and inherited traditions of the British Government which had preceded it; and, acting, as it did, in the name of popular constituencies no longer at an indefinite distance, could and must needs personate the whole people in providing for the urgent wants of the still immature settlement.

In the meantime the constant sale of government lands, and the incoming rental from pastoral leaseholds, brought money into the hands of the Government which, there being as yet no debt, it could not but expend on the improvement of the colony. The consequence was the incessant struggle in Parliament between the representatives of one district or township and another, for works such as roads, harbours, railways, bridges, waterworks, public buildings, and public libraries, to be done at the expense of the central colonial government. The times of this surplus national wealth and freedom from debt are rapidly passing away in all the colonies, and perhaps the effect may be the adoption of new principles of regulating government intervention.

The real province of government in opening out a new colony rather belongs to a subject already discussed,—the 'Government of Dependencies.' But it may be said here that while the habit of leaning on Government for every kind of public enterprise which could be undertaken better, more cheaply, and with less friction, by private co-operation is demoralising in the extreme, there are some classes of works, such as roads, railways, and the convenient planning out of new towns which, if left to the chances of a fluctuating and partial demand for them, instead of being well made once for all in the common interests of all, posterity included, may entail disastrous consequences in the future which can never be undone.

From this review of the actual position of the oldest and newest communities in the world with respect to government interference, it results that all States are largely committed in practice to governmental intervention in a vast number of matters which certainly could be undertaken by private persons, acting either individually or in voluntary combinations.

Thus the question can hardly be treated as though it were a new one now propounded for the first time. The case rather is, that a practical answer has long been given to it, and the world has been fashioned in habit and sentiment to the artificial conditions thereby created. It may be bad to recognise the legal right of the poor to relief at the hands of the State; but if such right has been recognised for generations, and if economical and social conditions have adjusted themselves to this state of things, it may be impossible to annul the right, or to do more than restrict and rigidly define it, or, at the most, to ascertain the true conditions on which alone it can be any longer recognised.

So with the right to have all classes of contracts enforced by law. It might have been a question once whether the legal enforcement of all contracts was really favourable to public morality and did not tend to substitute an outward and more easily evaded sanction for an inward and more searching sanction of inexorable authority. But, as things have been from the foundation of existing States, contract-law has been a prominent part of all law; and society, commerce, industry, and civil relationships of all kinds, have been built up on the supposition that contracts will be enforced in Courts of Justice. Thus this expectation of the intervention of the State for the support of the validity of contracts must now be treated by the statesman as one of the ultimate,—even though artificially produced,—facts of man's nature; and as such he must provide for its claims, though he may slowly attempt, if he pleases, to modify this expectation.

To understand how it comes about that, at a certain stage in the history of a political community, the limits of Governmental interference may have to be readjusted, it is necessary to make some historical reflections.

At the outset of political life, when the population has become settled within definite territorial limits; when agricultural habits have succeeded to those of a nomad or pastoral type; when the coalition of tribes is developing a monarchical form of Government, and when the civilisation is becoming refined and established by the foundation of towns, there are present certain predominant political conditions, which gradually fade away as the community advances, and, at a certain stage of its progress, wholly disappear. Such conditions are, first, the indefinite amount of available land in proportion to the needs of a population, sparse, and as yet indisposed to steady agricultural pursuits; secondly, the equable distribution of such elementary kinds of wealth as are alone appreciated at this early stage of society, and the consequent absence of a large pauper class; thirdly, the eminent superiority of the small governing class in respect of knowledge, practical capacity, and political foresight, over all the rest of the community ; fourthly, the ignorance, which prevails generally and extends to the governing class, of the laws of wealth and of all those scientific principles of Government which nothing but long experience could discover or historical reading communicate.

As the community advances, all these conditions undergo continuous, though scarcely perceived, changes till at last they are almost reversed. Except in the rare case of incessant colonisation or annexation of fresh territory, the population gains on the land, while the national improvement at all points enables the larger population to demand far more of the same land than the simpler resources of early society could even suggest. Wealth becomes more and more unequally distributed, till the physical and moral power of the society is shifted from the few to the many, the principles and basis of Government undergoing a corresponding transformation, and a pauper problem being always at hand, and ready to attain alarming proportions.

Gradually, too, the knowledge and thought of the society, even in respect of purely political matters, is found also outside the group of persons on whom the task of Government devolves, and these persons have increasingly to take their instruction and even their orders from the outside public, rather than to impose on others the unquestioned results of their private lucubrations. Lastly, economic principles are discovered, false doctrines are finally exploded, and the reign of capricious conjecture as to the consequences of large classes of legislation,—such as that relating to crime, taxation, health, sumptuary matters, and religion,—is at end.

It is not making too large an assumption in favour of many modern States, including nearly all the European ones, to assert that the later stage here indicated has been already attained. In such States as England, France, Germany, and Italy land has become inconceivably precious when viewed in the light of the population which in these several countries claims to have its residence upon it and its support out of it.

The reciprocally opposed conditions of the few who are very rich, of the many who are just free from solicitude about the means of existence, and of the too large class of the very poor, present problems, social and political, which strain to the utmost the sagacity and scientific acquirements of the modern Statesman. The governing class, again, are finding themselves no longer masters but servants, and are bound to learn of others rather than to propound what doctrines they please. In the meantime Political Economy, in spite of its unscientific treatment in many quarters, has laid down principles of taxation, of currency, of commercial freedom, and of poor relief, which no statesman or legislative assembly could any longer dare either to remain ignorant of or to disown in practice.

The result is that, while existing facts, and conditions or predispositions resulting from the past, must be recognised by statesmen as the material with which they have to deal, it is no argument for the retention of any principle of Government that it suited a different and earlier state of society. In mapping out afresh, in these days, the province of Government, it is of the utmost importance to bear this in mind, because it is here, perhaps more than anywhere else, that the reversed condition of society has its most important bearing.

For instance, the only apology which could be made in England, in the reign of the later Plantagenets and the Tudors, for the sumptuary laws and the laws regulating wages and Poor relief was, that the Government which devised the laws knew better than the persons to whom the laws were addressed what was the fitting private expenditure for dress, what was the right rate of wages, what were the best means of restricting pauperism. It is now established as a scientific fact that in all these matters the Government was wholly mistaken either in its apprehensions of economic principle, or in its interference, and generally in both; so that it erred, in interfering for an object which was itself bad.

In the present day, neither the executive government nor any popular assembly in an European State would affect to act independently of reference to principles of political economy established elsewhere, though often misconceived or mis-cited; nor would they assume that they contained within their own body an exclusive monopoly of the wisdom of the country. The whole representative system of popular government is opposed to any such conception; and, as government becomes more and more popular, and the people better educated, the proportions of knowledge between the governing classes and those they represent will be more and more altered, in a way unfavourable to the former. Those who govern will need to be specialists in their own art, but, for that very reason, they will be less and less well equipped with doctrines concerning broad masses of knowledge on which information is from time to time needed for their due co-ordination to a political end.

Hereafter those who govern will cease altogether to be presumed to be wiser or better than the rest of the community. They will merely enjoy the privilege of serving it. In the discharge of this task of service their first duty will be of the negative kind, implied in merely protecting the large but important classes of the community who, owing to the unequal distribution of wealth, are likely to suffer certain peculiar disadvantages from which they have a moral claim to be exempted.

Such disadvantages may come (1) from the absorption of the soil of the country in a few hands; (2) from accidental oversights in the modes of imposing or of distributing social burdens, particularly of a financial kind; (3) from monopolies of the means of locomotion or of communication; (4) from a neglect, on the part of the few, of the conditions of public health affecting the many; (5) from the weight of associations of persons forming influential commercial organisations, and having large amounts of capital at their disposal; and (6) lastly, from the pressure of large religious organisations which, through the hold they too readily obtain on conventional sentiment, are a continual menace to individual liberty.

With a view to the orderly examination of each of these possible subjects of a State intervention undertaken for the purely negative end of protecting the more dependent and numerous portion of the community against a variety of classes which, in a progressive society, tend to become increasingly influential and overpowering, it will be convenient to exhibit them in a brief tabular form, as follows:

State intervention may be justified on behalf of its *negative* purpose of protecting the dependent and more numerous portion of the community in respect of

(1) The absorption of the National Soil.
(2) The unequal distribution of Social Burdens.

LIMITS OF STATE INTERVENTION. 295

(3) The monopoly of the means of Locomotion and of Communication.
(4) Public Health.
(5) The power and undue influence of Commercial companies, Industrial organisations, and large Capitalists.
(6) The power and undue influence of Churches and Religious Associations.

(1) THE NATIONAL SOIL.—It has already been pointed out that, in default of incessant annexation of adjoining territory or special facilities and aptitude for colonisation, the amount of available land always tends to become disproportioned to the wants of the population. Superior organisation of the modes of living, the growth of towns, the introduction of superior methods of cultivating the soil, and, most of all, free commercial intercourse between country and country,—especially in respect of the necessaries of life,—make it possible for this growing insufficiency of the soil to be long overlooked.

But, at the same time that these facts are disclosing their consequences, the growth of capital, and its inevitable tendency to get concentrated in a few hands, lead to the land being absorbed into the hands of an ever diminishing class. Here again the phenomenon is long disguised through the general improvement in all classes of the community, and the more diffused acquisition of small landed properties, though at a far slower rate of advance than the rate of accumulation of large properties in the hands of a few. Of course, in countries such as those still partially feudalised, like England, where the policy of the law is in favour of hereditary ownership, and the transfer of land in the market is hampered by artificial fetters, the concentration of land does not strictly follow the concentration of capital, although, so far as the competing claims of the bulk of the population go, it proceeds just the same, and this, too, in a form still more unserviceable from an economic point of view.

The logical and necessary consequence is, that the mass of the population not only cease to be landholders themselves, but, owing to the necessity they are under of living on the soil and,—in the case of a large proportion of them,—of earning a livelihood by its cultivation, they are in an ever growing danger of being servilely dependent on the proprietors of the land. This dependence, which is brought about by the play of purely economical conditions, is of a very different kind from that dependence of serfdom or villenage which is found at an earlier stage of society, and which is due to a very different class of causes.

In that relationship of agrarian dependence which results from nothing else than the absorption of the national soil by a limited class of the community, there are no sentiments of moral reciprocity, of personal allegiance and protection, to soften the grating hardness of economical competition. There is not even, of necessity, the difference of education or of social antecedents to interpose a sort of natural and impassable barrier between the proprietor and his tenant or labourer.

Apart from new laws made to meet the new emergency as it arises, there is little to prevent the land proprietor,—whose command of the market which supplies tenants and labourers is only restricted by the possible rivalry of an easily assignable number of other proprietors like himself, and whose interests are identically the same as his own,—from accepting what tenants, exacting what rent, making what bargains, or paying what wages, he pleases.

In one and another country of Europe a condition such as this has been nearly attained through the mere regular operation of the causes,—such as those of over-population and the concentration of capital,—which have been just adverted to.

In some countries, such as France just before the first Revolution, and Germany before the reforms usually attributed to Stein, the persistent endurance, in a semi-fossilised form, of feudal institutions and relationships, helped to precipitate a catastrophe which the mere development of modern commerce would, of itself, have in no long time brought about.

In some provinces of British India a similar crisis has been reached by the mere agency, for the most part beneficial, of the Government itself. It has not been so much that population has grown out of proportion to the available supply of land, as that the greater preservation of life, brought about by exemption from war and from other means of wide-reaching destruction, has been equivalent to a sudden growth of population. The British Government itself made the mistake of prematurely dissolving the system of village proprietorship, and of substituting the practical proprietorship of an intermediary,—a tenant, on the one hand, of their own, but, on the other hand, an independent capitalist, who, by advancing money on exorbitant terms to the sub-tenants, gradually brought them wholly under his power. It is to this state of things that the Government has recently been addressing itself, by measures of land-reform favourable in an almost unprecedented degree to the sub-tenants and actual cultivators of the soil.

The land problem in Ireland is only a small fraction of the general problem here stated, and it is owing to some exceptional historical incidents in the relations of England and Ireland that it has, perhaps prematurely, been thrust into prominence, and attained such portentous proportions.

In Ireland all the causes which, in other countries, have usually worked singly, or by twos or threes, towards producing a disproportion between the claims of the people and the supply of land, have worked in combination and contemporaneously. Owing to physical peculiarities, the land available for cultivation is comparatively small in quantity, the uses to which it can be turned are limited, and the improvement of which it is susceptible is less than in most other countries having an equal population at the same stage of civilisation.

It also happens that both imported feudalism in respect of the hereditary proprietorship of large estates, and the concentration of commercial capital, have combined together to aggravate each other as causes for the withdrawal of the soil from the hands of the people. It further happens that, whether from the indestructible instinct of territorial clanship, or from an inherited indisposition for all pursuits other than a superficial cultivation of the soil, the 'hunger' for land on the part of the bulk of the Irish population seems to be of a peculiarly insatiable kind.

All these conditions, taken together, have precipitated in Ireland a crisis which must come sooner or later in all old countries, though the absorption of labour in manufactures, the extension of towns, the popularity of emigration, or the sudden opening out of new fields of largely.remunerative labour, such as the construction of railways or the working of a new gold district, may long defer its arrival.

The universal problem is, of course, further perplexed by the fact that there are many points in which the analogy of movable property is not applicable to land, and therefore the duties and rights of government in the matter have to be considered now for the first time, without deriving any help either from ancient precedent or from recognised principles of policy in respect of other species of property.

The sentiment of an owner or even of an occupier of land is capable of acquiring a peculiar colour and intensity. It may, and does in countless cases, associate itself with the recollections of a lifetime and, through the practice of hereditary transmission, with the sense of continuity of relationship and with affectionate associations of the most ineffaceable kind. Nor can the State afford to treat sentiments like these as being of no account, or to tamper with them too recklessly in legislation. Such feelings, diffused throughout a population, afford the strongest guarantee for loyalty and patriotism. They connect together the successive generations of the life of the State, and are among the richest of the elements which contribute to mould the national consciousness of the people and to ensure stability for their traditional institutions.

· But such considerations as these are rather an argument for distributing the ownership of land as widely as possible than for acquiescing in its continued and accidental absorption by a few. True it is that, to arrest the process of accumulation, some stringent policy may have momentarily to be resorted to which will, in some quarters, awaken the cry of .' confiscation.' But, if the step is delayed, the problem can only increase in magnitude, and its solution be attended with ever greater difficulty and apparent, if not real, injustice and hardship. Happy are those countries in which the inevitable problem is seen afar off, and the absolute claim of the State to deal unrestrictedly with the national soil, in the interests of itself and of all classes of the community, is early recognised.

It is unfortunate that in the British colonies in Australia the rights and the duties of the State in respect of the enormous tracts of land within its control have been very imperfectly recognised ; and this too at an early era in the growth of the colonies, when the government could have taken its own way with the smallest possible injury to existing interests.

The general practice pursued in most of the colonies, including New South Wales and Victoria, has been, so far as the agricultural settlements have gone, to sell the land absolutely at a cheap rate, most favourable terms being devised for the payment of the purchase money. The result is that as time goes on, and unless the policy is reversed, all the best land for agricultural and building purposes will be in the hands of a limited number of persons, who, by natural processes of accumulation and concentration, will tend to become fewer and fewer.

The same problem which has racked the brains and strained the consciences of European statesmen will be always hanging over these colonies; and one day it will have to be solved, as elsewhere, either by confiscation, or by revolution, or by both together. A simple substitution of long leases from the State for absolute sales, with rights of renewal or re-valuation, coupled, perhaps, with provisions against undue accumulation, would have been open to no fair objection at the time, and would have prevented difficulties scarcely as yet conceivable in the future.

In contrast to these modern agrarian problems and to the now recognised mode of their solution by decisive State interference, it is instructive to recall the agrarian problems of Rome, which were due to causes both like and unlike.

In the later days of the Roman Republic the large national domains were for the most part occupied by rich capitalists who either paid a merely nominal rent to the State or evaded payment of rent altogether. These lands were cultivated by slaves, and the bulk of the free Roman people were being gradually excluded from the use and ownership of the land of Italy altogether. The successive agrarian movements and seditions which took place in consequence are remembered by all. Passing remedies were found in the acquisition and distribution of newly conquered or forfeited lands among the people, in colonisation, and in the absorption of the population in military expeditions and interests. But these remedies were insufficient, and the result appeared in the Servile wars, in the exhaustion of the treasury by grants of corn to the populace, and in the social disintegration which rendered the Republic an anachronism and the Empire the sole salvation of society.

(2) PUBLIC BURDENS.—One of the natural consequences of the unequal distribution of wealth, brought about, to an ever increasing extent, in the progress of civilisation, is the unequal distribution of social burdens, especially those of a financial kind. As society becomes organised the necessity for regular contributions, or at least of periodic contributions, devised on a systematic plan makes itself felt.

In very primitive times the mode of levying contributions for the expenses of the State is of the rudest sort and scarcely goes beyond free gifts in kind, personal military service, and the concession of peculiar rights in the soil. As tribal chieftainship develops into national kingship, and government acquires greater complexity, the king, as representing the government, attracts to himself a number of prerogative rights of the nature of monopolies, exemptions, pre-emptions, and personal dues, which it becomes the first business of a popular representative assembly, as it emerges into existence, to ascertain and to restrict.

There thus comes about a re-distribution of the functions which are directed to supporting the mechanical business of Government. Their course is no longer left to be determined by the accidental institutions of a primitive society. The popular will is consulted,— or, at least, a show of consulting it takes place,—and some broad theories of public obligation and of general taxation are acted on, if not formulated. Nevertheless, in the course of conducting this secondary adjustment, which will proceed slowly and almost unconsciously, it is always probable that the bulk of the population, that is the less moneyed classes, will be disproportionately burdened in comparison with the more moneyed classes.

According to any numerical statement of the mode of distribution, it may be hard to demonstrate the unfairness, because any numerical statement must proceed upon the basis that the elementary units of money, time, and labour, are of the same value for one person as they are for another. But there are large classes of society for which any taxation whatever, any increase in the price of the necessaries of life, any withdrawal of marketable time or labour, may mean either utter destitution or such loss and accompanying anxiety as can have no counterpart in the privations incurred by their more fortunate fellow countrymen through their share of the public burdens.

An illustration of this is supplied by France before the first Revolution, when some of the wealthiest classes of society were wholly exempt from taxation, and the poorest classes were crushed by its incidence in innumerable grinding forms. A sort of morbid congestion of wealth had set in, in consequence of long years of feebleness and corruption on the part of the central Government, and the causes must rather be sought in the continued impotency of the multitude than in any intentional policy of oppression on the part of the more favoured classes.

Another illustration equally apposite was found in the indisposition of the landowning and farming classes of England to risk any loss themselves for the purpose of saving a considerable portion of the population from the suffering, loss, and pauperism brought about by a purely artificial system of excluding the importation of foreign corn. The loss (such as it was) to the well-to-do agricultural classes meant, at the most, a deprivation of certain luxuries and comforts, and perhaps, in the case of the more needy among them, of some of the conveniences of life. To the mass of the population a difference in the price of bread meant the difference between sordidness and decency, penury and independence, health and sickness, life and death. Yet it required all the energy of a Minister of rare independence, and commanding a strong Government, to overcome the social and political influences which weighed so heavily against the many and in favour of the few.

It is sometimes said or thought that the progress of popular institutions will tend to adjust the burdens of the country in such a way that the richer classes will be overborne and the bulk of the people exempted even from their proper and equitable share. Such a state of things might be brought about under a dominion of pure mob rule, where all social and political organisation is lost sight of, and the voice of the loudest and most numerous has unrestricted sway. But this is a disease of the body politic which has its own special causes, symptoms, and remedies. It has nothing to do with the healthful condition of a State resting on the broadest basis of popular government.

In such a government, the highly organised, educated, and leisurely (because wealthy) classes will always tend to become supreme and to override all other classes in the community. It is, then, in such circumstances the most indisputable province of government to effect a counterpoise to these influences, and to secure an equable distribution of all kinds of burdens, so that the actual amount of sacrifice to the support of the State be, not only quantitatively but, really proportioned to the means of each.

(3) LOCOMOTION AND COMMUNICATION.—The question of the province of government in respect of locomotion and of communication is, again, one which must be treated primarily from the point of view of the claims of the more dependent classes of society. It is these classes which, in the conflict of the economical forces, tend to become proportionately the most numerous, and which, if revolution is to be avoided, most need protection at the hands of government.

The modern means of locomotion and communication by railways, by telegraphs, by telephones, and by steamships all tend, through the advantage they obtain from being conducted on a large scale, to produce practical monopolies. It needs no special concession of legal privileges to construct such monopolies. They spring up of themselves by the mere force of accumulated and concentrated capital. The result is a short-lived competition between project and project, company and company, and, at last, the survival of the strongest or an adjustment of terms between two or more of the rivals. The ultimate sufferer is sure to be the public, and it may be that large classes of the public may suffer so much from the monopoly-prices and conditions that, while losing all the primitive means of locomotion and communication now superseded, they are equally excluded from the use of the improved means which everywhere have taken their place.

It is here that the regulative duty of government finds its place. Government is bound to see that the bulk of the population, or even that considerable classes of the population, are not put at an undue disadvantage by the improvements of which the wealthier classes make so great and profitable a use. It may be a question whether this interference is best exercised by the government acquiring the actual proprietorship of the great undertakings in question, or whether it suffices to prescribe by general law, and by occasional legislation, and by acts of administration, what enterprises shall be permitted, and on what conditions, and within what limits of time and place.

The question of one or another mode of interposition will turn upon political considerations which must vary with the occasion and the state of society. There is one problem for a largely extended territory, like that of the United States, where official corruption seems at present beyond the reach of any popular censure or means of detection, and another for a small territory like that of Belgium or of Switzerland, where every official concerned may be always subjected to microscopic supervision by the public. The problem, again, is different for new countries like the Australian colonies, where the government is able to proceed systematically and is bound to prevent opportunities being lost for ever by the self-interest of a few, and different for an old country like England, where railways had already acquired a history and prescriptive rights before even Sir Robert Peel, in 1844, interposed to vindicate the claims of the State. The right of the State to interpose is indisputable. The duty, nature, and extent of its interposition at any particular time and place belongs to the Art, and not to the Science, of Politics.

(4) PUBLIC HEALTH.—The subject of Public Health, as belonging to the province of government, when scrutinised from the negative side, of protecting the

dependent classes of the community, presents some peculiar difficulties. On the surface there would seem to be no matter to which the force of the whole community, as wielded by government, could be more beneficially and safely directed than to the prevention of the indefinite spread of disease through the carelessness or ignorance of a definite number of private persons easily brought within the control of law. Nor, indeed, is any difficulty, theoretical or practical, experienced, so long as the intervention of government is restricted to those sanitary safeguards, or measures of precaution, as to the value of which a very large amount of popular agreement exists, and which in themselves are of so simple a nature that they can be carried out, or the neglect of them detected, without any undue intrusion on personal liberty.

The ordinary requirements of efficient drainage in towns, of wholesome and decent accommodation for the poor in towns and country villages, of suitable fever hospitals small and large, with due provisions for the insulation of cases, of a plentiful supply of pure water, for purposes of drinking, washing, and bathing, and of open spaces in towns, all fall within a range of subjects which government can conveniently take under its control with no more risk or loss than inevitably adheres to all government action, in the weakening of private energy, and in the autocratic, if not corrupt, agencies through which government must always do its work.

But the progress of medical science in the present day, and the extraordinary popular influence, even in the political field, which all specialists acquire through the confidence reposed in them because of their indisputable claims to attention in their own departments, have led to a dangerous extension of the province of government in this direction.

It may be granted that, if the whole population of a country could be handled like a regiment of soldiers or a company of prisoners, and could be subjected, at a doctor's will, to exactly equal conditions of life, not only might many of the worst diseases with which mankind is afflicted be kept at a distance, but many interesting experiments might be conducted for the purpose of elucidating the nature of certain diseases and of discovering their remedies.

The common tendency of medical practitioners is to treat mankind in this way. The political mistake committed is two-fold. In the first place, in spite of the rapid metamorphoses which medical science is constantly undergoing, and the very unsettled and unsatisfactory condition to which it has, as yet, attained, the medical profession are always so enamoured with a new theory or discovery that, if they can only agree among themselves, they are prepared to avail themselves of all the forces of Government to compel the nation to conform to it, and to try their new-fledged theory or crotchet on the largest scale.

In the second place, the medical profession, even when justified in recommending Government intervention for a sanitary end, are apt to pay no attention to the peculiar political dangers and inconveniences which this sort of intervention necessarily involves. For the doctor's purpose no sanitary measure is good for much if it is not universal and unflinchingly compulsory. But to make it either the one or the other there is needed an accomplished and ubiquitous police force, a vast extension of the magisterial jurisdiction, and a serious addition to that part of the law which, though not called criminal, has most of the penal character and consequences of criminal law without its solemnity of administration, and without jury-trial.

When it is considered that the extension of police agency means the necessity of drawing the police from a lower stratum of society in order to fill the enlarged ranks, and that the necessity of a comprehensive execution of the law means the large use of espionage and an absence of the securities accorded to an accused person in all real criminal proceedings, it is obvious that no sanitary measure of the kind here alluded to can be carried out without a very serious limitation of public liberty.

The evil is likely to be aggravated in practice through the imperfect scientific knowledge on which so vast an organisation is often set to work, and the small amount of popular attention and vigilance it usually attracts at its earlier stages. It is an incubus fixed on the neck of the people, like the Old Man of the Sea on the back of Sindbad, before they are aware of it, and it is long before they can shake it off. An army of salaried officials is called into being, deep-rooted interests are created, national habits and practices become adjusted to a state of things which has been crystallised by the silent operation of unquestioned law, and even science itself is scarcely listened to when it lifts up its voice to revoke its own decrees.

It must then, be laid down that, while the sanitary protection of the people against individual extravagances, recklessness, or perilous ignorance, is certainly within the true province of government, yet there should always be a strong antecedent presumption against the expediency of bringing any particular scheme within the range of governmental action; a presumption only to be removed when Science has said its last, and not only its first word, and when all the inconveniences of any government interference, for any purpose whatever, have been evaluated to the full.

(5) POWER AND INFLUENCE OF COMMERCIAL COMPANIES.—There is one special sort of pressure against which the bulk of the community need the protection best supplied by government, and yet which often eludes attention. The progress of society and the accumulation of wealth tend to bring about the amalgamation of the wealthier members of the community into groups which take the form of industrial or commercial associations. These associations, which, in their modern form of Joint-Stock Companies, often include a vast number of persons whose names are unknown, but whose interests are all one way, necessarily exert a considerable social and political influence, which may or may not tally with that of the bulk of the community. Their wealth and cohesion are pretty sure to secure for them a disproportionate amount of representation in Parliament, the result of which is that their interests are likely to be something more than adequately protected there.

The railway interest, in England, is said to be thus superabundantly represented in the House of Commons, a consideration which is often found to be of no small importance when a movement is made for compulsory legislation for the reduction of fares, the prevention of accidents, and the increase of the speed of workmen's trains. In the same way it has been found that the shipping interest is so largely represented that it is difficult to carry through any measure which benefits mariners at the expense of ship-owners. Similarly, the banking community is abundantly protected by its own representatives; and, both in and out of Parliament, the richer traders and shopkeepers make common cause for the suppression (if it might be) of the natural remedy against unfair prices found in co-operative stores.

Against all such undue pressure as this, exerted by the mere power of associated wealth and enterprise, it is within the province of Government to protect the great mass of the population who may be described as unmoneyed.

To accord such a protection might be a good reason in itself for a government to assume into its own hands the ownership and management of all the railways. It might also justify the institution of savings banks, insurance societies, and a vast class of institutions which would, or might, be just not remunerative enough to attract private capital, owing to the amount of labour required in collecting small contribubutions and performing small transactions, and yet which would involve very slight loss to the State. A vast number of such State institutions have long existed in Italy; and England has, of late, entered on the same path.

Of course it would be a misfortune if the intervention of the State in such matters went at all beyond the necessity of protecting classes which must always be too much weighted to compete with those who, in the race for wealth, have advantages which are in a measure due to the credit and security afforded by the

State itself. It may be hoped that the gradual improvement of the labouring class in all countries, the better distribution of profits, so as largely to raise wages, and the general improvement of the means of living, will enable workmen's unions, becoming ever larger and more intelligently managed, to do all that the State could do in these respects, and to do it better, because with a more elastic application to changing necessities. But in the meantime the task of protection cannot be deferred, and it indisputably falls within the province of government.

(6) RELIGIOUS ASSOCIATIONS.—The grounds of interference of the State with Religion have undergone a conspicuous change, in modern times. The change dates from the epoch of the Protestant Reformation; and the new system acquired fresh force in England during the Revolutionary period which intervened between the accession of Charles I. and that of William III. On the continent of Europe, the spasm of controversy between the Temporal and the Spiritual Power has lasted during the whole of the present century, having had its origin in the intellectual antecedents of the first French Revolution. It would seem that, so far as rational and scientific principles go, the time is approaching when the limits and grounds of interference by the State in religious matters will be definitely fixed.

In the meantime there are too many vested interests at stake, and too many deep-rooted sentiments, not to say prejudices, involved, for the application of newly established principles to be effected in practice, without friction and much recalcitrant opposition.

For some time to come the main task of European statesmen in reference to existing religious beliefs and organisations will be that of determining how far recognised principles ought to be applied, so as to do practical justice and satisfy reasonable and long-formed expectations.

It can only be by a slow and gradual process,—in default of revolution,—that a really logical relationship between Church and State can be attained, and it may be that in some States it never will be attained. Religious ties are so ancient,—more ancient, indeed, than the fabric of any existing State,—and their hold on the deepest elements in man's nature is so strong, and the capacity for effective organisation is so notable a characteristic of that Christian Faith which dominates in the Western world, that it must be very long before the purely secular State can place itself in a position of sheer antithesis to every form of religious association, and deal freely with them as with all other corporate communities.

The principles which, not so long ago, rendered the path of the State more clear, are beginning to be held with a wavering faith; and in countries such as France, Germany, and Switzerland, where Catholicism, Protestantism, and what may be called,—for want of a better name,—Agnosticism, exist side by side, and often in the closest civil intermixture, it is impossible for the State to do its duty to all by throwing all its moral weight into the scales of any one of the contending Faiths. In Italy, where the State is pitted against the Church in behalf of civilisation itself, and in England, where the absence of the more extreme religious antipathies and the dominant spirit of religious belief render the side taken formally by the State a matter of comparative political indifference, the problems are, again, of a wholly different kind.

But it is this very variety in the ecclesiastical problem in each of the older countries of Europe which demonstrates the impossibility of treating it by any uniform method of solution. The most that can be done is to disentangle the few broad political propositions which have been gradually evolved on the subject, and then to apply them in practice, as opportunity presents itself, it being of course the duty of the statesman, here as everywhere, to do what he can from time to time to hasten the arrival of such favourable opportunities of reform.

The main proposition on this subject which has attained the quality of an axiom, and which underlies all the ecclesiastical controversy with the secular authority in different States at the present time, is that the State is bound (1) to protect each of its individual members in the enjoyment of such religious freedom as is compatible with the religious freedom of all, and with the performance of their secular obligations by all; and (2) to protect both the mass of the population and small minorities of it against the superincumbent weight and influence of religious organisations, whether small or great.

The first of these tasks is tolerably simple in these days; though up to modern times and before the doctrine of toleration had been thoroughly preached and apprehended, it was the only problem recognised. The second task is hard; mainly because of the inordinate strength of the opposition organised to resist its being carried, and of the impalpable form of the obstacles which often have to be encountered. It seems sometimes as if the statesman were clinging with pedantic tenacity to a bare shred of principle, when he is really fighting a great battle for justice.

Thus the form the struggle takes in many European countries is, that the State claims of the subsistence of a civil marriage without Catholic rites; then the exaction from the Catholic schoolmasters of a certain minimum of secular training; the control of the Episcopate so far as appointments and discipline go; the right to inspect conventual communities and to disband disloyal confederacies; and the right to put a limit on the exemptions enjoyed by the clergy from secular burdens such as military service and taxation.

Now in all these matters it is obvious that religious bodies,—and pre-eminently the most highly organised body of all, the Church of Rome,—have indefinite opportunities of encroachment on the functions of the State, and that from the point of view of their own existence and aggrandisement they have every inducement to avail themselves to the utmost of these opportunities.

Indeed, even in England, where the ecclesiastical problem is a comparatively minute one, were the Anglican Church deprived of all the advantages which constitute it a State establishment; were the creed of the monarch treated as a matter of political indifference; were the Bishops excluded from the House of Lords; were the clergy qualified to sit, equally with nonconformist ministers, in the House of Commons; were the Act of Uniformity repealed; were Convocation substituted for Parliament as the only Church Legislature; were all special Church Courts abolished except as exercising voluntary and disciplinary jurisdiction; and even were the Church largely, or wholly, disendowed; yet, even after all this, the Church might still be the Church of the preponderant and most influential classes of English society and, by its wealth and organisation, exert an influence against which the secular State would find it very hard to contend.

It is of little use for the State to recognise a civil marriage if an influential church includes under a social ban all those whom its own ministers have not joined together. Intolerance may exist without formal law to support it, and law may even be practically impotent to grapple with it. So far as the English problem goes, it is probable that nonconforming influence and political strength will continue sufficiently united to resist any purely ecclesiastical combination which might threaten English liberty; and in any scheme of church-disestablishment and disendowment there is no doubt that pains would be taken to prevent the independent church from becoming an irresponsible social despotism.

In other countries, the problem is complicated by the extra-national aspects it has, owing to the foreign allegiance of Catholics to the Pope, and the international sympathy between Catholics in different countries which is roused into active and combined resistance when any State vindicates decisively the civil liberty of its subjects against ecclesiastical aggression.

It will not be questioned, then, that in marking out the negative province of State activity, there must be included in this province the protection of its citizens against ecclesiastical aggressions of all sorts, whether this protective power be exerted by provisional but

sharply-defined recognition, as by 'Concordats' and
'Organic Articles'; or by incorporation in the structure of the secular constitution of some parts of the
ecclesiastical organisation, for the sake of a more constant and subtle control, as in England now; or by
equally ignoring and equally permitting all forms of
religious organisation, as in Greece, Ireland, the
United States, and the British colonies.

It is more difficult to determine the province of
Government in respect of matters in which the *positive*
welfare and progress of the country is concerned, and
not merely the protection of large classes of the population against undue pressure due to the forces generated
by civilisation and by the social organisation themselves.
It is in respect of positive good to be sought by governmental intervention that all the general objections to
State action specially apply. It is here that the danger
is presented of paralysing private enterprise, and so of
arresting beneficial experiments and consequent inventions; of indefinite extravagance, waste, and secret
corruption, without adequate checks; of extending the
range of government patronage to a degree which not
only infects the moral character of the whole public
service, but reacts most prejudicially on the habits of
the executive authority at its very centre and tends to
make all government primarily a machinery for illicit
self-advancement.

In view of these dangers, not only must there be a
constant presumption against the expediency of government occupying itself with tasks which can be done
by private persons or associations, but there is need
for the exercise of the most unremitting vigilance in

respect of all the work of which, for one reason or another, government assumes the direct management. Furthermore, the consideration of the special dangers to be guarded against affords a means of marking out the class of operations to which direct government activity can be applied with least risk and most unmixed advantage.

Such will be those operations the conduct of which is simple and uniform and capable of being thoroughly and easily understood by the general body of the population. There must not be room for a great variety of rules and methods of work at different points. Opportunities for the exercise of discretion must be as far as possible avoided. If the matter have a financial side, the statement of accounts must be able to be mastered without special or professional knowledge. If patronage has to be exercised, the exercise of it should be rendered as independent as possible of irresponsible choice on the part of the central executive.

Subject to these tests, the sort of tasks which will profit most from being undertaken by Government will be those in which uniformity, certainty, punctuality, and the cheapness which may come from a monopoly without temptation to use it for profit, are such important considerations that they outweigh all the general objections against government intervention. Whether such considerations are in any given state and condition of society a counterpoise to such objections will depend upon the circumstances of the case. Thus in a very early primitive society, or in a growing and simply organised Colony, the people are so near to the government that the government is little more than a large commercial company of which all the population are members. In such a condition of things government can with advantage do much which, in a more complex stage of society, might become the source of indefinite corruption and national indolence. The main objection to government intervention in this case is, that the habit of relying on government is difficult to shake off, and becomes more and more vicious just as the difficulty of exchanging it for independent enterprise increases.

It will be admitted generally in the present day that the management of post and telegraph communication, and a very considerable control of the railways, satisfies the above requirements, as supplying a test of what work government should undertake. In speaking of the negative reasons for government activity it was noticed that government has a necessary function to discharge in guarding the national soil against absorption by a limited part of the population. One remedy for this was said to be the assumption of proprietorship of all the land of the country by the State itself. But, in this case, as in that of the ownership of the railways, if this should be resorted to it must be remembered that the government cannot itself act as a land-proprietor or railway-director (though this is done in many European countries) without leading to a transgression of the principles just laid down as defining the area of the positive functions of government.

The management of an agricultural estate, and, still more, of building land and household property, and only in a less degree the direction of a railway, calls for all that incessant personal exercise of discretion and of capacity for suddenly adjusting unpremeditated means to new ends, which implies, if the work is performed by an agent, the highest species of confidence on the part of his principal and employer.

When such delicate and varied tasks are extended all over a great country, according as the task of central superintendence comes to be delegated through an endless hierarchy of subordinates, the possibility of popular control by a representative Assembly is out of the question. The Government of the day is itself in the hands of the permanent officials, who alone hold in their hands the vast skeins of business so ready to be tangled and so difficult to pass on from hand to hand. If there is incompetency, fraud, or mismanagement, it may be only an accident which discovers it, and, as often as not, inquiry is checked, through the danger that in so intricate a system the wrong persons will bear the penalty of an exposed flaw. Thus popular criticism is either lethargic or spasmodically unjust, and the government becomes a huge organ of popular demoralisation and degradation.

The remedy, of course, is, for the government to retain in its own hands no industrial or commercial undertaking of the sort indicated, but in all cases to make fair and public contracts for their management by others. The terms of such contracts can be understood by all, and the modes of performance, expressing themselves chiefly in figures and accounts, can also be understood by most. Even in this case, inspectors of work and agents empowered to decide on questions of repairs, improvements, and prices, or fares, will have to be appointed and superintended by government. But they will be comparatively few in number and their reports can be systematically arranged and published at brief intervals so as to reduce the inevitable dangers from State-managed labour and capital to the smallest amount.

There is yet to be considered, in connexion with the positive functions of government, the practice common in most European States of imparting to the Executive government a certain measure of control over commerce and of giving certain legal privileges to a National Bank or Banks. The origin of these privileges, and perhaps the continuing justification of them, is the fact that not only is the government,—as was before seen,—the greatest capitalist in the country, but, in the case of most of the older States, it is the greatest debtor in the country. The result is that its financial movements, in making occasional arrangements with its creditors, altering its rates of interest, funding its debts, increasing them and paying them off and transferring them, constitute it, as of necessity, a Bank almost in spite of itself. The Government cannot avoid discharging many of the most important functions of a true Bank, and when a National Bank is constituted by law for the purpose of being the agent of Government in the investment of its capital, in the payment of interest (that is, of dividends) to its creditors, and in the receipt and retention on deposit of its revenue, this is only a mechanical expression of an existing fact,—an expression of the greatest convenience to the commercial public.

This is so because, through the Government allying itself with a Bank, or calling a Bank into being, or subsidising a Bank for its own purposes (as was done originally with the Bank of England) it enables that

Bank to employ the government funds for the benefit of mercantile loans. This may seem a startling proposition, but it is a true one; and it will be found on examination that if the governments of England and France withdrew from all concern in the Banks of England and of France and established no substitutes, the loss to commerce of the amount of floating credit available at a moment's notice on trustworthy security would be almost incalculably great. Thus the interference of governments in banking is a necessary consequence of taxation, of national debts, and of expenditure on an enormous scale. The National Bank is only the material witness to this, which, by a sort of innocent legerdemain, is made profitable to all parties, and serves simultaneously the commercial public and the government.

It need scarcely be added to the remarks that have been made in respect to the management by government of land and of railways that all interference by government in commerce, except for the purpose of protecting, on principles already laid down, the more dependent and helpless classes of society, is to be looked upon with the greatest suspicion, and circumscribed and restricted wherever it has taken root. There is no doubt but that government will in the future be wholly expelled from this sphere, from which it has, during the last century, been everywhere slowly withdrawing.

Closely akin to the claim of governments to interfere in the supervision and control of commerce, is that to interfere in and regulate Navigation. Up to a recent date, when the domination of Free Trade doctrines finally abolished all the national privileges of a commercial kind formerly monopolised by the shipping of each

State, the governmental control of navigation was merely a necessary means of enforcing the policy of the State. At the present time the only grounds for exerting such a control are :—first, the importance of distinguishing national and foreign shipping in time of war; secondly, the necessity of carrying into effect customs laws, laws of quarantine, and harbour regulations; and thirdly, the protection of the dependent class of sailors against the effect of avaricious contracts of a fraudulent nature, against ill-treatment, and against hazards of the sea brought about by the carelessness or reckless loading of vessels by ship-owners.

The intervention of the State for all these purposes not only seems to be justified by common political considerations, but, being of a purely preventive and corrective kind, is little exposed to the abuses to which the direct management by the government of large concerns has been seen to be so obviously open. Nor is it plain that intervention of this limited sort weakens, in any considerable, or at least in a proportionate, degree, the independent energy of private ship-owners. There is, no doubt, the recurrent difficulty that superintendence of a large mercantile marine implies a vast amount of inspection and the employment of a large body of inspectors of different grades. Against this really valid objection can be opposed only the compensating advantages which are sought; and the evils which this objection recognises are much reduced when they are not ignored, and when the amplest opportunity is afforded for popular censure and for the detection and exemplary punishment of illicit transactions in the name of the government.

Of late years the duties of the State in respect of National Education have been much debated, and, in almost all countries where the question has arisen, the practical decision has been in favour of recognising the duty of the State to enforce on all its subjects the acquisition of the elements of primary education. The arguments which have finally prevailed have been that the children born into a State have a moral right to claim, first of their parents and, if they fail, of the State, to be put into a condition to understand the duties obligatory upon them and to earn an independent livelihood; and that the State has a corresponding moral duty,—as it has, furthermore, a cogent interest,—to provide the opportunity for the training thus claimed, and to vindicate the claim of the child, if need be, against the parents themselves.

These broad arguments have, no doubt, been perplexed in their application by the peculiar traditions or prejudices existing in different countries in reference to the necessity of including some kind of religious instruction within the range of primary education imposed by the State, and to the degree and kinds of compulsory force which may be legitimately exerted in order to render it effectual and universal. If once it is admitted that a certain *minimum* of education is the right of every child, and the duty of the State, the remaining questions as to where the *minimum* is to be fixed, of what it ought to be composed, and how the duty of the State in this matter ought to be performed in the special circumstances of each particular country, are questions of political Art and not of political Science.

There yet remains a class of topics in respect of which the functions of the State are more indubitable than any of those hitherto alluded to. These topics are such as directly concern the subsistence of the State itself, and its maintenance against disorder within and assaults or injustice from without. They are (1) the management of the Police and the administration of Justice; (2) the management of the Army and Navy; (3) the collection of the Taxes.

As to all these matters the objections to governmental management of large and complex concerns apply in the fullest measure, and it has been seen, while discussing the subject of 'Local Government,' that one of the advantages of decentralising government is that the means of inspection, and the direct responsibility of the administrative agents, are increased. Such local delegacy can be applied with marked advantage to the Police, to important departments of the administration of Justice, to some supplementary departments of the national Army, and even to the collection of Taxes for purposes of purely local expenditure.

But there will still fall on the shoulders of the central government a sufficient burden of direct administration, in respect of all these matters, to open out the floodgates of every form of abuse and corruption in default of incessant public vigilance. This vigilance, however, must be exerted in a way to co-operate with truly conscientious statesmen, and not so as to hamper endlessly, and thereby to weaken dangerously, all their best efforts. A strong government is one which can always rely on adequate and faithful popular support, even when it is exerting to the full its most centralised powers; and the best government is weakened indefinitely when every exertion of power is popularly mistaken for aggressive violence, and comprehensive activity within its appropriate limits for a treasonable conspiracy against popular rights.

427

CHAPTER XI.

REVOLUTIONS IN STATES.

THERE is something anomalous in the attempt to incorporate a treatment of the Science of Revolution into the study of the Science of Politics. It might seem, in the first place, inconsistent with the very notion of Revolution that it should be classed and organised, by anticipation, as an ordinary or necessary phenomenon; and the anarchical elements on which it rests might be held to exclude the possibility of its being made the subject of precise scientific statement. In the second place it might seem that no State or government could subsist if it contemplated Revolution in advance, and that the attempt to do so by including it in the provisions of the constitution deprives it of its essential character as an incalculable, and not a calculable and regular, phase of political existence.

Nevertheless there is no doubt that it is round the theory of the right or duty of revolution, and of the rights and duties which spring from it, that the most celebrated controversies on theoretical politics have been waged. It seems to have been during the Parliamentary struggle with Charles I. that the first notion of an abstract constitution was conceived and worked out by Harrington and his political associates. It was the revolutionary resistance to the claims asserted by the Stuart dynasty to have a 'right divine to govern wrong' that called forth the imperishable arguments of Hobbes and Locke on the basis of all government and on the Social Contract.

It was the revolt of the American colonies which called forth the political propositions broadly formulated in the Declaration of Independence and elaborated in argumentative detail by the authors of the 'Federalist.' It was the French Revolution which in 1791 originated the Declaration of the Rights of Man, and which suggested Burke's 'Reflections' and the replies of Thomas Paine and Sir James Mackintosh.

It is, again, the American Secession War which has, in our own day, established on deeper bases than ever the doctrines of political right and duty in a constitutionally-governed State, and has given a new spring to theoretical speculations on the true nature of the constitution of the United States, as distinguished from that of a federal government. The recent revolutionary movements in Poland, Russia, the provinces of the Ottoman empire, Germany, and Ireland have kept alive political controversy on the profoundest topics of constitutional existence, but without, as yet, obtaining any complete or satisfactory solution, even in theory, of the problems raised.

This indisputable connexion of revolutionary facts with the history of political speculation in modern times certainly suggests that the study of some of the most notable revolutionary agitations of the past two or three centuries may be expected to throw light upon the class of permanent truths with which scientific politics alone deals. It may be that revolution itself will, as constitutional government grows, become an anachronism. There is reason to suppose it will, because the characteristic of every good constitution is to provide, by anticipation, for its own gradual amendment, and to supersede the necessity for violent and cataclysmic demonstrations of the popular will.

But, while these happier times are still being expected, it may be profitable to turn to account the chief revolutionary epochs which have been of late both the occasions and the tests of political controversy, and to endeavour to remove from their history the spurious coating in which party spirit and popular ignorance have enveloped it.

It is not necessary to go further back than the seventeenth century of the Christian era, and it would be unprofitable to dwell on any revolutions which have arisen in States having no shadow of constitutional government. The revolutions of Greece and Rome, and of early monarchical France and England have, no doubt, their important lessons. But the more recent revolutions in constitutionally-governed States, or,—as with France at the close of last century,—in States infected by a revolutionary spirit manifested in other States with which they had political relations, convey all these lessons, and others besides.

While, then, the history of the world's political revolutions in their entirety would be full of profit as a contribution to political science, the field it would cover would be too large to form only a part of another treatise. It is sufficient for purposes of scientific exactness to concentrate the attention on those revolutions which have a distinct bearing on the characteristic aspects of modern political society in some of the most advanced and advancing States.

Such revolutions are that of England, beginning with the Parliamentary Wars against Charles I. and ending with the establishment on the throne of the Orange, and afterwards of the Hanoverian, dynasty; that of the American thirteen colonies, concluded by the recognition of their independence by Great Britain; that of France, beginning in 1789 and concluded (to fix a purely arbitrary date) by the battle of Waterloo in 1815; the American Secession war from 1861 to 1865; and the revolutionary movements at different epochs in the present century in Poland, Hungary, Russia, Germany, the Ottoman empire, and, it is almost necessary to add, Ireland.

By way of preface, it is necessary to notice that revolution is of three kinds, each of which is usually strongly marked, so as to render it clearly distinguishable from either of the others.

A revolution may be, first, essentially anarchical, that is, it may proceed from a general undisciplined temper in the revolting population, and be directed to the upsetting of the existing government, or government and constitution combined, without those who conduct it having any views as to substitutes for one or the other, and being in fact other than indifferent as to the political prospect of the future. This form of revolution is likely to be chiefly manifested in a primitive stage of civilisation, when the advantages of orderly and settled government have not been long experienced, and when these advantages, indeed, only exist in a moderate degree, from the political weakness of the government and from the imperfectly organised state of society.

A second form of revolution is when no thought is entertained of reverting to anarchy, but the object of those who take part in it is, primarily, either to change the personality of the government or to resist some legislative or executive measure. This measure may presumedly be in accordance with the constitution, in which case the movement is directed to bring about a new interpretation of constitutional rules, or a modification of the constitution, or a better use of discretionary powers on the part of the authorities complained of: or the measure complained of may be contrary to the rules or spirit of the constitution, in which case the object of the movement is to re-enforce the constitution and establish it on surer foundations.

A third form of revolution is where the object, conscious or unconscious, is to change the constitution itself from its foundations and to introduce a new form of government.

The confusion of these different forms under the general name of Revolution has been rife with much political misapprehension, having, at times, serious results.

A caution has, however, to be interposed, to guard against the supposition that any revolution can be readily classed under one or other of these heads without looking below the surface, or even, in certain cases, reverting to recent historical conditions. Thus it seldom happens that the leaders of a revolutionary movement and the great mass of their followers are exactly of the same mind, or that they continue long to be of the same mind, if they were so momentarily; or that the facts resulting from the movement itself do not undergo such a change as to produce divisions of parties and to alter the entire complexion and object of the revolution.

In fact, this is one of the most calamitous incidents of a revolutionary period,—that, the usual landmarks being removed, all the anarchical and undisciplined dispositions latent in the community have free course, and assume a positive energy which is injurious to the cause of wise political reconstruction. There ensues for a time a condition of flux and chronic instability highly favourable to fanatical parties, to usurpers, to pretenders to power of all sorts.

Every historical revolution, both secular and religious, has witnessed phenomena of this sort,—from the incessant changes of leadership which took place during the protracted revolution during the last hundred years of the Roman Republic, to the Anabaptists of Münster, the two Napoleonic *régimes* and the 'Commune' in Paris, and the more extreme modern Separationists in Ireland.

It may happen, indeed, that this very tendency of revolution to generate within itself a temporary organisation, having its roots, not in the broad political instincts and exigencies of the country, but in some superficial and partial sentiment, may act as a preservative against prolonged anarchy. It is possible, too, that the man, or party, or section of opinion, which for the moment comes to the top may represent some valuable truth or long despised cause, which is recalled to life with lasting benefit to the State. He or it teaches his or its lesson, leaves his or its impress, and passes away.

There is, too, a really close connexion between the grounds of revolution above distinguished which prevents them from being always separable in theory or in practice. Thus in cases where a reigning dynasty represents particular principles of government, a change in the dynasty may necessarily involve a change in the constitution. In autocratically governed States this is likely to be especially true, and the truth of it is the only conceivable apology for political assassination.

Furthermore, the change of a dynasty as a consequence of a revolution, whether democratical or aristocratical, is itself not without necessary effects on the constitution. There is always a doubt as to the theoretical foundation of an existing form of government, and this doubt is most prevalent and harassing when a dynasty has long occupied a throne on no other pretext except that of hereditary descent.

In one sense this is the strongest foundation of all,—so long as popular criticism is not aroused,—because it carries all the pretensions due to a mysterious origin in the far past, and to a traditional reverence almost amounting to superstition. But when once popular criticism is fairly aroused, and, owing to some conflict, the person of the Sovereign is treated with contumely, and the dynasty displaced in fact, a new condition of the popular consciousness supervenes. Government goes on without interruption, and it is found that its basis is not in a person, or in a family, or in an historical accident, but in the will of the people, or, it may be, in the will of some narrow and autocratic section of the people, who represent themselves, and are really felt to be, the vicegerents of the people.

Thus, in the course of changing the personality of the government, a constitutional change has also been effected. It is likely enough (as has happened over and over again) that the new dynasty, sovereign, or ruler, introduced to take the place of the old, will be formally bound to recognise the new source of power, and to repudiate the principles of his predecessor. This new obligation and act of repudiation becomes henceforth a constitutional bulwark, and is the starting point from which future revolutions take their rise.

In the same way there is a genuine anarchical element present in all revolutions, inasmuch as they can only be distinguished from mere local seditions by proceeding from a broadly diffused popular determination; and this implies the co-operation of a vast number of persons who can appreciate (like the Kentish men in Jack Cade's time) the misgovernment from which they suffer, but are ignorant of the necessary conditions of government to which they owe the security of their lives and property and the maintenance of their political existence.

It is the main function and duty of revolutionary leaders to avail themselves of their inordinate influence to check the extravagance and fanaticism which comes from this ignorance, and to do their utmost to teach their followers to distinguish the evils they are entitled to rid themselves of, from the equable and inevitable pressure which belongs to the very existence even of the best and best-administered Government.

The fact that rational efforts after change open the door for irrational impulses in the direction of mere disorder is aggravated by the presence, in every community, of a certain class, not numerically important in quiet times, who have a direct personal interest in relaxing the bonds of society, and in weakening the action of the Executive Authority.

In the continental countries of Europe, where the boundary lines between State and State are usually of a very artificial kind, prolonged anarchy in one State results in its collecting within its territory all the outlawed scum of surrounding States. Life and property become unsafe, the police become impotent, and the magistracy overawed; the taxes cannot be collected, and the army is recruited by foreign adventurers; while, all the time, the attainment of the real political object which is at the root of the revolutionary movement is impeded, rather than advanced, by these wholly extraneous incidents. The worst is, that the revolutionary reformers, however good their cause, have to suffer from the obloquy properly attaching to such needless disruption of order. This was especially the case during the time of the Paris Commune in 1870, and has occurred repeatedly in the revolutionary movements in the European provinces of the Ottoman empire.

In the light of these observations, bearing on the distinctions between the leading causes of revolution and on the modes in which these causes often co-operate or simultaneously present themselves, it will be expedient to refer to the chief characteristics of the series of revolutions already enumerated, which, in the aggregate, may be said to have prepared the way for the existing constitutions and mutual relationships of the chief modern civilised States.

In English politics, the revolution period,—extending from the breaking out of the Parliamentary War against Charles I. to the accession of William III.,—has supplied the main principles which have been applied by statesmen and political authors to the discussion of the subject of revolution generally. It was Thomas Paine who pointed out that this limitation of view was the main ground of the erroneous reasoning which underlies Edmund Burke's otherwise magnificent 'Reflections on the French Revolution.'

It would seem, in much of the reasoning contained in these Reflections, that the author conceived no other way of effecting a revolution, and no other just cause of revolution, than those which could be illustrated by the history of what has been called the Whig Revolution, of 1688: In fact, Burke does not seem to have connected in his mind and in his arguments the whole of the revolutionary events, extending over more than half a century, of which the final expulsion of the Stuarts in the person of James II., and the establishment of a new dynasty by Act of Parliament was merely the climax. If he had looked at all these events in their sequence and connexion, he would have seen that the lessons they taught were wholly peculiar to England at that time, and might have little application either to another country or to another age.

From the first distinct outcry against the high-handed proceedings of Charles I.—expressed in the refusal of 'Ship-money' and in the 'Grand Remonstrance'—to the trial of the seven bishops, the foundation of the English Revolution was a conception, right or wrong, of an English constitution to which the King and the Parliament were equally subject.

It was, indeed, no new thing to make such appeal to laws and customs which the monarch could not violate with immunity. The reiterated enforcement of Magna Charta and similar constitutional formularies of ancient repute; the repeated use of the impeachment of Ministers of the Crown for acts done in the monarch's name; the dethronement by a quasi-judicial process, however rough and irregular, of Edward II. and Richard II.; the successful resistance to the aggressions on Parliament attempted by Queen Elizabeth, and the disallowance of torture as applied by the Privy Council for the purpose of obtaining evidence; and, finally, the stern check imposed on James I. in the matter of monopolies; all these were but anticipations of the practical belief in the existence of a constitution to the requirements of which King and Parliament, as well as the people, were all equally amenable.

It is true that, as is the case in all revolutions, soon after the purely constitutional position had been taken up by the Parliament, and public order was suspended in consequence of the King's firm stand against concession, religious differences played an important part both in widening the feud and in determining the form of the temporary reconstruction. The Puritan movement, whether in the form of mere non-conformity or in the more organised character which it assumed in the hands of the Presbyterians and the Independents, co-operated with the purely constitutional movement, but did not merge it in itself.

No doubt, in the early days of the Commonwealth, a rage for positive legislation set in, which was rather an anticipation, by some two or three centuries, of the progress of the constitution than a denial or contradiction of it. But a passion for positive legislation is a result of such a disturbance of a familiar national routine as brings people face to face with long-seated but real evils and gives them a novel experience of the act of law-making. During the past half century in England the spirit of legislation has been almost rampant, and the Acts of Parliament probably far exceed in volume and mass all previous legislation from the time of the Conquest. Yet the constitution has been maintained on the same general lines, and has always been regarded, by the most opposed political parties, with almost superstitious reverence.

Of course it is true that the establishment of the Protectorate involved a very distinct alteration in the form of government; but the founders of it were, probably, incapable of estimating how great was the constitutional change. For them the true English constitution was not so much to be found in the hereditary monarchy, and in a House of Lords, as in the general principle of a popular representative assembly; in broad intelligible principles concerning the free exercise of religious worship, and free speech; and in exemption from illegal taxation, from arbitrary imprisonment, from central executive usurpation, and from unjust State trials.

These principles were patently essential; and were guaranteed by ancient traditions; though one Sovereign and another, and, most of all, the Stuarts, had in practice outraged them all. So long as they were vindicated, the constitution, or all that was vital and precious in it, was maintained inviolate. If they were impaired, there was nothing worth maintaining.

The result of the Catholic proclivities of James II., following upon the moral laxity of the reign of Charles II., was to recombine the secular and religious revolutionaries. The only points round which they could momentarily meet were the elementary constitutional principles which were independent of any particular dynasty, as they had already nearly proved themselves to be (and in truth are) even independent of the institution of an hereditary monarchy and a House of Lords.

The Whigs who, in a somewhat cold and dispassionate manner, conducted the final negotiations which resulted in the abdication of James II., were in fact intermediaries between those who were earnest on both sides, whether as ardent protestants or as clear-sighted republicans. As a dominant faction, they cared little for spiritual religion, and had the reverse of any class interest in abolishing social and hereditary distinctions. Their natural object was to rehabilitate the constitution with the help of more ardent reformers than themselves, whilst retaining the direction of affairs in their own hands. Thus the revolution ended in reinstating the essential principles of the constitution as finally embodied in the Bill of Rights, and in perpetuating the outward forms of monarchical and aristocratic institutions as a testimony to the claims of formal continuity.

It will be convenient for purposes of contrast, though at the cost of chronological order, to oppose to the consideration of the English Revolution of the seventeenth century the consideration of the French revolution at the close of the eighteenth century. Burke committed a double error in first supposing that the French in 1789 had anything deserving the name of a constitution to appeal to, as against the depravation of monarchical institutions in the person of Louis XVI.; and, secondly, in assuming that all political disorders can be cured by orderly processes recognised and implicitly provided for within the limits of the constitution itself.

It is true that the latent political discontent flamed out into revolution before the third Estate had had an opportunity of making its constitutional voice fairly heard. But an Assembly which has not been summoned for some three centuries can only by force of a strained antiquarian superstition be reckoned as part of the existing constitution.

The act of summoning it was a desperate measure devised to stave off national bankruptcy with some show of political regularity. That it was alien to the spirit of the despotic and aristocratic rule which, by long prescription, in fact governed France, was instantly proved when it tried to set itself to work to express the real voice of the people without allowing itself to be swamped by the privileged classes already in possession of the Government.

Thus, while the old feudal constitution, which recognised the political and representative rights of the freemen, had long been dead, the joint aristocratic and monarchical constitution, which had gradually superseded it, was in the act of perishing by its own corruptions. It was found, by the experience of a day, that what was dead could not be made alive again, and what was dying could not be saved. There were too many distinct and reasonable causes for local disaffection throughout the country for a moment's delay to be brooked.

In the case of the English revolution the House of Commons had not only been continuously sitting, even in the reigns of the most despotic and overreaching monarchs, but it had, amidst all obstacles, retained and enlarged its right to control taxation and to check the action of the executive. The usurpations of the Plantagenet and Tudor kings were conducted, not by rendering the House obsolete, but by domineering over it, or by corrupting it, or by unfairly influencing some of its prominent leaders. Thus the way was kept clear for a reformation of government; and neither the king himself nor the ingenious crown-lawyers and judges, whose courteous services he usually succeeded in purchasing, could deny the broad claims of the House and of its members to independence. The true constitution can thus scarcely even be said to have been in suspense,—not even when Henry VIII. succeeded in procuring Act after Act of Parliament for his own personal and family aims, or when Charles I. appeared on the floor of the House and ordered the seizure of the Five Members. The constitution might be outraged, but it could not be ignored.

In France, on the other hand, a constitution could not be established by galvanising a mummy. New political sentiments had to be created among the people, new machinery had to be constructed, and new relationships between the people and the government had to be established. And this all had to be done while the crumbling edifice of the discredited constitution had not yet quite disappeared; while the mass of the population were hungry, excited, and ignorant; and while surrounding nations were becoming fearful and aggressive, from the belief that the revolutionary doctrines prevalent in France would shortly extend to themselves. It is obvious that no analogy whatever exists between this condition of things in France and the condition of things in England a century earlier.

A natural question is suggested as to whether the

revolution in the American colonies,—which only preceded by a few years the first French revolution,—inclined rather to the English type in the seventeenth or to the French type at the close of the eighteenth century. Everything points to the fact that the English and not the French type was before the eyes, and in the hearts, of the leaders of the American War of Independence; and that in the conduct of their revolution they were more English than the English themselves. There is less of religious fanaticism, less of the effect of mere personal influences, less disregard for the consequences of violent political change visible in the American revolution than in the English. In every step of the American revolution, there is a conspicuous appeal to unassailable principles (though often wrongly formulated and dangerously wide), and the recognition of existing ties, obligations, and conventional relations, which betoken calmness of head and deliberateness of intention. The American people rebelled,—but it was in order (as they took it) to repel novel and tyrannical invasions on their long-established and often-chartered rights of Local Government and self-taxation, not to obtain a licentious independence, and still less to enjoy the supposed sweets of anarchy, or even of a newly invented form of government.

An instructive contrast to all three revolutions is afforded by the history of the Secession war. The best arguments alleged by the Southern slave-holders for seceding from the Union were, first, that the right of dissolving the Union by withdrawing from it was an inherent right of every State, and had never been expressly withdrawn by the constitution; and, secondly, that in every free government, each member of the State is entitled, as by an indefeasible right, to withdraw from connexion with it in case he regards the conduct of the government or the nature of the constitution as incompatible with his own physical and moral existence.

Mr. Calhoun had formulated the first of these positions as early as December 27, 1837. In his speech upon the Rights of States ('Works,' vol. iii. 155), he said :

" The only remedy is in the States Rights doctrines ; and, if
" those who profess them in slaveholding States do not rally
" to them as their political creed, and organise as a party
" against the fanatics in order to put them down, the South
" and West will be compelled to take the remedy into their
" own hands. They will then stand justified in the sight of
" God and man, and what in that event will follow, no mortal
" can anticipate."

So far as relates to the federal constitution of the Union which Mr. Calhoun here treats of, no general question on the abstract right and nature of revolution was involved. And events have decided on an interpretation of the constitution adverse to Mr. Calhoun's views.

But, as to the larger proposition included in Mr. Calhoun's statement that a mere discontent (however profound) with the conduct of the government in power, with the working of the constitution, or with the constitution itself, can of itself justify revolution, either as a matter of political expediency or as one of morality, to maintain the affirmative is to go far beyond the most extreme revolutionary doctrines which have ever prevailed in France or now prevail anywhere in Europe.

No reasonable person attempts to justify or recommend a revolution except as a last and desperate resource. It must be the only conceivable remedy; a probably successful remedy; and a remedy for an evil so great as to be incompatible with moral and political existence deserving of the name.

To cite the language of one who was a trenchant reformer of political abuses and who wrote before the Secession War:

" The evils must have become intolerable before the resist-
" ance is to be attempted; the parties whose rights are invaded
" must first exhaust every peaceful and orderly and lawful
" means of redress. An insurrection is only to be justified
" by a necessity which leaves no alternative; and the proba-
" bility of success is to be weighed in order that a hopeless
" attempt may not involve the community in distress and
" confusion."

Every one of the tests was decisively against the case of the Southern States. It is only necessary to read the Declaration put forth by the Southern Congress at Richmond, and to compare it with the liberal provision for representation of the whole population of all the States in the House of Representatives, and of each State equally in the Senate, and with the equal share of all in the election of the President, in order to see how wide is the difference between the position of the Southern Confederacy and their forefathers who founded the American Union. The Declaration says that

" we fell back upon the right for which the Colonies main-
" tained the War of the Revolution and which our heroic
" forefathers asserted to be clear and inalienable."

DECLARATION OF THE SOUTHERN STATES. 445

It further says:

" Compelled by a long series of oppressive and tyrannical
" acts, culminating at last in the selection of a President and
" Vice-President by a party confessedly sectional, and hostile
" to the South and her institutions, these States withdrew
" from the former Union and formed a new Confederate
" alliance, as an independent government based on the proper
" relations of capital and labour."

The truth is that according as popular institutions grow, revolution should become more and more needless and impossible. Representative government, of a broad and really effective kind, combined with ample facilities for its own amendment, and for any amount of constitutional reconstruction, must secure the adoption of every change which is really an object of determined, persistent, and general desire. Movements for the carrying out of partial ends, for the abrogation of laws injuriously affecting special classes, and objections to the policy of government, felt (it may be) throughout large sections of the community, will always continue to manifest themselves; and they are signs of health rather than of disease. The public press, the right of public meeting and of free association, will test the sincerity of agitators, and accustom them to patient and deliberate, as well as mutually tolerant, habits of action. Sedition will always be possible, though more and more rare.

The only cases in which these principles and prospects seem out of place is where a distant—or even a near, but alien—dependency (such as Ireland, or it might be the Channel Islands) is governed by a popular legislature sitting at a distance. In such a case, no doubt, a widespread movement of discontent may partake rather of the character of revolution than of sedition, and deserve proportionate respect, not to say precautions. Whether a particular revolution satisfies the tests just laid down, is a question of practical politics and does not belong to political science. The current revolutionary movements in Russia, Poland, the European provinces of the Ottoman empire, and Germany all belong to the type of the first French revolution, the object being rather to found a new constitution than to re-establish a lost or weakened one.

CHAPTER XII.

RIGHT AND WRONG IN POLITICS.

THERE is no serious thinker at the present day who, if pointedly questioned, would deny the applicability of the terms *Right, Wrong, Duty, Conscience, Morality,* and *Immorality* to the conduct of States and governments as well as to that of individual men and women. It is true, indeed, that,—if these terms are used loosely and thoughtlessly enough in pronouncing on the conduct of private persons, where the problem, if any, is tolerably simple in its elements, and where most of the conditions of it are capable of being ascertained and reduced to a certainty,—in the larger political field the inquiry is highly complicated, and large classes of the most essential facts are wholly out of the reach of the judicial investigator.

Nevertheless it is manifest that in all quarters in which public criticism resides—whether in the newspaper press, in the more laboured and deliberate magazine, on the election hustings, or in the political text-book—the rightness or wrongness of the acts of legislatures or administrators is brought to the bar of a strict public opinion with quite as much decision and explicitness as is the expediency or prudence of the same acts. This use of language is at all events a testimony to the existence of a widely diffused consciousness that States and governments have no immaculate conception.

The fact is, indeed, so obvious, when thus stated, that it is almost forgotten how wholly absent from the ante-Christian theory and practice of politics in all Western communities was the notion of a purely moral standard of action, and that perhaps Christianity has triumphed almost as signally in moralising secular politics as in spiritualising individual and domestic life.

The readers of Coleridge's lay-sermon on 'The Bible the Statesman's Manual,' as well as of the late Professor Maurice's ' Prophets and Kings of Old Testament History,' will recall the lesson, nowhere more impressively taught than in the writings of these authors, that the Bible has had an almost incalculable influence in swaying political judgments, that it was providentially designed to have that influence, and that political judgments for all time can never escape from an obligation to the immutable principles pre-eminently, if not exclusively, revealed to the Jewish Church.

In spite of these incontestable facts, there is a difference of some importance and magnitude between the ethical standard and even the ethical motive, when it is applied to vast communities consisting of an indefinite and indiscriminate number of individual persons organised for the ends implied in the complex notion conveyed by the term *State*, and when it is applied to the individual life of private persons.

It is obvious, for instance, that in a despotically governed community, where the king or emperor is above the law, and makes the law as he wills, and executes it when and how he pleases, the rightness and wrongness of acts of State are in fact synonymous with the rightness and wrongness of the autocrat's acts; and the critical problem is reduced to the same mode of determination as in ordinary judgments on the acts of private men.

But where the government is of a more complex kind, or perhaps of an extremely complex kind—depending, say, in the case of each of its acts, on a concert of chambers, of representatives, and of various executive authorities, there being much discussion and finally broad divisions of opinion—the unity of conduct seems to be so disturbed or confused as almost to exclude the idea of moral responsibility as residing anywhere in the nation at large.

Considering that the tendency of modern times is certainly in the direction of an increase of complication in the machinery of government, partly on account of an access of intricacy in the concerns to be provided for, partly on account of a higher susceptibility to the claims of a distributive justice, it would be a most grave conclusion to arrive at, that moral judgments were to be paralysed just at the moment when they need to be quickened into more active life.

Fortunately, experience is the other way; and there is no doubt that the very same causes which have made modern political constitutions intricate in their structure, and perhaps somewhat slow and cumbrous in their action, have vitalised the moral energy of the critical public everywhere, and are compelling governments to comply with a purely moral standard of action to an extent which even a hundred years ago, and à fortiori, in pagan times, would have seemed to the moralist a mere gorgeous dream.

M. Rénan[1] has pointed out, with a force which he might have borrowed from some of the most orthodox modern Christian apologists, that the interval of the Roman Empire was in fact an interpolation of a cosmopolitan and denationalised society between the intensely patriotic worlds of the Roman and Greek republics and those of the modern European States.

But M. Rénan and Christian apologists place very different interpretations on the phenomenon they combine to illustrate. Whether the interval was a merely human cause of the growth of Christianity, or was a divine and necessary preparation for it, there is no question but that, as the new Christian States arose, an ethical element was found to be indissolubly bound up with them, for which no place was found in republican Rome or even in philosophical Greece.

Mr. Ward, in his 'History of the Law of Nations,' has attributed much direct influence on the growth of international morality first to the Councils of the Church and then to the action of the Papacy. But,—apart from their direct operation on such matters as the observance of treaties, the treatment of prisoners of war, the restriction of private wars, the observance of the 'truce of God,' and the censure of the private lives of rulers,— there was a far greater though long-hidden change manifesting itself in the nature of the standard to which a final public appeal was made.

The Christians from the orthodox south met the Arian Christians of the north, and amidst all the clinging barbarism, the crass inconsistencies, the individual outrages manifest everywhere, the name of God and the supreme obligation of a moral law occupy a place

[1] Hibbert Lectures. London, 1880.

in the thoughts of the soldier, the colonist, the serf, the barbarian chief, and the popular assembly, which was wholly new in the growing world.

The story from that time to this is indeed a checkered one; and during it the seed of the moral life has been hidden, sometimes for generations together, in the cell of the monk; or wasted in the untimely visions and utterances of the fanatical enthusiast; or religious wars have seemed to drown in blood the precious inheritance for which they were waged; or violent persecutions have simulated the portents of heathendom: till at last there dawns some hope that the nations of the West are to have free course, with all the gains and with all the help of finely adjusted moral criticism for which they have so long struggled and waited.

Of course in these remarks it is not intended to depreciate the aspirations and criticisms of such of the nobler spirits of old as Plato, Aristotle, Cicero, and Plutarch; nor, still less—to deny that motives of the most purely ethical kind were all along determining, however unconsciously, the action of statesmen and the lives of patriot citizens. It is only alleged that the conscious application of a moral test in the region of politics, not by a few of the more highly trained minds, but by the general and intuitive apprehensions of the multitude at large, is a growth and attainment coeval with the appearance of what may be characteristically called Christian States.

The application of an ethical standard and motive to politics sheds an instructive light on the curious fortunes of modern Utilitarianism, and, when properly considered, is capable of helping forward the solution of the problem to which the existence of that theory owes its rise.

Modern utilitarianism reached its fullest, or only logical, development in the teaching of Jeremy Bentham. It has indeed had a history since his time to which the late Mr. John Stuart Mill has largely contributed. But in the countless modifications and explanations which have attended it, it has lost what at its first birth and mature growth was its chief recommendation—the excellence of simplicity and consistency.

In the last chapter of his treatise on 'Early Institutions,' Sir Henry Sumner Maine has drawn attention to the fact that Jeremy Bentham was a legislator more than anything beside; and his taste and genius as a legislator determined his habits of thought on all subjects whatever. But, at best, legislation is, on one side of it, a rough practical remedy for the evils of the world. Each person legislated for counts as one and no more. And between two alternative remedial processes, that generally has to be preferred which benefits more persons before another which benefits fewer.

Bentham's celebrated treatise on 'Morals and Legislation' is nothing more than a logical expansion of this principle and its application to the whole field of human life. The legislator transforms himself into the moralist, and he brings with him into the new universe he has invaded no other implements and mechanism than the coarse materials which fully sufficed him for his previous work.

It needed but a superficial criticism to show that, whereas such an idea as that of happiness (or rather the restriction of pain) may have an intelligible meaning for the political reformer, it is far too impalpable and indefinite to be of the slightest service in indicating the aim and standard of all moral acts. The measurement, again, of this happiness, and the calculation of the number of persons who may be affected by any specific scheme devised for imparting it, again imply materialistic conceptions of number, quantity, and weight, which, in connexion with the thoughts and feelings, as well as with the singular phenomenon of conscience (with which morality is alone concerned), are singularly irrelevant and inappropriate.

Nevertheless it has been well pointed out that the opponents of utilitarianism have afforded a handle to their adversaries by ignoring, or appearing to ignore, the truly materialistic and calculable elements that often must enter into moral acts. There are many cases in which the moral agent who is scrupulously desirous of conforming to the dictates of conscience must balance the claims of diverse alternative duties by reference to the number of persons whose interests may be affected, according as one course or the other is adopted, or by the degree, quality, or quantity, of the interest which is at stake.

The late Professor Grote, brother of the historian of Greece, in his exhaustive 'Examination of the Utilitarian Philosophy,' was among the first opponents of that philosophy who recognised the real utilitarian element, inseparable from any complete moral theory; and he did more to close the controversy for ever than any other writer in the same field.

It is undoubtedly in the world of politics that whatever utilitarian element really belongs to a science of abstract morality will be pre-eminently found. Mr. John Austin, indeed, was so impressed with this fact, and so desirous of reconciling the teaching he derived from Bentham with the promptings of a reverential view of Divine Providence, that he based his utilitarian structure on a theocratic foundation. God loves all His creatures, argues Mr. Austin, and designs for them the utmost happiness possible in their mundane circumstances; in fact, the greatest happiness of the greatest number of all members of the sentient creation. By an inversion of this thought, Mr. Austin holds himself entitled to conclude that if the happiness can be weighed, and the number of persons affected counted, the arithmetical elements would be provided for ascertaining in any given case the will of God and the path of duty.

Unfortunately there are, in the ethical regions, products which are less ponderable even than pleasure, and as heathenism certainly failed to regenerate the world by the law of competition, it is still being seen whether Christianity has done or can do more for it by the law of sacrifice.

As an instance of the curious transmutations which moral ideas and terms properly undergo when transferred from the life of individual men to the existence of the State—or rather from the lives of men in a non-political, to the lives of men in a political, aspect—there will at once recur to the memory the persistent problems as to whether and under what conditions patriotism, ambition, national rivalries or antipathies, are virtues or vices.

It would be said at once that it depends on the circumstances; that what is a virtue up to a certain point becomes a vice if practised beyond that point; and that the fact that the State is the object of action cannot really alter moral estimates from what they would be if smaller and more insignificant corporations were alone concerned. And yet this is not exactly true. It is felt at once that for a man to devote the whole of his energies towards advancing the material interests or even the safety of a narrow circle with which he is identified—be it his family, his clan, his club, his village, or his political party—scarcely differs, as a matter for moral evaluation, from an entire devotion of a man's life to what is in the narrowest sense himself. Not, indeed, that the moralist will forget that some of the hardest and most perplexing duties and those least well remunerated, being inward rather than outward, may be said, however fallaciously, to be performed solely in reference to a man's self.

In this sense the constantly-extending groups of his fellow-creatures with whom he comes into relation during his earthly life represent only an ever-enlarging and enriched self. He may be called upon at different epochs to consecrate himself wholly to one or other of these groups, or he may run in advance of his duty—and so really lag behind it—by preferring at the wrong time and place the claims of one group over those of another. These claims cannot be measured nor adjusted by any rude appreciation of the numbers of persons affected, or of direct effects of conduct. He may need a lifetime of cultivated moral sagacity to determine rightly and justly, and no bare rules or recorded experience of others can do more than supply him with principles or stimulate him by example.

But when the transition is made from all the smaller societies to the State, the moral atmosphere seems to have undergone a transformation and old things to have become new. Duties which were relative become absolute. Actions which were, or seemed, partly virtuous and partly vicious are exposed in their true colours to the light of day. The whole judgments of mankind seem to have become concentrated and enlightened, and the experience of the race to be laid under tribute for the purpose of clearing moral action and propagating throughout society straightforward and perspicuous popular sentiments. *Cari sunt parentes, cari liberi, propinqui, familiares; sed omnes omnium caritates patria una complexa est; pro quâ quis bonus dubitet oppetere mortem si ei sit profuturus.*

In such sentiments as these are gathered up a world-history of philosophy, which has been not only filtered into popular truisms, but transfused into the most inexpugnable of emotions and aspirations. It is believed to be right to make sacrifices for the State which no other cause—scarcely even the interest of a man's self and his home—could justify.

It is asked why a State or nation differs, beyond possible comparison, in the dignity and authority of the claims which it makes on the individual human component of it, from what is made in the case of any other or smaller organisation, or even by a wider organisation, such as an empire (that is a levelling assemblage of divers nations or States); it can only be answered that the State occupies, in the constitution of the world, a position *sui generis*, and to which there is nothing which presents any exact resemblance or analogy.

So far as our knowledge extends, it is in the life of the State, and only there, that human life, in all its ramifications, can obtain the nourishment it needs for its appropriate expansion and development. This is equally true, indeed, of the family, and we believe it to be true of some still higher and less materially constituted society which, amidst all the limitless interpretations which have been placed upon the name, still retains for Christians the profoundest significance—that is, the Church.

Each of these organisations has an essential contribution to make to the perfection of human society and to the perfection of individual life in that society. Each lays claim to the devout allegiance, within proper limits, of the persons who compose it; and each, on the other hand, owes to those persons the maintenance of its own peculiar character and the faithful discharge of its tutelary duties.

It is thus that the largest-minded heathen philosophers, such as Aristotle and Cicero, discerned that in a life of public activity on behalf of the State something more was concerned than the accomplishment of narrow personal aspirations. In the same way, even with all the refinements of modern ethical criticism, it is intuitively felt that the self-seeking of such men as Henry VIII. of England, of Frederick the Great of Prussia, and even of Napoleon Bonaparte, has to be submitted to a very different,—though perhaps not more indulgent,—ordeal from that which is applicable to ordinary men acting in a more circumscribed area.

The root of this feeling is, no doubt, a true consciousness that the mere contact with State affairs, and the lively apprehension it carries with it of the innumerable and lasting interests which the conduct of a single man affects, have of themselves a sobering influence, which, by tending to dwarf into insignificance all mere personal cravings, forces even the most narrow minds into a certain largeness of action which suggests a dominant sense of accountability to something other and better than a temporary and vacillating public opinion.

The faults of this moral inquisition, as applied in the pagan world, were due in a large degree to the constitution of the pre-Christian States, in which a slave population vastly exceeded in numbers the population of enfranchised citizens. The result was that even the most scrutinising philosophers had no types presented to their eyes or their memories of phases of society in which common civic virtues and, still more, prominent civic excellences were demanded of more than a limited fraction of all the persons in the State. Thus attention was fixed far more on the signal examples either of virtue or vice in individual citizens of note than on that general standard of public self-renunciation to which even the humblest and most indigent citizen would, according to a modern standard, be expected to attain.

Another cause of this altered spirit of criticism is to be found in what is sometimes regarded as the greater gravity of modern life as contrasted with ancient, but which is really the expression in the world of politics of the ideas of individual conscience, of duty, of right, and of wrong, to which the training of eighteen Christian centuries has, with all its terrible drawbacks, given such a magnificent extension.

In the older world duties were distinct, separate, manifold, and, as it were, dislocated. There was no tie to bind them together, and none to explain the connexion which the duties of one person, or of one class of persons, in a community had with duties of a different kind elsewhere. Thus the duties of a man to his country were artificially contrasted with duties to his family, to himself, or to mankind at large, and any impetus that might be given to one order of these duties simply terminated there, without diffusing any fresh light or heat beyond itself.

The essence of Christian civilisation and of morality, on the other hand, is to impart to all duties a mutual connexion, and further to link every group of duties to a comprehensive and unique spirit of obligation and self-devotion, in the harmonious oneness of which the commonest uses are strengthened and quickened by alliance with all the rest. Hence, when once it was recognised in modern consciousness that a man owed a duty to his country, and could commit a sin by neglecting this duty, the duty in question was instantly enforced by all the sacred and persuasive sanctions by which the whole of the reformed society was kept together.

It will be well at this point to remark upon a few of the concrete manifestations of this change of moral attitude. Instances are supplied by the familiar moral formulæ now universally adopted as defining the duties of individual citizens in respect of (1) frauds on the revenue, (2) corruption at elections, (3) revolution.

(1) The prevention of the class of offences to which belong smuggling and false returns to taxing assessments, might be expected to be easier in modern communities, into the government of which the idea of representation enters so largely, than in States in which the governors and the governed were for almost all purposes polar opposites.

Yet the extension of the range of modern government from that of the city to the aggregate of cities and landed territory composing the modern State-unit, has of itself, apart from the mere growth of moral ideas, introduced a new class of difficulties in the application of common morality to the relations of a taxpayer and his government. The smaller and more concentrated the State system, the more nearly does it approach, in the popular apprehension, to a purely communistic society, in which the end of the organisation is understood by everybody concerned; in which the supports derivable from a clear and uniform public opinion are of the strongest; and in which the loss occasioned by individual defaulters is most obviously connected with the undue burdening of all other persons in the community.

In the present day the financial machinery of States,—complicated and magnified as it is by enormous public debts,—has attained to a portentous size and breadth, which in other ages would have seemed scarcely compatible with the continued existence of a State. But the productive resources and the extension of commerce by land and sea could also never have been foreseen. The general effect, however, is that such taxation as there is is spread over almost innumerable classes and orders of persons, none of whom are exempt, none (theoretically) unduly burdened, and no one subjected to exactly the same amount of pressure as another.

Thus, where legal contrivances for detecting evasions fail, as little help as possible is provided by a rigorous and keen-sighted tribunal of public opinion. Every one knows that, if he were the only defaulter, the loss to the State and the access of burden to other persons would be incalculably small. Every one also, when arguing with himself in his own cause, is too prone to adopt a sophistical suggestion that a self-governing community leaves to private citizens a greater licence to do as they like—that is, not to be governed at all, and consequently to be governed at their neighbours' expense—than is granted in less popularly-governed communities.

Hence,—what with the privacy which the very extent of the taxing operations involves, the unequal incidence of the taxes, and the impotence of executive organisations for buoying up the popular conscience,—a sentiment too easily grows up, and is rapidly diffused, which is inimical to stern convictions of the treachery to the State and the real moral turpitude and shameless cowardice which is involved in evading the discharge of money debts to the State.

Such a sentiment is in fact one of the deepest political heresy, or rather amounts to political infidelity. It is one thing openly to refuse to pay a particular tax in the spirit, say, of John Hampden, or even, as some persons have done even in England of late, to take the first step in revolution by refusing to pay all taxes, on the ground of dissatisfaction with the representative system, or with the conduct of the government. It is quite another thing to continue openly to draw all the advantages of civic concert and to breathe the air of a full national life, and yet at the same time to turn to private account the necessarily infirm efforts of the State to grapple with its perplexities, and to batten in secret over prey—however small—filched from the common treasury.

There is growing up on every side a far higher morality than heretofore, with respect to the relations of a private citizen to the State on its financial side; and if scandalously lax doctrines still prevail in many quarters, this is mainly owing to the greater rate at which modern States have grown in population, in territorial extent, and in financial liability, than in an ethical intelligence adequate to meet the new demands upon it.

(2) Some of the same reasoning and the same historical consideration applies to the case of bribery and electoral corruption. The case here is no doubt a somewhat more complex one, inasmuch as the possibilities of wrong-doing in the matter of giving a vote by no means stop at the point of merely refusing a pecuniary payment for it, but travel through the whole scale of unworthy motives up to those which are just short of an ideal and scrupulous conscientiousness.

In some countries—as in England, for instance— the very structure of the State has almost inevitably connected a base personal interest with the discharge of the highest representative functions. Under the nomination-borough system, which prevailed before the English Reform Act of 1832, it was almost inevitable that the right to send, and therefore to choose, a member of Parliament was, in the popular consciousness, an essential ingredient in the aggregate of property rights vested in the local potentate whose will determined the election. So soon as these boroughs were abolished, it might well have seemed that the new constituencies were the 'universal heirs,' for electoral purposes, of the aristocracy whose place they took.

This dangerous and confusing notion is even still supported by the anomalous circumstance that Peers of Parliament are constitutionally and legally entitled to make monetary contracts with railway companies in respect of their vote for or against a proposed railway-scheme before the House of Lords. They are not held to be representatives of the public, and on behalf of the interests of themselves and their families they may do what they choose. Thus, just after the passing of the Reform Act of 1832, it is probable that not only did corruption reach its highest point in England, but the popular conscience in respect of it was at its weakest.

The great extension, however, of the suffrage has been gradually working its own cure, and the House of Commons has only reflected, however tardily, the promptings of the national conscience, by improving the machinery for trying imputations of bribery by a judicial process closely resembling that of a criminal trial, conducted on the spot by one of the judges of the High Court of Judicature, as well as by instituting the ballot.

As to this last institution, indeed, some controversy has taken place among critical moralists as to its direct and indirect bearing on the public sense of honour and of political responsibility. It has been said that voting is discharging a trust, and that every trust ought to be discharged openly and courageously. To shelter a voter from the consequence of his vote is said to be merely nursing in him habits of political timidity, not to say cowardice.

This reasoning, however, is certainly opposed to the universal experience of the action of the ballot both in the United States, the British colonies, and in Great Britain itself during the years in which it has already been in operation. The relief which the ballot secures from immediate and surrounding pressure, or rather intrusiveness, of all sorts, and the quiet and decent order thereby secured for the performance of the most solemn and deliberate of all political functions, constitute an almost priceless boon. The ballot need not of itself involve any concealment of a voter's political character, intentions, or acts. All it does is to prevent the forcible exposure of a political act to the eyes of persons who have no claim whatever to be acquainted with it, and still less to control it.

If the only sort of corruption which had to be denounced were that which takes a directly pecuniary form, there would be a fair prospect of its shortly becoming an anachronism. Experience, however, has been showing of late years that one of the main difficulties, which popular government,—especially when extended over a wide area,—has to contend with, is due to corruption of a less palpable kind, and one which, on the face of it, less easily falls within the reach of moral obloquy.

The individual voter in the smaller constituencies or the more remote districts of a country, cannot but have all sorts of private interests of himself, his family, his township, or even his religious sect to serve by returning one candidate to the Legislature rather than another. It is difficult to say that it is in all cases base to give a preponderant weight to one or other of these interests as contrasted with the whole claims of the State, which are, perhaps, very imperfectly known, and still less duly estimated at their true value.

To give just the right degree of regard to the narrower interest,—which ought not to be wholly neglected,—and to the wider interest,—which ought to be of supreme concern,—requires a finely-cultured conscientiousness, which can only be the growth of long and arduous national training, and indeed of individual education. It is none the less proper, however, to denounce in the strongest terms the more flagrant kinds of preferential regard for private over public, and for local over national objects in the selection of members of the legislature.

It does not seem possible in such countries as England, with its antiquated traditions the other way, and the United States, with its federal system and its enormous area, to dispense with the prominence of the local and territorial element in representation. Efforts, indeed, have been made (as was seen in a former chapter), by some such machinery as Mr. Hare's method of proportional representation, to add the minorities together over a considerable district, and so, among other advantages, to reduce the openings for corruption. But the primary basis of the representative system, especially in widely scattered territories, will probably always be local; and therefore the best securities against corruption must be looked for in a quickened sensibility to the true relations of near and distant demands, and to a penetrating conscientiousness in preferring, on proper occasions, the general to the more particular interest.

(3) The moral duties of citizens in respect to Revolution have at all times opened out an unbounded field of debate. The opinions of most persons are coloured

by reference to some recent experience either of their own, or their own nation, or their own times; and in proportion to the gravity of the subject is the heat of the passion with which the discussion of it is usually approached. In Europe, indeed, it happens that, for the last two hundred years, the breaking up of the pretty uniformly distributed pressure of the feudal system has been attended by a series of revolutions of an almost uniformly and obviously beneficial character in each of the European states.

The experience of America has been of a more ambiguous kind. Enough, however, has happened to range, on the whole, the friends of political progress with the advocates of the extreme rights of revolutionists, and in their eyes to erect the right of revolution into almost as dignified a position as was once occupied by the 'Divine right of Kings.'

And yet if the modern politician could find time to ponder at leisure on the history of the last hundred and fifty years of the Roman republic, he would learn that there are states of society in which there may prevail a facility of creating a revolution—now by the help of the mob, now by that of a professional soldiery, —which may constitute at once the most tempting seduction to an unconscientious citizen, and become the main peril to the stability of any government at all. Bad and reckless as was the Roman government at the beginning of the time alluded to, and flagrant as were the breaches in the constitution habitually made by the constitutional authorities themselves, still the first violent occupation of Rome by Sulla with an armed force,—for the purpose, indeed, of maintaining or restoring formal order,—marks the moment from which the true constitutional reparation of Rome became for ever impossible.

Probably the actual revolution perpetrated by Sulla was rendered unavoidable by preceding constitutional events, including the innovations of the Gracchi, and the choice was only between the permanent rule of successful soldiers and the intermittent despotism of street mobs led by capitalists.

Such memories are wholesome as checks on any predisposition to glorify a revolutionary spirit as synonymous with patriotism. When popular government is completely established, it rests with the people themselves—*ex hypothesi*—to control the action of the executive, to determine the policy to be pursued by the legislature, and, if necessary, to recast entirely the formal mechanism which is interposed between the popular will and its interpretation in action—that is, to reform the constitution. It may not be able to do any of these things in a day, and from personal and accidental causes the impediments to the full exertion of the popular force may be greater at one time than at another.

But after a sufficient interval has elapsed for bringing the public mind to bear on a subject requiring attention or a defect requiring amendment, and after full discussion has taken place, and after all the legitimate influences of all sorts have sufficiently played upon and counteracted each other, there does arrive a moment at which it may be truly said that people have come to a definite determination and know their own mind.

It is the part of a good citizen, who is possessed by even the most frenzied eagerness for achieving some particular political improvement, to attain his object by a legitimate use of the multiform means legitimately at his disposal. He will do his utmost to bring the world —that is, the ultimately effective portion of the whole body-politic—round to his views; he will resort, it may be, to all the instrumentality of the public platform, the public press, and of what is implied in the right of association and combination. It is not till every one of these resources has been tried and has failed that the question can so much as present itself as to the comparative duties of a citizen to acquiesce, for the sake of order, in a hopelessly bad state of things, and that of encountering the certainty of present disorder, with the possibility of bringing about a catastrophe, involving good and evil alike, in pursuit of a good not otherwise, if at all, to be attained.

The plea for revolution in a popularly-constituted State must rest on the allegation of there being some accidental obstruction to the free action of the popular will. This obstruction may be owing to the preponderant and maliciously-exercised influence of some individual person or group of persons, who, by the existing forms of the constitution, happen to be placed out of the reach of popular control; or it may be due to the unexpected failure of some check or balance-wheel which time and circumstances have rendered futile; or, again, it may be due to a deliberate conspiracy, in some quarter or other, by which the forms of the constitution are complied with, while its spirit is perverted or treacherously invaded.

Even in such contingencies as these, recent examples,—of which France at the close of Marshal MacMahon's Presidency was a signal specimen,—have shown that there may be an outlet for the reassertion of the true popular will short of either mob or military violence. Anyway, it is a crime of the deepest dye for any man or assemblage of men to contemplate revolution, so long as remedies may still presumably be found either within the normal range of constitutional action, or by means of popular amendments of the constitution, conducted after a regular and orderly fashion.

Not, indeed, that severe and scrupulous limits can be assigned to the excitement and even ebullient fury which are likely to accompany the disturbance of things long settled, and the stir of strong passions heated by fervent appeals to them, and by a consciousness of corporate sympathy. But the fire and fume of a healthy political life and growth are distinguishable at every point from the wanton abuse of the free mechanism of popular government for the sake of precipitating results, which, either are achieved only in appearance, or, if achieved in reality, do, by enthroning the principle of premature, capricious, and needless revolution, bring with them infinitely more loss than gain.

If, as has been seen by the above brief illustrations, the conduct of the individual citizen is properly exposed to a moral criticism, on the ground of its conforming or not conforming to a purely moral standard, it is still more true that the State itself, in its relation towards its citizens and towards other States, is properly subjected to a like censure. The acts of the State are determined by its executive authority for the time being, by its legislature, and, in a popularly governed

State, by the people. It is in the interaction of these three elements that the form and working of the constitution consist; and though, for one purpose or another, one of these elements may have to take the initiative, the action of the constitution, whatever its form, must tend to bring them all into harmonious cooperation sooner or later, and so to make each department of the State, and the aggregate people above all, responsible for what is wrong and fairly to be accredited with what is right.

It is in this way that when the conscience of the nation is spoken of, and the sins of a nation are denounced, this is by no merely loose analogy to the moral conformation of the individual human being. Man is gifted with such an inherently social constitution, that numbers of persons admit of being so organised as to take up into themselves, as it were, even the most spiritual elements which characterise each one of the component atoms. The perfection to which this sort of moral incarnation reaches will depend, in a State, on the constitution of that State, coupled with the facilities which exist for amending, controlling, or continuously inspiring that constitution.

In whose soever hands the supreme political authority of the State at a given moment rests, that authority has cast upon it, as its first duty, the completion of the State itself, by the development of all the moral possibilities latent in the people, and by, to this end, facilitating the acquisition of that organised force which enables the real proclivities and intuitions of the people most easily to express themselves, and most effectually to be converted into action. Certain practical corollaries follow from these positions.

In the first place, the existence of *slavery* in a State is a certain sign either that the State has its conscience as yet only very imperfectly developed, or else that it acts habitually and persistently in defiance of the promptings of conscience. Wherever true slavery is found, there the cardinal political sin, as Coleridge pointedly described it, is committed of turning a person into a *thing*. The denial of human rights thereby implied, even if confined to ever so small a fraction of the community, and even if accidentally attended by every kind of modification and even humane compensation, is an outrage which can never be extenuated.

The history, indeed, not only of the most enlightened Pagan nations, but of modern nations otherwise Christian, has shown the terrible inertness of the ruling portion of the community when brought face to face with classes of persons who, either by past conquests or by long-inherited traditions, are found in a condition which is very favourable to the present wellbeing, or at least to the material enrichment, of all other persons but themselves.

Experience has shown that the temptations to moral self-delusion, and even to religious casuistry, for the purpose of forging pretexts for an institution incompatible with every idea of a true humanity, including all the free moral and spiritual elements comprised in the term, are facile and ever at hand to an extent which will probably dismay our posterity even to a greater extent than it does our more hardened selves.

What is true of slavery is true in an only less conspicuous degree of every denial of full political rights which is based on any other necessity than those contained in the disabling infirmities of age, mental infirmity, and penal disfranchisement. If the State has, in truth, all the essential elements of a moral and spiritual structure, this structure can only be composed out of the contributive humanity of every individual atom of the population, and not of only a portion of those atoms, and still less of any capriciously or invidiously-preferred portion of those atoms.

No doubt the course of historical development has been that of extending the suffrage downwards so as to embrace wider and wider classes, less obviously marked out at first as concerning themselves with political action, rather than of starting with the widest suffrage and limiting it afterwards. It is no exception to this that the first English Reform Act of Henry VI.'s reign, by which the county suffrage was restricted to forty-shilling householders, was a disfranchising act. This was a special enactment for the purpose of procuring order in the county court at election time, and for substituting a definite for an indefinite constituency.

The notion of universal suffrage, or of manhood suffrage, never prevailed at any time in England, in which country, as in all other feudal States, the original basis of the suffrage was that of doing suit and service at the county court as a vassal of the king. The borough suffrage, again, had a distinct history of its own.

The modern extension of the suffrage is usually treated not as a moral requirement, but as a matter of mere political expediency, or, at the utmost, of compulsory necessity. When once, however, it is apprehended that, for any classes in a community in full possession of political rights,—and therefore theoretically, as well as

to a great extent practically, in command of the State,—
to refuse a concession of like rights to any other classes
of persons not demonstrably incompetent, constitutes in
the State an offence parallel to that of fraudulent misappropriation in the individual person, it is probable
that political measures for a reconstruction of the
franchise will be considered in a somewhat less exclusive and selfish spirit than is common. Corresponding
to this duty on the part of the State is the duty of the
citizen to exercise his right to vote, and to exercise it
righteously.

Assuming that the State has reached a constitutional
extension which affords a sufficient opening for the full
exertion of the national voice, and for the effective
manifestation of the national will, the first concern of
those who are for the time being the legislative and
administrative organs of the State will be that of
asserting at every point the truly moral constitution
of the State itself as a supreme instrument for the
evolution of all the fairest constituents of individual
character and life.

Among the institutions which even in Pagan societies have been regarded, and are regarded, as of cardinal
importance for the sustenance both of individual existence and of the State itself, is that of family life and
of monogamic marriage, on the rigorous maintenance
of which true family life can alone ultimately depend.
In every wide national society very great latitude may
properly be allowed for private associations of all kinds,
whether for mere social purposes or for the higher ends
of economic, industrial, scientific, religious, or political
co-operation. But the character and circumstances of

the initial family groups,—on the vitality, strength, cohesiveness, and modes of reciprocal interaction of which the healthiness of the whole body-politic turns,— are of so momentous an importance that they cannot be left to individual choice or to the vagaries of scientific experiment, without the gravest dereliction of duty somewhere, and—if such a state of things is allowed to continue—everywhere.

In the older feudal monarchies of Europe, penetrated as they are by the crystallised spirit and formal institutions of Christendom, monogamic marriage is so unassailably established, and contains so many conservative guarantees, that the main difficulty in some of these countries is to make just provision for unavoidable divorces, and to provide equitable arrangements for the unhampered marriage of persons belonging to different religious societies.

The phenomenon in the United States of a large, well-populated, industrious, fertile, and otherwise highly organised district—always aspiring to be a State—being professedly built up on a foundation of polygamy, is a portent which can only fail to astonish and alarm the home, as well as the foreign, critic because of that long familiarity with an evil which is at once its most dangerous consequence and its sorest punishment.

Repeated indications in Presidents' Messages, in desultory acts of Congress, and in intermittent sallies of the central executive government, have always had at least the effect of making an overt confession to the world that the wrong is one the flagrancy of which is nowhere denied, and to which the government is entitled and morally bound to apply a stringent and effective remedy.

A problem of a peculiarly modern kind has been presented by the practice, long habitual in European States, of utilising by Lotteries the speculative tendencies of the mass of mankind, in order to enrich the State without apparent pressure in the way of taxation. This practice is now being abandoned in those States in which a liberal constitution has brought the conscience of the people adequately to bear, and it will at no distant time probably go the way of all other desecrating stains on the ideal dignity of the State.

It does not require any refined ethical analysis to demonstrate the viciousness of the practice. Not only are the vices of men rendered tributary to the State, and therefore inevitably regarded with political favour —an objection which so far equally applies to raising a large part of the revenue from the consumption of spirituous liquors; but,—over and above this operation which it has in common with excise duties on spirits fixed at a point which shall carefully fail of being prohibitory,—State lotteries stimulate to the utmost the vices on which they repose, extend the temptations to them over vast classes of persons of all ages and positions to whom they would otherwise be strange, and, by the mere force of associated interest and a sort of riotous conspiracy in ill-doing, affect to build the stern fortunes of an immortal State on the most sandy of all foundations—public excitement for a flagitious cause.

What is here said of State lotteries properly so called—that is, the practice of raising revenue directly by the institution of all the mechanism of general contribution, a few great prizes, a vast number of blanks, a widely extended system of advertisement, and all the glamour capable of being imparted to it by a superficial decorum in the elaboration of details, all under the direct executive administration of government,—applies with little less force to all public patronage of gaming-tables, to fixed institutions for the direct encouragement of gambling, and to the permission, whether legislative or executive, of even occasional lotteries which are on a scale extensive and pretentious enough to entrap and delude those innocent classes of society which, from their previous experience, are least likely to be able to save themselves from a wholly novel infection.

Nothing, indeed, short of a determined recognition of the illegality of all public gaming-tables or institutions, permanent or temporary, which rest on a gambling basis, can vindicate the honour of the State in this matter. And it will not be sufficient for the State to make laws, however severe, unless it practically secures that they are consistently and effectually enforced.

There are other modes of raising a revenue or of temporarily increasing the national resources, which, however supported at the moment by the popular voice, and however successfully they may evade the criticism of even the more sceptical members of society, are none the less tainted with immorality, and, to the extent that they prevail, are fraught with danger to the stability of the nation.

To this class of expedients belong all remedies for current evils which really partake of the nature of confiscation of property, of repudiation of debts, and— what usually involves both the one and the other—of depreciation of the coinage. This is by no means saying that revolutionary crises may not arise in which measures of these kinds, which usually must be characterised as suicidal, may not be morally justifiable, as courses to be preferred to an instant plunge into anarchy. If these desperate adventures were only reserved for such epochs, they would scarcely come within the ken of the general moralist.

It needs, however, only to glance around at the actual practice of some States, otherwise enjoying a reputation for justice and public honesty, and at the language occasionally used in the legislative assemblies, and even at diplomatic correspondence with other States, to see that the current line drawn between justice and injustice, truth and falsehood, right and wrong, in the case of such financial topics as those adverted to, is far too often shamefully flickering and indistinct.

There is indeed one special abuse in this direction which is a peculiar growth of modern times, and is a product of the very increase of stability and of moral reputation to which, on the whole, modern States, as contrasted with ancient ones, have attained. This is the disposition to meet financial emergencies, deficits, or pressing and accidental claims, by creating national debts, involving indefinite charges on the remotest posterity.

The general principle is, indeed, publicly avowed, that a moral rule does apply to determine the cases in which it is, and which it is not, legitimate to burden posterity. But the facility of obtaining money in this way often presents a seductive temptation to statesmen and to political parties desirous of carrying out a policy of their own, and for a ready and persistent adherence to which they cannot steadily rely on the bulk of the population, nor expect to meet with all the sacrifices which the policy—if paid for at once, as is said 'within the year,' that is, by simple taxation—would involve.

Yet not more in political circles than elsewhere is the facility for obtaining money always a moral justification of the means resorted to for obtaining it. That State is most truly a State which carries to the highest pitch the notions, so tardily and hardly acquired, of its own integrity, continuity, and immortality. Where the State shows itself reckless in regard to its future constituents, it not only demolishes its own public credit at home and abroad, sets a pernicious example of reckless prodigality in the sight of its own subjects, but, to the extent that the financial operations go, impairs its own existence by a sort of constitutional suicide.

A more perplexed topic is presented by a very universal practice among modern Christian States, as well as among the States of antiquity, of organising sexual vice by providing a special police machinery in the greater towns of a country, and not merely for controlling the excesses or marking out the local boundaries of vicious indulgence, but for the purpose, or certainly with the obvious result, of encouraging and facilitating it, at all events, within those boundaries. The fact that the whole topic does, from its nature, escape the sifting discussion and public criticism to which every other class of questionable policy is in free States exposed, has had the effect of withdrawing it in a considerable degree from the unfettered and direct action of the public conscience. It is difficult to draw the line between the legitimate province of the State as occupied in curtailing the outward exhibition of vice, and even in restricting the far-radiating physical inconveniences brought upon the innocent by the guilty, and the undoubted trespass beyond the limits of that province committed in giving any, even the minutest, impetus to vice itself, in degrading one sex for the presumed gain of the other, and in lowering everywhere the standard of moral perfection which the laws of the State, though incompetent directly to produce, must invariably confess and undeviatingly tend to bring about.

When the history of these laws is thoroughly examined, it will be found that the defences of them are wholly *ex post facto*, that they rest on imagined benefits, which either do not follow at all, or are due to some casual operation of the police system which has nothing intrinsically to do with the licensing and medical inspection which is the essence of it; and that, lastly, the whole method owes its origin to countries and states of society so far already sunk in universal profligacy as to make for them the thought of even average purity and self-restraint seem a mere utopian vision. But it cannot be admitted that the morality of the future should be 'cabined, cribbed, confined' by the dwarfing shrouds in which the dead past has buried its dead.

There is yet one topic which must be noticed as affecting the State's conscience of right and wrong—that is, the legitimacy of the use of certain punishments for crimes. It is now generally recognised that there are certain kinds of punishments, such, for example, as those which involve torture, mutilation, and certain forms of infamy, which no circumstances whatever can justify as available. There are others, such as capital punishment, on which opinion may be said to be sharply and decisively divided. There are others, such as flogging, on which public opinion may be said to be wavering and unsettled.

Two principles of moral criticism have, however, clearly emerged of late years. One is, that there are certain moral and personal attributes which constitute the human nature of every one, and that there are kinds of outrage on this nature which no end whatever can justify the State in resorting to. Again, it is getting recognised that, in all criminal punishments, the moral improvement of the individual offender must be always maintained as one of the ends in view, so far as it is compatible with the protection of society.

The application of these principles in detail is indeed not easy, and will long continue to promote debate among philanthropists and reformers. But it is no small gain to the cause of morality to have for ever altered the aspect of criminal punishments from being violent, vengeful, and retaliatory conflicts with the defenceless wretch for whose crimes society is at least as much responsible as himself, to a deliberative and cautious essay how far the minimum of pain to one may be combined with the maximum of profit to all the parties involved. The majesty and authority of the State is far better manifested in using its giant strength with precision, with gentleness, and with caution, than (as was once supposed) in surrendering itself to the promptings of angry passion and of a capricious vindictiveness better befitting children or madmen than rational human beings called to share in the divine task of government.

The aspects towards right and wrong of the individual citizen and of the State, in its domestic relations, have hitherto attracted less attention than the more obvious moral constitution and responsibilities of the State when brought into contact with other political or imperfectly civilised communities.

In this last case the unity and integrity of the State is pre-eminently conspicuous, and the complexity of its action, as well as the counter-movements of opposed parties, from the ultimate reconciliation of which every determinate course of proceeding springs, is cloaked under the form of decisive administration and simple diplomatic utterances.

Indeed, in very ancient times, the good or bad faith of States towards each other in respect of the strict observance of treaties, of engagements towards commanders in the field, of promises to ambassadors, and of capitulations of all sorts, were held to stamp the community with a permanent reputation of the highest or the lowest kind. It cannot be said that in modern times the stringent exactions of moralists in respect of ordinary good faith between State and State, as between other moral beings, is in any degree relaxed. A wholesome difference and improvement, however, is observable in the greater extension to which the moral scrutiny is carried out, and the more precise details to which it is held practically to apply.

It is especially in the transactions of a stronger with a weaker State,—or with a State which, through the momentary event of an unsuccessful war, finds itself in the condition of a weaker State,—that the force of a purely ethical canon of action is most decisively put to the test.

Not to dwell on the more perplexed and ambiguous history of British policy in the East Indies during the last century and a half, and the current treatment of hopeful aboriginal communities by British colonists,—only too often aided by a mass of unscrupulous prejudice and guilty ignorance at home,—the treatment of the great, though unhappily, for too many purposes, impotent, Chinese Empire, is a deplorable illustration of the quantity of iniquity which, even at the present day, one State may wreak on another without exciting animadversion or odium either at home or abroad.

From the numerous examples which have been above adduced of the application of a strictly moral standard to the political acts of citizens, and to the executive, legislative, and international acts of States, it will have been sufficiently seen where the main difficulty lies in applying in detail the best acknowledged general principles. In all policy there must be a certain element of conjecture, of calculation, of comparison of ends, of the adjustment of means to ends, and, in a word, of quantitative measurement, which, in the more simple and spontaneous domain of individual life and action, would be irrelevant, and might seem even base. But at the best, and when the State is idealised to the utmost as an independent and responsible moral being, it still retains certain of the qualities and conditions of an artificially constructed machine.

The State can only be called into dynamical action by a concert of forces producible by a more or less complex series of casually co-operating, but more frequently conflicting, agencies. Much of the healthiest part of political life is concerned with bringing the latent opposition of persons and parties face to face, and with reducing the points of final divergence to such an extent that a clear line of common and united action may be discovered. But all this process implies delay, hesitation, uncertainty, and, even in some way, concession and compromise. In State life there are mental conditions which, on the face of them, are alien to those prompt and, as it were, intrusive as well as decisive suggestions, which in the individual person of healthy moral organisation are never lacking, and are deferred to with unquestioning obedience.

But the fact that prudence and calculation, as well as a peculiar complexity of action, distinguish the conduct of a State from that of any one of its citizens when dealing with his own private affairs, is only an aggravation of the difficulty of the moral problem so soon as it is presented, and is no reason for ignoring its existence, and still less for a precipitate and nugatory attempt to solve it.

In the region of individual life and existence the triumphs of Christian morality have, after centuries of ecclesiastical vagaries, been finally vindicated. It is now pretty universally confessed that no distinguishing line can be drawn between the consummated perfection of nature, for which the Pagan moralist longed and longs, and the spotless holiness of the Christian who deems himself bound to be perfect as his Father in Heaven is perfect. The last triumphs of the same morality will manifest themselves in the building up for each temporal State of a finely and exactly adjusted polity, or, in other words, of a city which 'lieth four square,' of which ' the length is as large as the breadth,' and the slow and struggling formation of which will be then, and not till then, fully vindicated when, in the spiritual region, the kingdoms of this world are transformed into a new and larger city-State, having everlasting foundations, and whose builder and maker is God.

INDEX.

ADM

ADMINISTRATIVE, the term, history and explanation of, 100

Agrarian problems, account of Roman, 401

AMERICA, history of Party in, in reference to political organisation, 189-191

American Colonies, problems suggested by history of the, 316-318

— Revolution, its place in the history of political science, 46

— Secession War, criticism of grounds of, 442-445

— War of Independence, comparison of, with the French Revolution, 441, 442

ARISTOTLE, place of his works in the history of political science, 23, 24, 181

Army, problems relating to the management of the, 257

AUSTIN, his views on centralisation, 289

— his Utilitarian theory, 453

Australian Colonies, connexion of England with her, 332-334

— — their disposition to extend the province of Government, 386

— — history of Party in, 191, 192

BALLOT, use and moral justification of the, 464

Bank Charter Act, the, its political bearings, 267, 268

CHU

Bank of England, the, its political position, 267

— of France, the, its political position, 267

— functions of the State in relation to a national, 421

Bribery, grounds of immorality of, 462

British India, land policy in, 397

— — recent changes in administration of, 340

BURKE, his 'Reflections,' place of, in political science, 49, 124

CABINET, constitutional character of the English, 249, 250

CALHOUN, Mr., his 'States Rights' doctrine, 443

Capital punishment, arguments on, as illustrating logical methods, 121

Centralisation, analysis and history of term, 289, 290

Chamber, problems relating to a Second, 202, 236 *sq.*

CHINA, causes of its commercial exclusiveness, 368

— its place in the modern political world, 135

Christian Church, the, its relation to political organisation, 174, 185 *sq.*

Church Councils, their relation to political organisation, 187

— of England, the, its constitutional position, 415

CHU

Church and State, the relation of, considered, 413 *sq.*
Codification, place of, in the history of law, 81-84
Colonies, American, place of, in the history of political science, 47
— — problems suggested by history of the, 316-318
— Australian, connexion of England with her, 332-334
— the British, in America, as illustrating the history of constitutions, 175
— land policy in British, 400
— possibility of representation of, 334 *sq.*
Colonisation, political aspects of, 324 *sq.*
Colony, Crown, what is a, 176, 177
Commercial Companies, relation of the State to, 410-412
'Commune,' bearings of the history of the French, 256
Communism, account of modern, 379
Companies, commercial, relation of the State to, 410-412
COMTE, M. AUGUSTE, place of his treatises in political science, 52, 53
— — — his views on the relation of women to men, 141
Constitutional, the term, history and explanation of, 60, 176
Constitutions, general account of, 174 *sq.*
Contract law, an occasion of Government intervention, 389
Contract, the Social, place of the idea of, in the history of political science, 45, 124, 182
Crimes, moral questions affecting punishment of, 479

DEBTS, moral questions respecting national, 477, 478
—, public, functions of the Executive relating to, 264 *sq.*
Dependencies, Government of, 311 *sq.*

GOV

EAST INDIA COMPANY, political development of the, 319, 320
— — — its policy, 369
Education, national, functions of the State in respect to, 424
Electoral franchise, examination of principles relating to the, 198 *sq.*
Emigration, political aspects of, 323 *sq.*
Executive, the term, history and account of, 87 *sq.*
Executive Authority, the, its relation to the Legislature, 246 *sq.*

FAMILY, the, its relations to the State, 166
'Federalist,' place of the, in the history of political science, 48
Federation, ancient and modern attempts at, 279
Feudal system, bearing of the, on land tenures, 156
Feudalism, its place in the history of politics, 37
Foreign relations, political problems involved in, 342 *sq.*
FORTESCUE, place of his works in the history of political science, 41
FRANCE, history of Party in, 193-195
Franchise, electoral, examination of principles relating to the, 198 *sq.*
French Revolution, influence of the, on political theory, 375
— — its place in the history of political science, 49-52
— Senate, organisation of the, 309

GAMBLING, policy of laws for the prevention of, 475, 476
Geographical area, the, of modern politics, 126 *sq.*
Government, the term, history and explanation of, 67-69

GOV

Government of Dependencies, problems relating to the, 311 *sq*.
— investigation into the province of, 371
— local, problems relating to, 277 *sq*.
GREECE, history of the States of, its scientific bearings, 25–29
GROTE, Mr., his views on Athenian character, 233
— Professor, his treatise on Utilitarianism, 453

HARE, Mr., scheme of, for the representation of minorities, 224
— — — as a corrective of corruption, 465
Health, the public, functions of Government respecting, 406 *sq*.
History, Sir G. C. Lewis's remarks on the use of, in politics, 114
HOBBES, his place in the history of political science, 42
HOOKER, his Ecclesiastical Polity, place of, in the history of political science, 38
HUMBOLDT, Wilhelm von, his treatise on the province of Government, 372

INDEPENDENCE of a State, what it means, 351 *sq*.
India, British, duties of English Government to, 333
— — recent changes in administration of, 340
— — land policy in, 397
Intervention, its connexion with the independence of States, 353, 354
Ireland, the land problem in, 398

JAPAN, its place in the modern political world, 135
Jewish State, the, its relations to family life, 161

MAZ

Judges, their constitutional functions, 275
Judicial authority, the, its relation to the Legislative and Executive Authority, 246, 248

LAND, State intervention in respect of, 395 *sq*.
— tenure of, as an element of political life, 147 *sq*.
Law, the term, history and analysis of, 69 *sq*.
Legislative, the term, history and account of, 87 *sq*.
Legislative authority, its relation to the Executive, 246 *sq*.
LEWIS, Sir G. C., estimate of his 'Methods of Reasoning in Politics,' 109, 114
— — — — his remarks on political Utopias, 22, 23
Liquor traffic, problems relating to regulation of, 300, 301
Local Boards, problems relating to the organisation of, 307
— Government, problems relating to, 277 *sq*.
— — of towns, 304
Locomotion, functions of Government respecting, 405
Lords, House of, problems relating to, 236 *sq*.
Lotteries, immorality of State, 475, 476

MACHIAVELLI, his place in the history of political science, 36
MAINE, Sir H. S., his views on the introduction of English tenures into India, 151
MALTHUS, illustration from his population theory, 376
Marriage, history of, as a political factor, 159
— monogamic, political grounds of, 473, 474
MAZZINI, place of, in the history of political science, 54

Medical profession, political disqualifications of the, 408
MILL, Mr. J. S., on the administration of British India, 340
— — — — on relations of women to men, 139, 140
— — — — his remarks on experiments in politics, 113
— — — — his views on the province of Government, 372
Minorities, problems relating to representation of, 219 *sq.*
Mohammedanism, its polygamic aspect, 160 *sq.*
Monogamic marriage, political grounds of, 473, 474
Mormonism, its polygamic aspects, 163, 164, 474
Municipal Corporation Act, political aspects of the, 308

NATIONALITY, influence of doctrine of, 345, 358
Navigation, functions of the State in relation to, 422, 423
— — Laws, political aspects of the, 317
Navy, problems relating to the management of the, 257
NEW SOUTH WALES, how its constitution was founded, 387
Nihilism, its influence on political theory, 379

OTTOMAN Empire, the, question of its political vitality, 132, 133, 136, 137

PARIS, Treaty of, 1814, political consequences of, 343, 344
Parliaments, problems relating to duration of, 217
Party, his'oric bearings of, on political organisation, 188 *sq.*
Party, various uses of the term, 6!, 62
PEEL, Sir Robert, his railway policy, 406

PLATO, his place in the history of political science, 22
Plébiscite, the, its constitutional aspects, 201, 202, 226
Police, problems relating to the management of, 254, 298, 478
Political economy, its influence on political theory, 375, 376, 392
— reasoning, inquiry into, 107 *sq.*
— terms, account of, 56 *sq.*
Politics, science of, its nature and limits, 1 *sq.*
Poor law administration, as a topic of local government, 296, 297
— laws, their indirect political influence, 377, 382, 389, 392
Prerogative, explanation of the terms, 105
President of the United States, constitutional position of the, 201, 248
Press, the, as a political influence, 234
Prime Minister, constitutional position of the English, 251
Privy Council, its constitutional character, 251
Province of Government, investigation of the, 371 *sq.*
Provincial Government, Roman, problems suggested by history of, 314, 315
Punishments, moral questions affecting criminal, 479, 480

RAILWAYS, Government policy relating to, 405, 406
Religion, functions of the State in relation to, 412
RÉNAN, M., his historical views, 450
Representation of colonies, possibility of, 334 *sq.*
— — minorities, problems relating to, 219 *sq.*
Revolution, the American, its place in the history of political science, 46

Revolution, the English, compared with the French, 439-441
— — French, its influence on political theory, 375
— — — its place in the history of political science, 49-52
— moral duties in respect of, 465 *sq.*
— period in England, account of the, 435-439
Revolutions in States, inquiry into causes of, 427 *sq.*
Right, the term, history and analysis of, 100 *sq.*
ROMAN Provincial Government, problems suggested by the history of, 314, 315
— Republic and Empire, place of, in history of political science, 31-34, 131
ROME, account of the agrarian problems of, 401
— as an exhibition of senile failure, 131
ROUSSEAU, his views on a state of nature, 117
RUSSIA, effects of its extent of territory, 323

SCHOOL BOARDS, their political aspects, 295
— — method of election of English, 227
Science of Politics, its nature and limits, 1 *sq.*
Secession, American War of, criticism of the grounds of, 442-445
Senate, French, organisation of the, 309
— of United States, its functions in foreign policy, 355
Slavery, its immorality, 471
— its place in the history of political science, 25
Social Contract, place of the notion of, in the history of political science, 45, 124, 182
Socialism, account of modern, 379, 380
SPENCER, Herbert, Mr., his views

on the province of Government, 372, 381, 382
State, the term, history and analysis of, 63 *sq.*
— Church and, relations of, considered, 413 *sq.*
— elements and growth of a, 138 *sq.*
— independence of a, what it means, 351 *sq.*
Statistics, their modern use in political inquiries, 18
SUEZ CANAL, policy of English purchase of shares in the, 270 *sq.*
Suffrage, extension of the, as a moral question, 472

TAXATION, immorality of fraudulent evasions of, 459
— principles of policy affecting, 403
Towns as areas of local government, 302 *sq.*
— problems relating to the representation of, 212 *sq.*
Trades Unions, their bearing on State organisation, 171
Treaty of Paris, 1814, political consequences of, 343, 344

UNCONSTITUTIONAL, history and explanation of the term, 60
UNITED STATES, constitutional position of the President of the, 201, 248
— — constitutional problems relating to the, 179, 180
— — growth of the, its place in the history of political science, 46
— Senate of the, its functions in foreign policy, 355
Utilitarianism, its place in political theory, 451 *sq.*
Utilitarians, place of English, in the history of political science, 54, 55
Utopia, Sir T. More's, place of, in

UTO

the history of political science, 38

Utopias, Sir G. C. Lewis's remarks on, 22, 23

VICE, legislative policy respecting, 478, 479

WOM

VICTORIA, colony of, how its constitution was founded, 387

WAR, prospects of its continuance, 361

WARD, Mr., his account of the influence of the Papacy, 450

Women, their political relation to men, 139, 182

www.ingramcontent.com/pod-product-compliance
Lightning Source LLC
Chambersburg PA
CBHW021420300426
44114CB00010B/571